The DUNDEE Book

An Anthology of Living in the City

Edited by
BILLY KAY

MAINSTREAM
PUBLISHING

For my wife, Maria João, who shares the view

This edition 1995

First published in Great Britain in 1990 by
MAINSTREAM PUBLISHING COMPANY (EDINBURGH) LTD
7 Albany Street
Edinburgh EH1 3UG

ISBN 1 85158 795 0

A catalogue record for this book is available from the British Library

Design and layout by Jim Hutcheson and Paul Keir
Typeset in Great Britain by Blackpool Typesetting Services Ltd, Blackpool
Printed in Great Britain

Contents

Acknowledgments

The editor would like to extend grateful thanks to all the people who have given of their time and expertise to help this book come to fruition. In particular I would like to thank Mr Ramage, Miss Foster, the photography department and the staff of the Local Studies department of Dundee Public Libraries; the staff of Dundee University Library and the Photographic Department; Adam Ritchie, David Stockdale, for permission to use transcripts of his interview with Joseph Paterson, Clara Young, David Scruton, Janice Murray and the Photography Department of Dundee Museums and Art Galleries; Claire Watts, Penny Clarke, Janene Reid, the directors and staff of Mainstream Publishing; Paul Keir for layouts; Jim Hutcheson for cover and design; Katherine Law for painstaking copy editing.

Charles McKean for access to the R.I.A.S. photographic collection, Eugenie Fraser for permission to quote from her books, Ron Fraser for the photos; Mrs James Cameron for permission to quote from her late husband's work; Clara Young for permission to quote from her father's writing; John Gibson for the photocopier; the Islay Street Brothers for Dundonian advice; Ken Sharp for his magnanimous gesture of the photographs and Joe Austen for his magnanimous donation of the drawing; Grant Lindsay for the books and the Alliance Trust photos; Graeme and Jean Burns for the books; Marion Quinn and Lesley Brennan for proof reading; João for keeping the show on the road.

Cover pictures courtesy of: Bruce Pandrich; *Tay Bridge from my Studio Window*, J. McIntosh Patrick, Dundee Art Gallery and Museums; J. D. Saggar (standing) with Guru, India *c.* 1919; Dundee District Libraries; *Brown Ochre on the Crumbling Walls*, by Joe Paterson, Dundee Art Gallery and Museums.

Preface to the
1995 Edition

The preface to the first edition of this book, published in 1990, began: 'Dundee's story is as fascinating as her setting is beautiful. Few people outwith Dundee know this. Even though there is intense local pride within the city, most Dundonians themselves have little more than an inkling of the richness and diversity of their distant and recent past.' The positive response by Dundonians to my exploration of their history in the book and companion BBC radio and television features made for the Dundee 800 celebrations has been gratifying. I always believe that if you get something right in the eyes of the community, you will also get it right for the outside world. This was proved when my musical history of the city *The Road and the Miles to Dundee* won a bronze medal at the New York Radio Festival in 1992.

Since 1990, the city has naturally gone through changes, positive and negative. The Timex dispute proved that the commitment and loyalty of even the most dedicated workforce are sadly dispensable. The city's major spectator sport, football, is in the doldrums with neither club playing in the top flight. More ominously, neither would appear to have directors with the vision necessary to get them back up there. In contrast, the culture of the city is thriving. So much so, in fact, that an entirely new chapter on the literary scene had to be written for this book to account for the tremendous work coming from Dundonian writers in the past five years. A positive attitude to the culture and what should be its central place within education has been shown by Tayside Region's pioneering promotion of the Scots language. Their provision of resource materials like *Tae Be Yersel* and the literature anthology *Fair Upon Tay* to all the region's schools gives status to the culture and pride in it to the pupils. It is also satisfying to see an increasing awareness among local councillors of the important role that history and culture can provide in creating civic awareness and promoting the city. The production of a video on medieval Dundee and the establishment of the annual George Kinloch memorial lecture are two recent manifestations of a phenomenon which I hope will gain momentum.

For Dundee needs to project itself. Within Scotland, there are still many journalists content to respond to the city with ignorant stereotypes, rather than give it the dignity of genuine analysis. Like Pavlov's dugs, feed in the stimulus of the word 'Dundee' and they'll slaiver out dated negative images which bear little resemblance to the actuality of the place today. In a recent university survey conducted to find the best urban environment in Britain in which to live, for example, Dundee came third from the top in the category for intermediate-sized cities. Despite such positive evidence, many hacks will still resort to the cocoon of negative cliché.

Findings like that of the survey, however, are testimony to the successful improvements in the urban environment undertaken by the city leaders in recent years. The public art input into the planning process has reaped great dividends in the way the streets of the city present themselves. The eyesores of the Overgate Centre and the even tattier function suite of the Angus Hotel, however, still blight the city centre and detract from the improvements in the Murraygait and elsewhere. Having seen how war-devastated cities in Germany and Poland can be rebuilt in all their historic dignity and integrity, I feel strongly that as we approach the millennium Dundee should undertake a great civic project: that of rebuilding the ancient Overgait. This would put the heart back into the city for the citizens, and create a major tourist attraction to complement Discovery Point. The scars from the dire development mistakes of the 1960s and 1970s can be healed. Dundee can again have a centre which reflects her medieval heritage and matches her beautiful setting, one in which her historical heart, the Overgait, is given pride of place, restored to her former glory.

Billy Kay,
Newport-on-Tay,
1995

Dundee

An Introduction

by BILLY KAY

On this dreich winter's day, looking from my window over to Dundee, the auld grey toun is living up to its name, happed in haar, smoored in shades of slate grey, dank browns and dull whites. The drabness of the grim juteopolis is the stereotyped image of the city borne by most folk who do not know the place. We who have the good fortune to live here, know better. The same view at night with its shimmering lights is Manhattan from the Staten Island Ferry or Naples from the Bay, and when the sun beats down and the estuary is dotted with sailing boats and waterskiers it's very much L.A. on Tay, without the smog. The view is constantly changing, and the more you know of Dundee, the more the stereotype is fragmented and replaced with pieces of a jigsaw which build up into something very unique, very idiosyncratic, very Dundee.

As an outsider, I inherited the negative, stereotypical view. It was shattered during my first visit to the city, on a Friday evening in the spring of 1980. I wanted to include a feature on the Angus area in my oral history series *Odyssey* on Radio Scotland. My contact was Jim Reid, the outstanding traditional singer from the city. Discussing possible subjects such as the Angus bothies, or the Auchmithie fishing, the strength of the songs probably settled us on the subject of the jute industry. I had reservations whether such a mundane subject could be enlivened to make a good forty-five minute programme, but with the series committed to telling the urban working-class experience as well as the rural, we arranged to begin recording that Friday night. My wife, Jim Reid and I visited two ex-spinners, Sarah Craig of Lochee and Mrs Cockburn of Dura Street, and left both houses exhilarated by the quality of the interviews and impressed by the directness, humour and strength of these two very different Dundee women. It was they who first kindled my fascination for Dundee's recent history: the reversal of the usual social roles between the sexes in a town in which women were the wage earners, and men 'kettle bilers'; the status feuds between weaver and spinner; the maverick politics of a hard-drinking city electing a candidate committed to the total prohibition of alcohol in preference to Winston Churchill; the family contacts with Ireland and India; the contrast between fabulous opulence and grinding poverty resisted with little more than the people's concept of respectability. All of this and more

The Law and East Dundee from Fife, 1990.
Ken Sharp

The making of the Trojan ruins. *Joseph McKenzie*

emerged, told in that very Dundonian mell of self-effacing understatement and bone-dry humour which has attracted me to the people ever since. Eventually, I wrote the play *They Fairly Mak Ye Work* and based the character of the heroine on Sarah Craig's recollections of political involvement during the Depression, and one of the mill characters, Meg, on Mrs Cockburn. Mrs Cockburn was not politically active, and her reason for not voting for Churchill went straight into the playscript: 'Eh never voted for him, Eh never voted at a'. Never did, didna hae time! For washing bairns, an washing claithes an looking after a bluidy boozy man!'

To understand Dundee properly you have to know the history of the place and the conditions which formed its character. That character has not been constant. If buildings tell a story, the contrast in outlook of the city's civic leaders of, say, the 1460s and the 1960s is perfectly illustrated in the magnificence of St Mary's Tower and the ugliness of the Angus Hotel's function suite which obscures part of it from view. One is confident and permanent, the other is shoddy, parochial and impermanent. One is fit for what was the second city of Scotland and a great European port, the other is scarcely fit for a housing scheme in a decaying mining village, let alone the centre of Scotland's fourth city. Many towns were devastated by the new building boom of the

8

1960s and 1970s – I myself witnessed Edinburgh University's philistine destruction of George Square, and the rise of the appalling St James Centre at the East End of Princes Street. Dundee had less it could afford to lose. The Hawkhill and Overgate were destroyed and replaced by parking lots, high rises, and an instant slum masquerading as a shopping centre. The destruction of buildings which constituted people's sense of their city, showed disdain and disregard for their feelings. This feeling of powerlessness and its expression in cynicism is ingrained in most Scots; it is embedded in the Dundee character. The black humour saves them. The tearing down of old Dundee was carried out by a firm called Trojan Demolition. The areas they devastated were called the Trojan ruins!

Part of the Angus Hotel and The Tower of St Mary's, Nethergait. *Ken Sharp*

Jim Boyd, the former Director of the city's museums, recalls arriving to take up his post in the late 1940s. He found the ordinary people enthusiastic about preserving their history and culture, the civic leaders less so. 'Mr Boyd, remember you are no longer in Glasgow, you are in Dundee,' said a prominent councillor. 'In Glasgow they get things done, in Dundee we dinnae!' They regarded culture as an irrelevance to their development plans, in which private and public benefit often got confused. Self-seeking politicians imposed their dubious stamp on the city, and exacerbated the alienation of the Dundonians. These politicians took over the mantle of power from the industrialists of the earlier twentieth century. They too cared little for the people and environment which gave them their profits.

The novelist David Walker recalls the attitude of the jute barons in his autobiographical book *Lean, Wind, Lean.*

> When I was a boy, the poverty among the mill-people of Dundee was terrible. The barefooted urchins in their only playground, the dirty street, were called 'keelies', a term of contempt. Looking back now, I feel shame at the way the likes of us must have exploited them. But to my parents' generation, the other half (a massive half) were not quite the same kind of human beings as ourselves. Even my sensitive liberal-minded mother, who never harmed anyone and spent her life doing kindness, would speak of 'those people'. They were the lesser orders who, if a generous employer installed a bath for them, would be sure to use it as a coal bin.

The legacy of the textile barons can be seen in the institutions, buildings and parks they endowed in the city – from the University of Dundee to the Caird Hall and Baxter Park. But much of the profits of the late nineteenth and early twentieth century were invested abroad – in the development of the ranches and railways in the American West. With its staple industry declining rapidly, the Depression of the late 1920s and 1930s left huge numbers of the city's working class destitute. The man responsible for

9

Sarah Craig. *Ken Sharp*

the provision of poor relief then, Bobby Allan, had a reputation for unfeeling coldness towards the people's plight which was probably deserved. The extent of the misery at that time can be gauged by the words he expressed at his retirement speech: 'I have witnessed scenes in Dundee which would make the angels weep.' The psychological and physical scars of these hard times are what Dundee folk have had to recover from.

Dundee is the fourth largest of Scotland's cities but it is far more isolated than the other three. Its projection to the rest of Scotland is limited by the fact that it is the only Scottish city without major television studios, while its local news is almost totally controlled by the introspective D. C. Thomson & Co. Dundee's reticence in publicising itself is mirrored in, or is perhaps a mirror of, the behaviour of this major communications firm. When you think of the flamboyance of major newspaper proprietors elsewhere, and contrast it with the publicity-shy Thomsons, you have the Dundee dilemma in a nutshell. The realisation that skilful marketing of successful products like Oor Wullie and Dennis the Menace actually benefit the company, will perhaps bring D. C. Thomson & Co. out of its shell, and in doing so increase its promotion of Dundee.

This strong provincial introspection, combined with the homogeneity of experience brought about by the predominance of the jute industry over the working life of the town, has given Dundee a very distinctive and tangible local identity. The identity is heightened by the uniqueness of the local dialect of Scots, a racy, irreverent, urban mell of the rich Angus tongue, levelled in the roaring clack of the mills to an acceptably stieran lingua franca by the influx of folk from places as far apart as Sligo, Vilnius, Badenoch and Buchan.

Jute is the reason why all these people came to Dundee and why the population more than quadrupled in the course of the nineteenth century. Even though there are only a handful of mills working now, it, more than any other factor, moulded the character of the modern city.

In Juteopolis, a breed of strong, independent-minded women was forged and more than any other place in Scotland certainly, possibly in Europe, Dundee is very much a matriarchal society. The strength of the Dundee women came home to me again when I was researching my play about the city's jute workers. I was dismayed to learn that my main informant, Sarah Craig, had been admitted to hospital to have her leg amputated. It was with some trepidation that I entered the ward, the day after an event which would have killed both body and soul of most octogenarians. I had not counted on the woman's spirit and mordant humour: 'Och, Billy,' she said, 'if they gie me a stick an a parrot, Eh'll get tae play Long John Silver!' Sarah, like many of her generation, had started work in the mills, using false documents, at the age of ten, so they had to develop hardness

10

from an early age. The spectre of destitution was never far away for the city's working class, and women bore the brunt of the struggle from childhood to old age. Mrs Cockburn's recollection is typical:

> When I got married an' athing, ye ken, ye were aff tae hae bairns, an then ye were back again, an then ye bid aff tae hae anither bairn (laughs) – Bloody Dundee men was murder Polis! (laughs) Meh God, ye worked tae ye were near fadin awa. My grannie was near seventy an she was still in the jute, an auld woman!

Many people find the story of Mary Slessor inspirational. She was the Dundee mill girl who trained as a missionary and had a tremendous influence for good in the West-African region of Calabar which had been brutalised and degraded by the corruption of the slave trade. Knowing the women of Dundee makes you realise that her strength of purpose did not stem from her faith alone. Eugenie Fraser's riveting description of the confrontation between her mother and a commissar, during the Russian Revolution, proves that the strength of purpose extended beyond the working class. And it is a trait which is still there today. Who can forget the way Liz McColgan bore Scotland's last hopes of glory in the recent Commonwealth Games, to win with that single-minded determination which is characteristic of the women she stems from? Who can forget the dignity and bravery in adversity of Veronica Lynch following the tragic death of her daughter?

The prominent economic role of women differentiates Dundee from Scotland's other cities. With its similarly rapid and traumatic industrialisation, the city Dundee should most resemble is Glasgow. The presence of the same Scots/Irish mixture in their populations should also have contributed to the similarity between the two cities. The fact that many of the Irish who settled in Dundee came there via Glasgow, makes the conundrum all the more puzzling. Yet the character of the two cities is totally different. In a way, it is Scotland's east–west divide exaggerated and heightened beyond this description in George Douglas Brown's novel *The House with the Green Shutters*:

> The East throws a narrower and nippier breed. In the West, they take Burns for their exemplar and affect the jovial and robustious – in some case it is affectation only, and a mightly poor one at that. They claim to be bigger men and bigger fools than the Eastern billies. And the Eastern billies are very willing to yield one half of the contention.

Discussing the similarities in the histories yet the differences in the character, the sports writer Roddy Forsyth told me that Dundonians lacked the 'spark' of Glaswegians. While

11

acknowledging the differences – especially among football fans from the two cities – I pointed out that the 'spark' he referred to was often kindled by sectarian prejudice, a phenomenon which had never taken root in the more tolerant and more homogeneous communities of Dundee. Personally , I wish Dundonians had a bit more of that Glaswegian ability to blow their own trumpet, and Glaswegians had a moderating graft of Dundonian understatement and modesty!

The battle of the sexes in Dundee often comes out in the city's humour and the women usually come out on top. Typical is the story told by David Phillips, of a young man passing comment on a woman breast-feeding her baby while sitting outside her house one summer afternoon: 'Here, that's affy clever,' says he, 'daein twa things at the same time – feedin the bairn an warmin the step!' 'Na, son,' says she, 'Eh'm daein three things, feedin the bairn, warmin the step an coolin meh erse!' The unashamed confidence in their sex Dundee women possess by nature is brought out in a story I got from the poet Ellie McDonald. Ellie's father was going from door to door in Lochee, collecting information for the census. At one house he was confronted with a harassed woman with a howlin bairn at her breast. Unable to feed the fractious child, and unable to hear the visitor's questions over the skraichin, the woman's exasperation finally boiled over, and looking down at the wee sour face she addressed the bairn with the memorable words, 'Haud yer wheesht an souk, you, or Eh'll gie it tae the mannie!'

The humour is nippy with a distinctly black twist to it. An old lady I know, living in a block of flats in Lochee, was not very happy with the quality of service given by the regular window-cleaner, and he was less than courteous when she complained. The next time he returned, she saw her opportunity for getting her own back. A neighbour upstairs had died, leaving the flat empty. When the window-cleaner enquired after her, my friend told him to go ahead and clean the windows as she was 'juist awa for a whilie'. Unpaid, he came back to the flats later, and still finding no one there, called at my friend's. 'Where's she awa til?' he asked. With a gleam in her eye, the octogenarian replied, 'She's awa tae the Hullie [the cemetery on Balgay Hill], she's no comin back an you're no gettin peyed!' The same person is as rich in warmth and human kindness as anyone I know, but cross her and ye'll ken about it!

Dourness is another Dundee characteristic, and examples of it are exchanged with glee. A Dundee lady, back in the city for the first time after seventeen years in Australia, could not resist going into the bakery for her first fresh Dundee pie. The following dialogue ensued: 'Could Eh hae a peh, please?' 'Eh, dae ye want a het ane or a cauld ane?' 'Oh, Eh'm no sure, whit dae ye recommend?' 'Please yer bluidy sel!' But for every dour shopkeeper there's nine cheery ones and shopping still tends to

Allan Braithwaite in the Coffee Shop. *Ken Sharp*

have a familiar small town feel to it, with people asking how members of the family are getting on. That old-fashioned feel is retained also in the quality of service provided. Braithwaite's in Castle Street, for example, is the only coffee shop left in Scotland which still roasts its beans every day – sending a heady aroma wafting into the city centre, to the delight of coffee snobs like me. Scotland's description as the 'Land o' Cakes' is emblazoned on the sign of one of many excellent bakeries in the city centre. In the matter of pastries, teabread and pies, Dundee is the undisputed capital of the country.

If dourness is a characteristic, it is balanced with a genuine warmth and caring for folk. Football supporters are a maligned breed elsewhere in Britain, but in Dundee they're the berries. Which other fans could see their team beaten in a European final, and still give the victors a spontaneous standing ovation as they paraded the Cup round the park? That genuine Dundonian gesture of warmth and appreciation for the other side, is such a rarity in the modern club game that FIFA instigated a Fair Play Award in recognition of the example United's fans had shown European football.

Dundee men know their women are a hard act to follow, and generally, they do not try to compete. In fact, they exaggerate their ordinariness as any kind of self-promotion is seen as

Andy Pelc – St Andrew. *Ken Sharp*

extremely bad form. The song 'Hermless', by St Andrew of
Woollen Mill fame, is a Dundonian male anthem, sending up the
ordinary bloke with nothing going for him, who goes through life
and affects nobody.

> Hermless, hermless, ye'll no catch me hurtin a flee.
>
> Eh ging tae the Library, Eh tak oot a book,
> An then Eh come hame for meh tea.
>
> Eh save up the coupons that come wi the soup,
> An when Eh huv saved fifty-three,
> Eh send awa fufty, put three in the drawer
> An somethin gets posted tae me.
>
> Hermless, hermless, there's never nae bather fae me.

(Dick McTaggart, Bobby Boland and Freddie Tennant
hermless? Aye, hingin mince!)

While this kind of 'hauden doun' character exists everywhere
else in Scotland, he is particularly apt in Dundee, where even the
brilliantly witty, erudite and urbane often hide these characteristics and affect a persona which they present to the world as

14

'hermless'. The result of this thrawn, perverse characteristic –
'Eh'll only be brilliant amang consentin Dundonians in the
privacy o meh ain hoose' – is that more than any other place in
Scotland, you are constantly being surprised by people who let
their talents slip. Sandy Kidd, modestly inventing a gyroscope
which defies Newton's and everyone else's laws of physics, in his
garden shed, is very Dundee. It is a city which has constantly
produced great characters, but because of the reasons outlined
already, only a chosen few know about them and their Dundee
connections. James Bowman Lindsay was the pioneer of electric
light and electric telegraphy; James Chalmers invented the
postage stamp; Neil Paterson played for Dundee United and
D. C. Thomson and won an Oscar for his screenplay for the
movie *Room at the Top*. Dundee has produced great scholars and
intellectuals: the philosopher George Elder Davie, whose book
The Democratic Intellect profoundly affected my awareness of
Scottish culture, came from the Hilltown, and R. L. Lorimer,
the translator of the New Testament into Scots, hailed from the
Strathmartine district. It is a city which provokes strange happenings: Mary Shelley gave birth to Frankenstein near Peep o'
Day lane; Patrick Blair dissected the first elephant to be
dissected in Britain on the Broughty Ferry Road; and Jack
Johnson, the American heavyweight champion of the world was
initiated into the rites of freemasonry up a close off the Blackness
Road! The world should know of such things.

Dundee has had an image problem to overcome, not as
extreme as the old Glasgow myth of hard men and slums, more
ugly duckling and nondescript, but one heightened by the city's
isolation from the rest of Scotland – few non-Dundonians know
Dundee. Within Dundee, the problem has been helped by a
growing interest in the city's history and a revival in its culture,
in the 1980s. The Dundee Oral History Project did excellent
work in giving ordinary Dundonians confirmation that *their*
history is the city's history. The desire of all sections of Dundee
society to celebrate their culture was made manifest when my
play *They Fairly Mak Ye Work*, before it even opened, broke
box-office records at the Rep. And the play's success was due to
the tangible bond between the actors and the audience. Dundee
has a huge pool of talented musicians who play together, and one
of the joys of living in the area is walking into pubs and discovering great music being played, be it Scottish, soul or jazz. With
the University, several colleges of further education, and the
College of Art, it also has very much the buzz of a students' town,
especially in the lovely West End. The visual arts, too, are thriving. Famous established painters such as McIntosh Patrick,
Alberto Morrocco, and David McClure live and work in the city,
while the College of Art has continually produced artists of
genuine quality in every generation: Neil Dallas Brown, Calum
Colvin and Keith McIntyre are just a few examples.

They Fairly Mak Ye Work with Grace
Glover as Sarah Craig. *Spanphoto*

15

Public Art – Whales Teeth by Alastair Smart. *Ken Sharp*

The exhibition, in the McManus Galleries, of Joseph Paterson's evocative paintings of working-class life in Dundee confirmed the growing belief that the arts in Dundee are not just the domain of a privileged few, but intensely relevant to everyone. Perhaps the most unique manifestation of that philosophy, is the dynamic Public Art scheme. The co-operation between planners and artists in every major development – something which does not occur in any other city in Britain – should ensure that Dundee's marvellous physical environment is never sold short again. Now, everywhere you go the eye is caught and held by arresting murals with images ranging from stags loupin ower dykes to whale's teeth with Oor Wullie scrimshaw details! They add even more surprises to a city already hoaching with them, and thrang with extreme diversity. The scheme also gives work to artists, so more and more are making Dundee their home.

In addition to all of this artistic activity, the return of Captain Scott's Antarctic exploration ship *Discovery* to its home port has acted as a focus for an important tourist development of the waterfront along the Tay and has given the Public Relations boys the gift of a promotional slogan, 'Dundee, City of Discovery'. Certainly, Dundee has been ignored for so long that anything which brings it positive publicity can only be good for the place.

Some Dundee people feel that the current projection of the city is little more than a cosmetic exercise. Because much of the Dundee Project's work has been based on the genuine history of the city, I have tended to disagree. As long as the working-class contribution is not lost or marginalised as the city seeks to present itself in new clothes, then the renaissance of Dundee can continue with, at last, an integrated community behind it. This is essential if the renaissance is to be complete and lasting. For Dundee this century has borne deep social divisions, with the vast majority of the population feeling that they had little control over the destiny of the city. They have tholed and endured, and remarkably, despite the dunts, still have a strong identity with the place. The last decade has seen tremendous cultural and artistic advances, and at last the politicians, the business community and the people are as one in their desire to regenerate this potentially beautiful city. The wounds caused by the old disdain, the old cynicism and the old divisions are healing. The environment has improved dramatically, and the image with it. There are hopeful signs that the vision that built St Mary's is slowly returning to Dundee.

But ultimately it is the character of the city's people which is its strength – a strong, often contradictory mixture of diffidence and undemonstrative warmth. If its reticence can be frustrating, its down-to-earth honesty and total lack of pretension tilt the balance decidedly in the city's favour. More than anything, I hope Dundee will continue to throw up characters and contradictions, for it is in its nature to be thrawn. As I hope this book

16

demonstrates, it is a delightfully maverick city, going merrily its own way and paying dearly for it for over 800 years. While writing, the weather and the view have improved dramatically. The Law, St Mary's Tower, Cox's Stack and the Hill o' Balgay are framed by the Perthshire hills and the magnificent expanse of the Tay. All are fringed with the glorious ochre and crimson of a setting winter sun. There may well be a few places in the world which match the astonishing beauty of Dundee's setting, but I know that there's no city population on earth with a character remotely resembling the Dundonian. That belangs Dundee fowk, an naebody else.

Broughty Castle and yachts in the Tay. *Ken Sharp*

A Hawkhill mansion, c. 1966. *Joseph McKenzie*

Earl David's Burgh

Dundee in Medieval Scotland

by GEOFFREY BARROW

Dundee occupies one of the finest natural sites of any city in the British Isles. The attraction of this site, even aesthetically perhaps, would have appealed to the earliest settlers: a south-facing natural harbour, comparatively sheltered, formed by St Nicholas Craig on the west, and the rocky outcrop on which the castle came to be built, and with two streams, the Scouring Burn and the Dens Burn, offering a handy supply of running water to supplement the local springs and wells. In the Pictish period a fort was constructed to give protection to some local ruler, possibly the King of Fortriu or southern Pictland himself. The fort acquired the name *dún Deagh*, 'fortress of Daigh', perhaps after some early warrior. The hinterland of this fort, reaching north to the ridge overlooking the valley of the Dighty Water (Strathdighty in the Middle Ages), west to Invergowrie and east as far as Craigie, formed a royal demesne whose component crofts and 'ferm touns', grazing land and tidal fisheries, would all have been required to produce tribute in kind – corn, hay, milk, butter and cheese, herring and salmon – to support the king and his family and entourage.

By the twelfth century this small district was known as the Shire of Dundee, a name which indicates that Dundee was already recognised as possessing some importance. Much of that importance would have been due to Dundee's extremely favourable situation close to the mouth of the Firth of Tay, on the sheltered side of the dangerous sandbanks which lie off the estuary. Even in medieval times, shipping was big enough to sail with cargoes of Scottish wool, sheepskins and cattle-hides to continental markets such as St Omer and Bruges in Flanders, Cologne, Hamburg and Lübeck among the Hanseatic towns further east, or to the far reaches of the Baltic. Of seaports north of the Forth, Inverness, Aberdeen, Montrose and Perth, all royal centres, seem to have got off the mark quickest with a favoured overseas trade, not only exporting raw materials (probably including a few valuable items such as pearls) but receiving appreciable imports of quality textiles, wine, and metal articles including weapons etc. Corn probably featured in a two-way trade: exported whenever the Scots farmers enjoyed a good harvest, imported in times of dearth.

c. 1107

Tradition has it that King Malcolm Canmore's son Edgar had his residence in Dundee. Andrew of Wyntoun's poetic *Origynale Cronykil* of Scotland written *c.* 1420 confirms the tradition and describes Edgar's death.

A thowsand a hundred yhere and sevyn
Fra Mary bare the Kyng off Hevyn.
Off Edgare, oure nobill Kyng,
The dayus wyth honoure tuk endyng:
Be-north Tay in till Dunde
Tyll God the spryte than yhald he.
And in the Kyrk of Dwnfermlyne
Solemply he was enteryd syne.

19

c. 1180

The founding of Dundee, part myth, part history, has come down to us in the Latin chronicles of one of the most eminent citizens of medieval Dundee, Hector Boece. It is quite possible that Boece drew from local oral tradition when he described the origins of his native city. Here is John Bellenden's Scots translation from Boece, of Earl David's escape from drowning at sea.

He was driven be unmerciful tempest nocht far frae Norroway with incredible danger. Finally, when he had BUILD made ane voit to *big* ane kirk to the honour of the Virgin Mary gif he war fortunate to escape the danger of seas, he arrivit in Tay beside Dunde not far WITHOUT frae Sanct Nicholas' Chapel, *but* ony rudder or tackle, and gave thanks to God and the blessit Virgin for delivering of him frae sic extreme peril. The place quhair he arrivit was callit BEAUTIFUL *Alectum*; but, after his cumming, it changit name, and was callid [Deidonum], quhilk signifies in our language the Gift of God.

The poet Stewart also translated Boece into Scots verse. Here he describes the founding of St Mary's Church, its association with Lindores Abbey in Fife, and the privileges the early town enjoyed.

Foundit ane kirk in ane field at that cost,
Quhilk at that tyme wes callit the Quhit Cross,
In to the honour of the Virgin pure,
Eternallie in that place till enduir.

. . . . .

This village dotit then hes he,
Quhilk he foundit that callit wes Dundie;
And mony uther privilege thame gaif,
That neidfull wes to ony town to haif.
Into this time remains yit to se,
That nobill town of greit auctoritie.
Sone efter this now that ye heir me sa,
Of Lundoris the nobill riche Abba
This Erle David foundit on Tay.

c. 1290

Dundee's role in the Scottish Wars of Independence of the late thirteenth and early fourteenth centuries was seminal, as the incident which brought young William Wallace into the struggle occurred there. The story of the patriot hero is told in an epic poem by Blin Hary, composed in the 1470s, also a time of turbulent relations between Scotland and

Although Dundee was as much of a royal demesne as Perth or Montrose, no king before William the Lion (1165 – 1214) seems to have thought of promoting Dundee as a main trading centre or burgh in the way that some of the other east-coast seaports were promoted. The reason for this may have been two-fold. First of all, the ships of the earlier twelfth century were quite small enough to sail all the way up to Perth without breaking bulk. There were real advantages attached to this in the days when markets were visited on foot or occasionally on horseback, and Perth stood firmly astride the main north-south route leading from the Moray Firth and Aberdeen, by Forfar and the Tay, to Stirling and on to Edinburgh or Carlisle. But as bigger ships came to be built during the thirteenth century the attractions of deeper water ports like Dundee became more apparent. A further point in favour of the city lay in the swing of Scottish trade away from France and the Bay of Biscay and towards the German cities and Baltic lands.

About 1178 King William I 'the Lion' made a big grant of lands to his younger brother David, clearly with the intention of establishing him as a principal magnate of the realm. Among the lands thus given was Dundee, including the whole 'shire', and within a few years Earl David – he had acquired the English earldom of Huntingdon in 1185 – was busy developing the port and settlement into an organised urban community and burgh. The Earl was no doubt responsible for building the earliest castle of Dundee, utilising the rocky outcrop now represented by the slight mound on which stands the Episcopal Cathedral of St Paul at the north end of Castle Street.

The first recorded reference to Dundee as a burgh occurs in two documents of around 1190 or 1191, one of them Earl David's 'foundation charter' for Lindores Abbey in Fife, the other his brother's confirmation of this charter, probably issued on the same occasion. Unfortunately both documents survive only in copies, although these are quite early in date and obviously accurate. We can envisage Earl David founding his burgh or 'new town' of Dundee during the twelve years between 1178 and 1190, laying out the site – mainly along the Seagait running east from the castle and the almost parallel Murraygait and Cowgait – fixing the line of streets and the size and alignment of house-and-yard plots or 'tofts' which would normally lie at right-angles to the streets.

Even more important than questions of physical planning would have been the matter of recruiting suitable merchants and craftsmen, appointing a grieve or alderman (equivalent of the later provost) and suitable leading men to form a council, and drawing up a scheme of laws, customs and privileges, along the lines of other Scots burghs, which would be attractive enough to bring in enterprising traders and craftsmen from far and near. Quite early in Dundee's history we know of burgesses whose by-names show they came from places as far apart as Aberdeen, Bedford and Dunwich, a prosperous English seaport in Suffolk which has largely disappeared into the North Sea.

The burgh may not have needed a parish kirk immediately, since there seems to have been a kirk of St Mary, precursor of the later 'Old Steeple', which had probably served the Shire of Dundee long before the burgh began. But it may be that the substantial and apparently parochial kirk of St Clement, standing where the Town House was later built, was erected towards the end of the twelfth century specifically to serve as the burgh parish kirk, much as the Holy Rude Kirk was founded at Stirling or the kirk of St Giles provided for Edinburgh.

The last decade of the twelfth century must have been a busy time for the new burgh and its burgesses. There is evidence that this period, although characterised by fairly sharp monetary inflation, was one of prosperity and expansion, and Dundee was poised to share in the process. Doubtless through the good offices of their lord and patron, the 'burgesses of Earl David's Burgh of Dundee' received from King John of England, as early as 26 October 1199, the valuable privilege of being able to trade anywhere in the English king's dominions, except for the City of London, without having to pay the tolls and customs normally collected by the king's officials.

Dundee seems to have grown steadily during the thirteenth century and developed an outward-looking attitude which may have been helped by the fact that it was not, like Perth or Forfar, a centre for royal government and administration with a resident sheriff. In the earliest phase the burgh grieve or alderman was almost certainly appointed by Earl David – in fact, the first alderman might have been the Earl's clerk, Philip, who was sometimes called 'Philip of Dundee'. But in course of time the office of alderman would become elective, and the civic dignitaries – the alderman, bailies, 'liners' (inspectors of boundaries), the kirkmaster, the 'feryngman' or treasurer, ale- and wine-tasters, inspectors of meat, bread and other foodstuffs – would be chosen once a year by the whole community of burgesses. In this way, and probably very rapidly, during Earl David's later years (he died in 1219) Dundee would have developed that corporate and communal spirit of which there is undoubtedly evidence by the last quarter of the thirteenth century.

The Earl himself, possessing scores of manors scattered widely across the eastern midlands of England, must be seen as at least as much an English as a Scottish magnate, a position symbolised as it were by the fact that he died at Fotheringay, where his direct descendant, Mary Queen of Scots, was to meet her end three and a half centuries later. But Earl David obviously valued his burgh on the Firth of Tay, the largest trading town completely under his control, and must have spent a good deal of his

England. Here Hary sets the scene of the Scotland of Wallace's youth, a country in thrall to a powerful and brutal army of occupation.

Scotland was lost quhen he was bot a child
And *our-set* throuch with our ennemys   SUBJUGATED
wilde.
His fadyr Malcom in the Lennox fled.
His eldest sone thedyr he with hym led.
His modyr fled wyth hym fra *Elrisle*,   ELDERSLIE
Till Gowry past and duelt in Kilspynde.
The knycht hir fadyr thedyr he thaim sent
Till his wncle, that with full gud entent
In Gowry duelt and had gud *lewyng*   LIVING
thar,
Ane agyt man the quhilk *resawyt* thaim   RECEIVED
far.
In-till Dunde Wallace to scule thai send
Quhill he of *witt* full worthely was   UNTIL WISDOM
kend.
Thus he conteynde in-till his tendyr age,
In armys syne did mony *hie waslage*,   BRAVE DEEDS
Quhen Saxons blud in-to this Realm
couth ring   COULD REIGN
Wyrkand the will of Eduuard, that fals king.
Mony gret wrang thai wrocht in this Regioune;
Distroyed our lordys and brak thar
byggynys doun;   BUILDINGS

   .   .   .

Willzham Wallace or he was man of armys
Gret pitte thocht that Scotland tuk sic harmys.
Mekill dolour it did hym in his mynd,
For he was wys, rycht worthy, *wicht*   VALIANT
and kynd.
In Gowry duelt still with this worthy man.
As he encressyt and witt haboundyt than
In-till his hart he had full mekill cayr,
He saw the *Sothroun* multipliand   ENGLISH
mayr,
And to hym-self offt wald he *mak his*   LAMENT
mayne.
Off his gud *kyne* thai had slane mony   KIN
ane.
Zhit he was than *semly*, stark and   HANDSOME
bauld,
And he of age was bot xviii zer auld.

The strongly nationalist sentiments of the Wallace epic have inspired Scots down through the ages. Robert Burns confessed that it 'poured a Scottish prejudice in my veins which will boil along there till the flood-gates of life shut in eternal rest'. Dundee has always been staunchly Scottish, with waves of immigrants inheriting the identity of previous generations. The sense of awareness of and continuity with Dundee's history is revealed in the campaign of Edwin Scrymgeour against Winston Churchill in the 1922 General Election. He is aware of the effect of a dig against the Englishman on the sentiments of his Scots and Scots-Irish electorate, when his supporters chalk the city's pavements with the words: 'Wallace struck his first blow for liberty in Dundee, – let Scrymgeour strike his first blow for liberty on Wednesday.' Scrymgeour would also have been aware that it was Wallace, in 1298, who granted his family the hereditary office of Constable of Dundee.

Here is Hary's description of the violent incident on the streets of Dundee, when the son of the English captain of the castle, Selby, mocks the gear of the gallous teenager Wallace, and tries to put him in his place.

	Wpon a day to Dunde he was send.
	Off cruelnes full litill thai him kend.
CRUEL	The constable, a *felloun* man of wer,
	That to the Scottis he did full mekill der,
HE WAS CALLED	Selbye *he hecht*, dispitfull and owtrage.
	A sone he had ner xxᵗⁱ zer of age,
EVERY	In-to the toun he vsyt *euirilk* day.
	Thre men or four thar went with him to play,
ARROGANT	A *hely* schrew, wanton in his entent.
	Wallace he saw and towart him he went.
HANDSOME	*Likle* he was, rycht byge and weyle beseyne
CLOAK	In-till a *gyde* of gudly ganand greyne.
	He callyt on hym and said,
	'Thow Scot, abyde.
CLOTHES YOU	Quha dewill *the grathis* in so gay a gyde?
IRISH/HIGHLAND	Ane *Ersche* mantill it war thi kynd to wer,
WHITTLE	A Scottis *thewtill* undyr thi belt to ber,
RAW-HIDE SHOES	Rouch *rewlyngis* apon thi harlot fete.
WHY ARE YOU SO WELL TURNED OUT	Gyff me thi knyff. *Quhat dois thi ger so mete?*'
	Till him he zeid his knyff to take him fra.
	Fast by the collar Wallace couth him ta,
DREW	Wndyr his hand the knyff he *bradit* owt,
	For all his men that semblyt him about,
	Bot help him-selff he wyst of no remede.
STABBED	With-out reskew he *stekyt* him to dede.
	The squier fell, of him thar was na mar.
	His men folowid on Wallace wondir sar.
CROWD, HINDERED	The *pres* was thik and *cummirit* thaim full fast.
	Wallace was spedy and gretlye als agast,
	The bludy knyff bar drawin in his hand.
	He sparyt nane that he befor him fand.
UNCLE	He knew the hous his *eyme* had lugit In;
	Thedir he fled for owt he mycht nocht wyn.

time there. As late as the end of the fifteenth century there was a tenement or hall on the south side of the Mercatgait (the later High Street) known as 'Erle David Huntlintoune [sic] Haw' – surely an indication not only of where the Earl had built his Dundee lodgings but also of what a prominent and well-remembered feature of the burgh the building was. It would have been in this hall that David's granddaughter, Dervorguilla, Lady of Galloway, spent her time when visiting Dundee, where she is traditionally credited with founding the house of Franciscans, the Greyfriars.

For Earl David, greatly respected in his day and apparently genuinely popular – 'he was a very gentle knight', sang one of his contemporaries, 'no holy church or abbey was ever robbed by him' – failed to found his own dynasty. By his wife Maud, a daughter of the Earl of Chester, David sired a large family, but only one son, John of Scotland, and three daughters, Margaret, Isabel and Ada, grew to adulthood. John married a daughter of the Prince of North Wales, but they had no children, and when he died, in 1237, the vast estates he had inherited from his father were divided, in equal shares as required by feudal law, among his sisters. How the Burgh of Dundee was carved into three parts we do not know, but carved it was, with only the castle remaining undivided, as the honour reserved by custom, for the first-born daughter Margaret. This lady had married the powerful Lord of Galloway, and although there were several children of the marriage the whole inheritance eventually fell to the youngest daughter, to whom, interestingly, the Gaelic name Derbforgaill (Dervorguilla) had been given.

Dervorguilla was without any doubt one of the outstanding Scots of the thirteenth century, among whose achievements being mother of the wretched King John (Balliol) was one of the less noteworthy. Besides endowing the Dundee Greyfriars, Dervorguilla founded the beautiful abbey of Sweetheart near Dumfries in memory of her husband John Balliol the elder. She was possibly also the founder of the Dominican friary at Wigtown. Most famously of all, Dervorguilla, following up the intentions of her husband about twenty years after his death, founded the hall in the Broad Street of Oxford, for teachers and students, which was eventually to become Balliol College. In any hall of fame, physically or figuratively treasured by Dundonians to commemorate notable individuals connected with their city, the Lady Dervorguilla certainly deserves a prominent place.

Although Dervorguilla seems to have used Galloway resources for the endowment of Balliol Hall, rather than income generated by the trade of Dundee, there seems to have been some enthusiasm for higher education among the Dundee community in the thirteenth century. Between *c.* 1220 and the 1280s no fewer than seven men who used the surname 'of Dundee' appear on record as university graduates. At this period, of course, there were no universities in Scotland, and the place with which these Dundonian scholars seem to have been particularly associated was Bologna, one of the great European centres for the study and teaching of Roman Law. It must have been a long journey from Dundee to Bologna in those days. The young Scots hopefuls setting off to broaden their horizons and better their job prospects were obviously not short of self-confidence, but, what was perhaps more to the point, they must have had exchangeable money in their purses and also plenty of Latin, knocked into their heads at the Dundee Grammar School. This school would have been an adjunct of the parish kirk of St Mary, and when we first hear of it in record, about 1224, the abbey of Lindores in Fife (to which Earl David had given St Mary's in 1190) was specifically said to have the right of appointing the master.

One of the enterprising Dundonians trained at Bologna University was Ralph of Dundee, the son of a local burgess called Gregory Long whose house was in the Seagait. Ralph and his elder brother must have been exceptionally bright pupils since they both attended Bologna, all the more surprisingly perhaps, since each in turn was heir to his father's property in an age when the eldest son was not expected to go on to higher education. Ralph, having obtained his Master's degree, entered the service of King Alexander III as a senior clerk ('secretary' would be a closer modern equivalent), and began to acquire a substantial estate as a result of the King's generosity. Disregarding the fact that he had already been appointed to canonries in the cathedrals of Ross and Glasgow, Master Ralph was made a knight and married a lady who was evidently the heiress of the mid-Argyll lordship of Glassary – the district containing Lochgilphead and Dunadd. Thus began a seemingly improbable link between Dundee and the West Highlands. It was one which continued for many generations, for Ralph of Dundee's estates eventually came into possession of the family of Scrymgeour, associated with Dundee since the thirteenth century, and the Scrymgeours maintained the link for many generations. It seems hardly too far-fetched to compare this medieval episode with the acquisition of vast ranching lands in Texas by Dundee and the cattle companies in the mid-nineteenth century, a remarkably far-sighted piece of investment which came to an end only in recent times.

Although Ralph of Dundee was one of the very first to declare his support for Robert Bruce when he made his bid for the throne, he was not really a politician or even a soldier. More prominent in public affairs during the first War of Independence was Thomas of Dundee, no relation to Ralph but like him the son of a burgess and trained in law at Bologna. Master Thomas rose rapidly through the higher ranks of the Church and by 1296 (the year war with England broke out) he was elected Bishop of Ross. Thomas played his part in several major events of the

An outlaw, Wallace eventually escapes in disguise and begins his campaign to galvanise the Scots into winning back their land. After the fall of Dunkeld, Wallace delights in waiting for the right moment to remove the English and their quislings from wealthy Dundee, and bring it back under Scottish control.

Quhen at the Scottis semblit on athir sid
Na Sotheroun was that mycht thar *dynt*   BLOWS
    abid.
Twa thousand *some*, was *fulzied* vndyr   SOON, TRAMPLED
    feit,
Off Sotheroun blud lay stekit in the
    streit.
Schir Ihon Sewart saw weill the toun
    was *tynt*,   LOST
Tuk him to flycht and wald no langar
    stynt;   HALT
In a lycht barge and with him men sexte
The water doun socht succour at
    Dunde.
Wallace baid still *quhill* the ferd day at   UNTIL
    morn
And left nane thar that war off Ingland
    born.
Riches thai gat off gold and othir gud,
Plenyst the toun agayne with Scottish
    blud.

A tradition surviving from medieval Dundee: the Kirking of the Trades at St Andrews Parish Church. *Copyright D. C. Thomson & Co. Ltd*

23

c. 1330

Dundee is also singled out for mention in an English poem from the time of the Wars of Independence. Written in 1333, Laurence Minot crows over the Scots may have won at Bannockburn back in 1314, but at least the English had the satisfaction of destroying Dundee Castle before they fled:

RAW-HIDE SHOES	Rugh-fute *riveling*, now kindels thi care
DWELLING	Bere-bag, with thi boste, thi *biging* es bare;
	Fals wretch and forsworn, whider wiltou fare?
BRIDGE [OF PERTH?]	Busk the unto *brig*, and abide there:
LIVE	Thare wretche, saltou *won*, and wery the while;
DESTROYED	Thi dwelling in Dunde es *done* for thi gile.

c. 1385

The French historian Froissart described the destruction of the early churches thus: 'The English burned Dundee and spared neither monasteries nor churches, but put all to fire and flame.'

c. 1402

The rise of Dundee as a great trading port was hampered by the claims of the merchants of Perth. They appealed to royal authority to verify their right to handle all the traffic that entered the Tay. The regent, Robert Duke of Albany rejected their request in a strongly worded declaration:

	We pronounce, determine, and decretis, that the burch and burchesses of Dundie, and yair successoris, have freedom to by ony schip or schihpps yat come in the water of Tay on a
BREAK BULK AT THEIR HARBOUR	venture, yat lykes to *lois at yair heaven*, notagainstandand ony privileges aledgat befoir us in the contrair, throuch the procuratoris of the burch of Perth. Quhairfore, we put silence to yame of Perth, and to yair successoris for evirmair.

independence struggle, at first supporting King John but by 1308 at the latest, coming over to Bruce, whom he seems to have backed loyally till his death in 1325.

It is a great pity that in the turmoil and conflict after 1296 the burgh seems to have lost the archives which had evidently been accumulating for a hundred years. When, in 1237, the town was partitioned among the three sisters of John of Scotland, the two families which shared the inheritance with the Balliols were the Bruces of Annandale and the English Hastings, Lords of Abergavenny. We have practically no surviving record to show how the Bruce or Hastings lords treated their portions of the burgh, but both families undoubtedly maintained a presence in Dundee and would naturally look upon the town, with its markets and fairs, as an important source of income. On balance, perhaps, Dundee was a Balliol-orientated community, and gained appreciably by the accession of John Balliol the younger as King of Scots in 1292, becoming at that point – and thereafter remaining – a 'royal burgh'. When war came in 1296 the English put a garrison in the castle, but within a year William Wallace and Andrew Murray had recovered the castle for Scotland. It may have fallen into English hands again in the aftermath of Falkirk (1298), but was in danger of being lost again, from an English point of view, by 1300.

It looks as though the Balliol influence was strong enough to allow local lords who supported King John, such as Sir David Brechin and Sir William Muschet, Lord of Cargill, to recruit and maintain a castle garrison which held out till the spring of 1312 – the year in which Robert I captured Perth. Whether they effectively controlled the town is another matter. Dundee's trade with the Flemish and German cities seems in fact to have helped the Scots escape the worst effects of the English blockade. In 1310 an important assembly of Scottish clergy supporting Robert I actually met in Dundee, at the church of the Greyfriars, in The Howff (conveniently at some distance from the castle). This meeting surely points to some pro-Bruce party among the burgesses, which would not be at all surprising in view of the Bruce presence in Dundee.

The fact that Edward II wrote a letter in 1312 praising the people of Dundee for courageously resisting his enemies, the Scots, should not, perhaps, be taken too seriously, especially as it was addressed to the 'mayor and community', not to the grieves or alderman. (We know that in the fifteenth century the correct designation of Dundee was 'the Alderman (or Provost), Bailies, Burgesses, Councillors and community of the Burgh of Dundee'). Only a few years later, in 1325, the Scottish king was setting up a commission to enquire into the rightful liberties and customs of Dundee, which its people had enjoyed in the days of Alexander III of good memory or even in the time of King William the Lion. This certainly does not suggest that Robert I

REMEMBER MAN AS FIOW GOES BY
AS FIOW ART NOV SO ONS VAS I
AS I AM NOV SO SHALD FIOV BE
REMEMBER MAN FIAT FIOV MOST DIE
The memoriall of the iuft fhall be bleffed
but the name of the wicked fhall rote

bore any grudge against the Dundonians. In due course (1328) he issued a solemn charter for the burgh which confirmed to it many of the customs of Berwick-upon-Tweed, including the privilege of having a merchant guild.

A century ago, historians of Dundee remarked on the phenomenal rapidity of its growth during the Victorian era – no town in Scotland, not even Paisley, Coatbridge or Airdrie, had expanded faster in population and area at the height of the classic industrial revolution, thanks largely to the import of jute from Bengal and the processing of jute in the vast pink sandstone mills which for many generations seemed to form the quintessential Dundonian landscape. It may not be so widely appreciated that the expansion of Dundee between the 1190s and 1300 must also have been extraordinarily rapid. The simple nucleus of Seagait backed by Murraygait-Cowgait, along with the Mercatgait which in time became High Street, was extended eastward and northward, but more especially westward. Northward, the Wellgait developed a line which would in due course lead to 'Hilltown'. But westward the Mercatgait bifurcated, the southern branch forming Flukergait, alias St Marygait or Nethergait, and eventually becoming the high road to Perth by

The Howff – one of many inscribed stones of wealthy Dundee burgesses, in the cemetery where they once held their meetings. *McKean*

25

Gardyne's House, Gray's Close, High Street. The only example of a 16th-century town house still standing. The Makaris Gild deserve support for their restoration plans for it. *McKean from Lamb's Dundee*

The Tower of St Mary's in 1846. *McKean*

way of Invergowrie and Longforgan. The northerly branch must, during the very earliest years of the burgh, have formed a suburb of Gaelic-speaking settlers, non-burgesses, mostly from the Highlands, for it acquired the name of Argyllgait. As at St Andrews and Glasgow, where a district named 'Argyll' also formed a western suburb, so at Dundee the Argyllgait would have formed a pool of urban labour, casuals or journeymen, a few of whose members in each generation might aspire to become master craftsmen or merchants and thus qualify for the coveted burgess-ship. St Mary's would have been their church, not inappropriately if, as already suggested, this was the old church of Dundeeshire. Even further west, around the source of the Logie or Scouring Burn, was the distinct district of 'Logie-Dundee', now Lochee, which already had its own parish church in the twelfth century. The burgh was evidently proud of its two churches, for its finely-designed seal showed the Virgin and Child on one side and the 'sign of St Clement the Martyr' on the other.

The English capture of Berwick-upon-Tweed in 1333 (it was hardly ever in Scottish possession thereafter, save for a brief period in the reign of James III) led directly to the economic decline of that busy seaport, which had for a long time ranked as the largest and richest town in Scotland. There can be little doubt that Dundee was one of the Scottish burghs which benefited from Berwick's misfortunes. The fourteenth and especially the fifteenth century saw Dundee enjoy considerable prosperity and hence political importance. It tended to rank third among the royal burghs of Scotland, after Edinburgh and Aberdeen. In the twelfth and thirteenth centuries the 'Four Burghs of Scotland' had been Berwick, Roxburgh, Edinburgh and Stirling or Perth; in the late Middle Ages they were Edinburgh, Perth, Dundee and Aberdeen. Parliaments and great councils were held at Dundee, and it seems that although Forfar was the head burgh of the sheriffdom of Angus the sheriff court quite often convened at the Tolbooth of Dundee. It is easy to see how Dundee and its burgesses came to play such a crucially important role in the Protestant Reformation of the Scottish Church. Its merchants were in direct contact with the trading communities of Germany and the Low Countries, where Lutheran ideas spread and multiplied so rapidly. Its inhabitants were relatively prosperous, well schooled, well informed and outward-looking. They enjoyed a buoyant self-confidence which in many ways, and despite many ups and downs, has been characteristic of Dundee and Dundonians throughout their history.

c. 1530 - 60 THE WEDDERBURNS, A DUNDEE DYNASTY OF POETS AND MERCHANTS

The intellectual vigour of Dundee at the height of her power in the sixteenth century is testified in the lives of the three sons – James, John and Robert – of one of the town's leading merchants, James Wedderburn of West Kirk Stile. A contemporary of theirs, and fellow Reformer, Professor John Johnston described the three brothers and the city which produced them, in glowing terms:

Harmonious minds and most distinguished ornaments of your race! Three equal in learning and in piety. Happy your parents and the land which gave us pledges so rare! Begotten in heaven, distinguished Alectum bestowed you on the earth, from whence I reckon it to have the name DEI-DONUM.

The eldest brother, James was admitted as a Burgess of Dundee in 1517. Like Sir David Lyndsay, he used popular theatre to satirise the excesses of the Catholic Church. Calderwood, in his History of the Church, *writes that:*

James had a good gift of poesie, and made diverse comedies and tragedies in the Scottish tongue, wherein he nipped the abuses and superstition of the time. He composed in form of tragedy the beheading of John the Baptist, which was acted at the West Port of Dundee . . . wherein he carped roughly the abuses and corruptions of the papists. He compiled the *Historie of Dyonisius the Tyranne*, in form of a comedy, which was acted in the playfield of the said burgh, wherein he likewise nipped the papists.

Unfortunately none of the plays mentioned have survived.

James's satires were sharp enough to raise the ire of the authorities, for he had to flee Dundee for France. He died in Rouen around 1553. Calderwood asserts that he passed on the spirit of Reformation to his son. 'When deing, he said to his son, "We have been acting our part in the theatre: you are to succeed; see that you act your part faithfully." '

The two younger brothers, John and Robert, entered the Church. Calderwood describes John's subsequent career: Being summoned [in 1538] he departed to Almaine . . . [where] he heard Luther and Melancthon, and became very fervent and zealous. He translated many of Luther's dytements into Scottish metre, and the Psalms of David. He turned many bawdie songs and rhymes in godlie rhymes.'

The songs which make up the 'godlie rhymes' show a remarkably broad range of styles. The tone of this one is spiritual.

We *trow* in God allanerlie,	BELIEVE
Full of all micht and Maiestie,	
Maker of hevin and *eird* sa braid,	EARTH
Quhilk hes him self our Father maid:	
And we his sonnis ar in deid,	
He will us keip in all our neid,	
Baith saull and body to defend,	
That na mischance sall us offend;	
He takis *cure* baith day and nicht,	CARE
To save us throw his godly micht	
Fra Sathanis subteltie and *slicht*.	CUNNING

We trow in Jesus Christ his Sone,
God lyke in gloir, our Lord alone;
Quhilk, for his mercy and his grace,
Wald man be borne to make our peace,
Of Mary mother Virgin chaist
Consavit be the Haly Gaist.
And for our saik on crace did die,
Fra sin and hell to mak us fre:
And rais from deith, throw his Godheid,
Our Mediatour and our *remeid*,   REMEDY
Sall cum to Judge baith quick and deid.

We trow in God the Haly Spreit,
In all distres our comfort sweit.
We trow the Kirk Catholick be,
And faithfull Christin companie,
Throw all the warld with ane accord.
Remissioun of our sin we trow;
And this same flesche that levis now
Sall stand up at the latter day,
And *bruik* Eternall lyfe for ay.   ENJOY

But the motivation behind this extract is decidedly political.

With huntis up, with huntis up,
It is now perfite day,
Jesus, our King, is gane in hunting,
Quha lykis to speid thay may.

Ane cursit fox lay hid in rox
This lang and mony ane day,
Devoring scheip, quhill he micht creip,
Nane micht him schaip away.

It did him gude to laip the blude
Of young and tender lammis;
Nane culd he mis, for all was his,
The young anis with thair dammis.

The hunter is Christ, that huntis in haist,
The hundis ar Peter and Paull,
The Paip is the fox, Rome is the rox,
That rubbis us on the gall.

This final one was left out of later editions of the 'Ballates' and is purely and simply a love poem, beautifully written by Robert Wedderburn, for his lover Isobell Lovell. The rhetorical question at the end of the poem contains a note of sadness, given the author's inability to marry the lady in question, due to the dictates of his Church.

Welcum fortoun! welcum againe!
The day and hour I may weill blis,
Thow hes exilit all my paine,
Quhilk to my hart greit plesour is.

For I may say that few men may,
Seing of paine I am [re]drest,
I haif obtenit all my pay,
The lufe of hir that I lufe best.

I knaw nane sic as scho is one,
Sa trew, sa kynde, sa luiffandlie;
Quhat suld I do and scho war gone?
Allace? zit had I lever die.

To me scho is baith trew and kynde,
Worthie it war scho had the praise,
For na disdane in hir I find,
I pray to God I may hir pleis.

Quhen that I heir hir name exprest,
My hart for joy dois loup thairfoir,
Abufe all uther I lufe hir best
Unto I die: Quhat wald scho moir?

28

Robert Wedderburn is also attributed with writing one of the great prose works in Medieval Scots, The Complaynt of Scotland. *In it the author rails against the English for their duplicity in invading Scotland to help the work of Reformation, then turning on the inhabitants with their customary savagery. Here he reproaches the Scots collaborators.*

Sum of you remains in your awen housis on the Inglismen's assurance [but] as sune as the Inglismen dreymis that ye have failyet to them, then thai repute you for their mortal enemies far mair nor thai repute ony Scottisman that was nevyr assurit; and, quhen ye have fulfillit the Inglismen's desire and hes helpit to destroye your natyve cuntre, yet the Inglismen sall nevyr call you ane uthir word bot renangant Scottis . . . [Our enemies] are vigilant to conques you nocht alanerly be gryt multitude of men of weyr and ane grit number of schipis be sea burde, bot as weil be secret machinatione to blynd you be avereis, presenting to you gold, silvyr, and grit promessis of heretages to persuaid you to commit traison contrar your faith, honour, and common weil.

c. 1580 - 1630

It is to another Wedderburn, David, who was admitted a burgess in 1580, that we owe a debt of gratitude for detailed knowledge of the life of the Dundee merchant class at the end of the sixteenth and beginning of the seventeenth century. He kept exact records which were eventually published as Wedderburn's Compt Buik.

The following list of 'vyvours', the family consumed, gives an idea of the standard of living enjoyed, food and drink:

Aitmeill, quhyt, beir, pes, wines – Alicante and Muskadellis, Bordeaux, Rouen, Clarit, white wine – aquavitae, Inglis cider, salmond, *grissillies*, YOUNG SALMON herring – Lochbroom herring – hadokis, dry fish, pik, confections, sucher, *scortschillis* comforts, quhyt sucher candee, *murmblade*, feggis, aplis, wyld SWEETS MARMALADE meit when the Earl of Mar wes here, lamb, scheip.

The richness of the cloth imported, is another clue to the lifestyle of the wealthier burgesses. Silks from La Rochelle and Naples, coloured velvets, crêpe, French and fine English cloths, hats with rich lining and velvet trimming, gloves, taffeta from Naples, sewed plaids, white woollen cloth and fustian.

The quality of the furnishings in the Wedderburn house – Flemish plates, Dutch spoons, silver cups, gilt pictures from Dieppe – also testifty to David's success, while other items tell us about intimate family life: 'A lite camp bed with my faher's and motheris armes thairon, my craidill to Effie my dochter, aikin [oak] cheir, an aikin frez pres [cupboard] with schottles of aik'.

Although spending his life 'gaitherin' gear', he did not neglect intellectual pursuits, and the book is replete with accounts, like this one, of borrowing and lending books:

Lent James Balfour sone to Michell Balfour of Monquhany Metamorphosis Ovidii in Laten with the pictouris bund in ane swynis skyn of werry braw binding sumtyme apertening to Robert Wedderburn my uncle with ane uther buik of Inglis of Emblemis in meter for the space of ane moneth.

The fables of Aesop, Homer's Iliad, Virgil, Socrates, Knox, Chaucer and the chronicles of his fellow Dundonian Hector Boece – just some works mentioned from what must have amounted to a substantial library of books. The intellectual vigour of the Wedderburn family, and the stimulation of living in an international port with connections all over Europe, made David Wedderburn half Rennaissance-man, half businessman. These extracts from the Compt Buik *show the range of David's business activities – trading from the Baltic to the Bay of Biscay!*

Send with Robert Schorswod to *Flanderis* xxx auld half merk peces to by me half FLANDERS a last of Ingzeonis and the remains on Aplis and to schip the same in the Swallow with him self

Send with Johne Roger to *Lupky* half a last hering with four auld rosnoblis a prince LÜBECK dolour and the eastwart fraucht to be of my part of the Thomas extending to half a quarter to be warit on *Suadins* gad Iron and oismontis equaly bot gif thai may geit SWEDEN pece gude chaip to wair the money on pece and mark the sam with my awin mark and to schip the same with him self in the sam schip

Send in the Falcon to *Spane* with Walter Renkene auchten scoir fourten elnis SPAIN lyning to be pakit in a new salmond tre markit with my awin mark at bayth the heidis and the middis and to be sauld and the fre money to be warit

29

3 October 1597

Send with Johne Scrymgeour mercheand to Spane in the schip of St Andros quhair he Robert Jak and David Heres sellis in

Twentie four ellis and a half of ell bred small lyning clayth cost the eln xvj^s

Item sex ellis eln bred small lyning cost the eln 24^s

Item xxiiij ellis eln bred small lyning cost the eln xij^s

Item xxiij ellis eln bred smal lyning cost the eln x^s

Item xxiiij ellis eln bred smal lyning cost the eln xj^s

Item xij ellis small lyning cost the eln 7^s

Item xx ellis a half lyning cost the eln 6^s 8^d

Item xxij ellis a half lyning cost the eln v^s

Item xxiiij ellis Hardin cost the eln 3^s

All thir peces bleitschit and markit with this my mark DW and the number and the prices wryttin on ilk pece and ar 9 peces

Item send with him Ane pair of pistollattis cost me xij lib Giffin him commissione to sell the sam in Ingland or ony uther port he thinkis best to my proffit or to bartir the sam or excheynge the sam on fisches or stockinges and thairefter with the fre money gottin for thir fischis or schankis wair it on gude alagant wyn or the fynest wynes in rubberis or fyn Muskedallis as ye think best and lyk as ye by to your self mark this geir with my said mark and schip the sam with your self nocht ellis bot the lord preserve You

Gif it be not barterit or sauld to proffit rayther bring it hame

His Compt Buik *also surprises you with occasional gems like his description of Black Saturday, 25 February 1597, when there occurred the total eclipse of the sun.*

Upoun the xxv day of Februar being Settirday, the signe In pisces 1597 Quhilk wes accomptit the ecclips of the sone and cheynge of the mone Betuix ten and ellevin houris befor nwn that day darkness overschaddowit the face of the hail earth that nane mycht knaw ane uther perfytly on the calsayis nor yit micht nae persone within thair houssis haif any lycht but candill Quhilk contenewit the space of half ane houre And the peiple with gryt fair fled aff the calsayis to houssis mourning and lamenting and the crawis and corbeis and ravenois foullis fled to houssis to our steple and tolbuith and schip tappis maist merveulously affrayit Quhilk sycht wes maist terreble and fairfull to all people young and auld And nane persone levand culd declair they ever hard or saw the lyk thame selffis in ony tyme preceiding.

DUNDEE CLARET

It is obvious from Wedderburn's accounts that wine was an important cargo for Dundee merchants. As late as 1620, it was the second port of Scotland for wine after Leith, importing 50,000 gallons compared to Aberdeen's 20,000 gallons. This is Cailean Maclean's account of the city's wine trade from the book, Knee Deep in Claret.

The wine trade made its mark in Dundee at an early date, her fairs being visited during the thirteenth century by King Alexander's henchmen on wine-buying missions. The Exchequer Rolls for Scotland detail Dundee's involvement in this trade from then till the sixteenth century. There were regular transactions between merchants of the town and the Royal households, even to the extent of shipping wine from Dundee through Blackness port on the Forth for the king's use at Linlithgow palace. The monks of St Andrews, Arbroath and Restennet were also in receipt of their essential supplies of wine from Dundee, as were the residences of the Countess of Strathearn, the Earl of Strathmore and other local gentry.

Probably the town's earliest wine merchant was one Hugo de Leyis, brother of Thomas de Leyis, a merchant-burgess of Dundee, whose premises stood on the south side of the Fluckergait. He appears to have met with good fortune as a wine merchant for among other substantial contracts his was the task of supplying the garrison at Stirling Castle in 1361. Another of his coups was the acquisition in 1365 of a safe conduct pass from Edward III for himself and four companions, authorising travels through England on business. Some two centuries later Dundee could boast a veritable army of merchants who had some involvement in the wine trade. The Register of the Privy Council for 1607 lists a score of Dundonian merchants who had defaulted on payments due on wine to the aggregate tune of £1376.1.8d. Among the worst offenders were the merchants Gray (owing £250.7.0), Mudie (£199), Caird (£76) and Robert Jak (£47).

30

At any one time there were colossal quantities of wine cellared within the burgh. In 1559 when English troops were asked to help out against Mary of Guise and her French Forces, a total of 200 tuns was requisitioned in order to supply Scotland's temporary allies. By way of compensation the Dundee merchants received £34 Scots or £8.10 Sterling on every tun appropriated.

Dundee's early advances in the wine trade were largely a consequence of her strategic location on the Firth of Tay. The River Tay, its associated strath, together with Strathearn and Strathmore, made penetration of consignments of wine upstream and into the Highlands relatively easy. The river itself was navigable as far as Perth, and all the wine required by the 'Fair City' could be landed at her quays. There were occasions however, when navigation on the Tay was impossible, but this was not to frustrate the movements of wine upstream. The Chronicle of Perth records an intense frost in 1624 which iced over the river and suspended all traffic. Undaunted some Dundee merchants transferred their cargo of 21 puncheons of wine into 13 carts and made the journey to Perth over the ice.

Beyond Perth wine was transported overland, most probably in skins slung between horses. To the west Breadalbane was supplied by way of Strathearn. Here Estate Books for 1536 itemise the arrival of claret and white wine brought from Dundee. The quantities delivered are described in terms of unusual measures – 'Barrekins' and 'Rubbours' – possibly ones which pertained to overland carriage in skins. Another curiosity in Breadalbane records was the arrival of 'Ulet' wines, thought to mean wine transported in flasks stopped by a layer of oil rather than rags or corks. Northwards, to Blair Atholl, wine would have been brought by way of Strathtay. Anything transported beyond Blair into Badenoch would have followed the precursor of the A9. This route was described in Gordon of Rothiemay's *Noates and Observations* made about 1650.

'There is a way from the Yate of Blair in Atholl to Ruffen in Badenoch made by David Cumming, Earle of Atholl, for carts to pass with wyne, and the way is called Rad-na-Pheny, or way of wine wheills. It is laid with calsay is sundrie parts . . .'

Rad-na-Pheny, or in its more correct form, *Rathad na Fiona* (The Wine Road), built by David Comyn in the thirteenth century, adopted a route to the east of the present A9; through the Glaick Forest, issuing just to the south of Kingussie. This marked the northern-most extent of Dundee's sphere of influence in the early wine trade.

Wine was brought to Dundee in exchange for local produce. Wedderburn was prominent among the town's merchants at the beginning of the seventeenth century and his practice was to export cloth and other local goods from there, entrusting the master of the ship contracted to barter these for wine

Dundee from the river, 18th century. *Dundee District Libraries*

and other exotic produce. In 1597 a quantity of linen valued at £90 was dispatched by Wedderburn and in his instructions to the master of the ship, John Scrymgeour, he suggests that the cargo be exchanged for 'gude Alagant Wyn or the fynest wynes in rubberis or fyn Muskedallis as ye think best, and lyk as ye by to yourself'. From the city's shipping lists at the turn of the seventeenth century it is apparent that any shipment of wine for the port had already been earmarked for one merchant or another. When the 'Hope for Grace' arrived from Bordeaux in March 1618 her cargo of 40 tuns of wine was to be divided among 19 merchants. Their share of the cargo was proportionate to the value of the goods they contributed to the outward cargo.

A list of Wedderburn's 'vyvours' – food and drink for his family's use includes an interesting range of liquors. Among the wines mentioned were Alicante, Muskedallis, Rouen, claret and white wine, but for the average Dundonian such variety of choice was exceptional. More often than not only two sorts of wine were available and both were shipped from Bordeaux. In the shipping lists they are described as 'Town Wine' and 'land wine', Dundonians making the distinction between 'vins de ville' and 'Haut-Pays' wines which the authorities in Bordeaux were at pains to maintain. They would have been delighted to learn that their policy of discrimination against the wines of the high country was having effect in the place of consumption also. But all was not as the Bordelais intended – according to the respective quantities of wine imported, Dundonians displayed a clear preference for 'Haut Pays' growths.

The arrangements for importing wine into Dundee could operate smoothly provided there was no state interference. As it happens they were constantly being confused by the avarice of successive Scottish monarchs, to the intense fury of the merchants involved in the trade. Perhaps because the Town Council of Dundee had sent King David II a couple of bottles of vinegar on his deathbed, no doubt precipitating his demise, relations between Dundonians and Royalty, particularly over wine, were generally at a low ebb. Towards the close of the sixteenth century the latter had engineered a situation requiring that all wine arriving in the port should 'remain with the ship onsellarit for four days' to allow His Majesty's taster or 'symeler' (from the french *sommelier*) sufficient time to assess their quality and select ones which should be appropriated for the Royal Household. Queen Mary made frequent use of this right and by way of compensation to the merchants for their losses, she allowed them to sell the remaining wines in the cargo at prices higher than those fixed by the authorities. Not content with having the 'pick' of the vintages, Mary on several occasions exhorted the Dundee council to provide for her household needs free of charge.

Wine could only be sold within burghs but before it could be released onto the market its quality had to be assessed locally, a requirement which created what must have been the most sought-after post in medieval Scotland – the 'taster' or 'sampler'. In 1523 the burgh records of Dundee mention two such *gustatores vinii* – George Pollock and Andrew Barry. As with other tasters their job was to check that newly landed wine was fit for the market, and whatever the sixteenth century equivalent of 'job satisfaction' was, they surely had a fair share.

Old Close off East Side, Tendall's Wynd, 1908.
Dundee District Libraries

From Second City to Juteopolis

The Rise of Industrial Dundee

by CHRIS WHATLEY

In one sense Hugh MacDiarmid was right to describe Dundee in the early 1930s as a 'great industrial cul-de-sac' and 'grim monument to man's inhumanity to man'. He saw it too as the most appalling example in Scotland of the operation of unfettered market forces. Jute had turned Dundee into something unique in Scotland, a one-industry city. None of the other cities were so dependent upon one product; nowhere else was subjected to such acute competition, largely in the form of the low wages that were paid to Indian spinners and weavers – most of whom worked with machinery and skills which had originated in Dundee. Unemployment in the city was higher than the Scottish average – amongst jute workers it reached almost 50 per cent in 1931 – and from the boardrooms of the great textile firms whose many, and often redundant, chimneys punctuated the city's skyline, only gloomy prognoses emerged. One dejected chairman could not see 'a single ray of hope in the business outlook'. Recovery came late and only partially, aided by government orders for sandbags as the Second World War approached. Otherwise, the 'utter degradation' of Dundee between the wars was relieved only by marmalade-making, the town's single flourishing industry.

This depressed image of Dundee was still current in the 1970s and was confirmed by my first miserable visit, for a job interview, in 1979. I didn't get the job at the university which many people didn't even know existed, or instead thought of only as an off-shoot of St Andrews. Dundee, I had been persuaded, was a broken-backed place, scarred by derelict jute mills. As I shuffled dejectedly down the Nethergate on the way to the station it seemed worse that that – I had noticed the water-worn and flaking freestone which gives much of Dundee's older building stock a run-down appearance – and was relieved to be heading back to Glasgow and the west.

Images, though, often only have a toe-hold on the truth. Jute did have a profound impact on Dundee. But its golden age was extremely short-lived. Jute did not replace linen as the city's 'staple' cloth until the mid-1850s, and as early as 1872 the *Advertiser* was asking publicly if 'King Jute' could rule forever. Wars,

c. 1410

The standing and wealth of Dundee is testified in verse in the early fifteenth century, when the English poet John Hardyng composed a Scottish travelogue, apparently for the benefit of an invading English army. Some things never change!

> Passe eastwarde with your army daye by daye,
> From place to place with small cariage,
> For your navy shall you mete in the viage,
> At *Portincragge*, shorte waye from TAYPORT Dunde,
> With vitailes to refreshe your whole armye;
> Beside the stuffe and vitaill of that lande,
> Which ye shall fynde in the countre as ye go,
> And market made alwayes to your hande,
> Of all theyr vytayles, althoughe they bee your fo.
> Now from S. Jhons towne, the soothe to say is so,
> Xviii myles it is to the towne of Dundye,
> The pryncypall burgh, by northe the Scotyshe sea.

c. 1540

Jean de Beaugue did a similar job in the 1540s for the French and Catholic forces gearing themselves for the coming religious struggles.

> DUNDEE – Dundee is one of the finest towns in Scotland, is situated on the river Tay, and capable of being easily fortified.

View from the Law. Reeking lums abound.
Dundee Art Galleries and Museums

c. 1535
The Dane, Peder Swave touring Scotland in 1535 discovered the Dundee area hoaching with friendly snakes!

Near Dondie there is an abbey round which to a radius of six miles there is found an innumerable multitude of serpents of a perfectly innocuous character. When hurt or wounded, they do no harm; they have no stings.

and the uses to which jute could be put as linoleum backing and in carpeting, kept it going however, and its grip on the city's economy was only slowly released. Indeed, considerable ingenuity was used by some jute firms in order to combat overseas competition and find new and secure niches for jute, in building and as a material for building road surfaces. In 1951 the industry still employed something like one in five of Dundee's workers, compared to 40 per cent in 1911. Today, although four firms in Dundee still spin jute, only one, Taybank Weavers at Taybank Works, weaves jute cloth. Most of the others who have survived and continue in textiles, make and weave polypropylene instead.

Since the end of the Second World War Dundee has been rebuilding its economic base and recreating its identity, casting off the hackneyed label of 'Jute, Jam and Journalism', and declaring itself instead as the 'City of Discovery'. It has undergone this process of reconstruction before.

In medieval times Dundee had been one of Scotland's leading burghs. It participated in national parliaments from the time of David II, for example, a role which was reserved only for those

34

burghs whose voices were supported by large purses. Dundee, in fact, was one of the four wealthiest towns in Scotland in the fourteenth century. The considerable rebuilding, and extension, of St Mary's Church which took place in the fifteenth century reflects this; one of the 'outstanding parish churches in Scotland', it rivalled Arbroath Abbey and Glasgow Cathedral for length, while the tower as it now stands is the hightest which remains from the medieval period in Scotland.

The abilities of Dundee's merchants in exporting hides and fells had by the sixteenth century raised the town to second place, behind Edinburgh, in the country's economic league. It would be wrong, however, to imagine that Dundee was simply a trading town: a large part of its success in the later medieval period was due to the extent to which cloth, mainly woollen, but notably too 'lynnen' (linen), was manufactured in Dundee. The growth in imports of hemp and flax from the Baltic *c.* 1580-1618 underlines the strength of Dundee's early association with linen-textile production. Dundee flourished and supported various other trades, including shoemaking, tailoring, bonnetmaking and glovemaking. In all there were nine, incorporated into the Nine Trades in the mid-sixteenth century, to be joined in the following century by masons, wrights and slaters, who joined forces as the United Trades in 1741. Luxury goods, though, and those requiring the highest levels of craftsmanship, as well as commodities such as wine and salt, were usually made abroad, and imported. Dundee's skills were invariably of the solid, utilitarian sort.

Economic prosperity was accompanied by physical developments in the town. More stone buildings were erected, such as the three-storey town house of the Earls of Strathmartine, although timber continued to be used for most domestic residences. Considerable rebuilding of Dundee's harbour also took place, a new tolbooth was built in 1562 and a more prestigious town cross put up in 1586. On the outskirts of the town, after 1580, Dudhope Castle, the mansion fortress of the Scrymgeours, was completely renovated, just as the fortified castle at Claypotts was nearing completion.

There is of course another side to this. Although there was not yet any evidence of the water shortage which was to lead to the nineteenth century 'Water War', increasing industrial demand put additional pressure on Dundee's two streams, the Scouring Burn and Dens Burn. Inhabitants of backlands near the former claimed, in 1597, that the dyers and skinners were poisoning the water which they wanted for 'brewing, washing and preparing of meals'. Still essentially a country town, Dundee's inhabitants were frequently pestered by livestock wandering freely through streets and yards. Sewage, of animal as well as human origin, was also a major problem. Dirt and inadequate sanitation made periodic visitations of typhus and bubonic plague more likely,

Tendall's Wynd, a 16th-century merchant's house. *McKean from Lamb's Dundee*

The Weavers

In the *Chronicles of Scotland*, Hector Boece describes Dundee as 'the toun qhair we wer born, quhair mony virtews and lauborius pepill are at makyng of claith'. He also detailed the source of the local wool and praised its quality: '. . . the vale of Esk is sa quhit and small wool, that it hes na compair in Albion'. Textiles, then, were at the heart of the Dundee economy from a very early date. After 1450 colonies of Flemish people settled in Scotland, particularly in the eastern ports. They brought fine weaving skills, and helped the Scots manufacture their own cloth. As late as 1601, the Convention of Royal Burghs was still importing Flemish craftsmen, twelve in all, of whom three settled in Dundee: Claus Lossier, shearer; Cornelius Dermis, weaver; and Henry de Turk, spinner and weaver. The power of the burgesses and councillors – usually the same people in Scottish burghs – lay in their ability to exclude rivals from trading in the city. The protectionist instincts of Dundee burgesses were riled with the growth of the wool trade and bonnetmaking industry in the Hilltown – just over the city wall but under the jurisdiction of the Scrymgeour dynasty of constables at Dudhope Castle. They constantly broke the Dundee burgesses' restrictive practices, and undercut their prices.

The acts made anent unfreemen resorting to the town to be put in execution but favour, and in special on them that dwell in the Hill and Rotten Raw, quha, without all order, as if they were freemen, handle with staple guids, in greit defraud of the freemen of the burgh, that do their duty to the King's Majesty for their freedom. . . The neighbours and inhabitants yet sustenit grite skayth throw certain unfreemen keeping open buiths and lofts at all occasions, and selling wool in mirk houses with unknown wechts, to the grite defraud of the puir and simple; [which is] forder liberty nor is grantit to free burgesses, although it is specially providit by diverse constitutions of the burgh that nane of the said persons sall be permittit to sell but in open mercat.

The Incorporated Trades, which still meet today, were particularly anxious about the problem of 'unfreemen' – in other words not Dundonian burgesses – depriving their members of their monopoly in the 'Brabanar Craft'. The use of the term 'Brabanar' to refer to the weaver or 'wabster craft' is itself interesting – Brabant must have been the region of

the latter being encouraged by the large numbers of black rats which infested the town. When plague arrived, its effect could be devastating: such was the severity of a visitation in 1585 that the magistrates thought it wiser to meet in the open air of Magdalen Green. A grim reminder that death was never far away was the presence near the centre of the town of the over-crowded graveyard, St Clement's. In 1564 this was replaced by 'The Howff', located on the northern boundary of the medieval town on land, formerly belonging to Greyfriars, which had been granted specifically for the purpose of burying the dead by Mary Queen of Scots. In moving the graveyard from the midst of the community, Dundee was following best French practice, according to which 'na deid' were 'bureit within borrowis'.

Nevertheless, to some degree or other all towns experienced difficulties of the sort just described. None, however, was to suffer as Dundee appears to have done in the mid-seventeenth century. Even before this, things had begun to go wrong. Trade with France, which had been second only to the Baltic in importance as a trading partner, contracted from the 1620s. Of greater long-term significance, the balance of economic power in Scotland had begun to shift westwards, as the Atlantic routes opened up.

The principal disasters which struck Dundee, however, were in the first instance military rather than economic. In 1645 Dundee was attacked by Montrose's royalist army and 'fearfully defaced and disabled'. This was followed by a further outbreak of plague in 1648. The hammer blow came in 1651, however, during the Civil War, when General Monk's New Model Army took the town, and engaged in two weeks of looting and burning. Hundreds of Dundonians, perhaps as many as 2,000 in all (including prisoners), lost their lives, to the extent that in the eight months which followed, of 159 babies born, twenty-five of them were to posthumous fathers. The town acquired a sizeable body of English immigrants, soldiers who stayed behind and married local girls. This was no compensation though for the loss, according to the most extreme (and almost certainly exaggerated) accounts, of up to 200 of the town's ships, which were either taken or sunk. Whatever the actual number, Dundee's commercial arm was severely weakened.

Not surprisingly, Dundee in the second half of the seventeenth century appeared a pale shadow of its former self. As for the future, much depended upon what Dundee made of the parliamentary union of 1707. Directly, it provided no assistance, and for some it may even have made matters worse. In 1717, for example, Charles Gray, a combmaker who had fallen on hard times, petitioned the town council for the post of town jailer. He claimed that it was well known, that he had had a 'very good livelihood . . . till the Union of the two kingdomes . . . effectually broke my trade'. Woollen-cloth manufacturing, which had been struggling before 1707, was wiped out, while superior Irish and continental linens threatened to drive the poor quality Scottish product out of the market.

The Union could, however, be made to work in Scotland's favour and concessions from Westminster were obtained. Of the greatest importance to Dundee were the establishment of the Board of Trustees for Manufactures in 1727, and the introduction, in 1742, of bounties on coarse-linen exports. This of course was the sort of cloth which Dundee had long manufactured, and the stimuli provided by the Board, which was concerned to raise standards, together with the bounties, enabled Dundee merchants and manufacturers to swell their sales of low-value coarse cloth to the Plantations. As a result, by 1820, almost two-thirds of Scotland's coarse linen which met the standards of the Board, was coming from Angus towns, of which Dundee was far and away the most important. In 1791 over eight million yards of cloth, mainly linen, were sent out from the town.

Dundee's growing prosperity in the second half of the eighteenth century was not based wholly on the manufacture of linen cloth. In 1783, for instance, 3,000 people were employed in making linen thread, while in the 1790s cotton and woollen cloth, leather, rope, glass, sugar and snuff were also being made in Dundee. Shipping, too, was said to have 'wonderfully increased', while new thoroughfares such as Crichton Street and Castle Street were laid out and villas built for members of the town's buoyant merchant class, such as Provost Alexander Riddoch, whose house in the Nethergate still stands. Dundee in the eighteenth century was no cultural backwater. Nor were its leading citizens burdened with any sense of provincial inferiority: at a time when most other Scottish towns people were making do with their older semi-fortified tolbooths, William Adam, architect to several of Scotland's leading landed families, was called upon (in 1731) to design a grand new townhouse, later known as 'The Pillars', (it was pulled down in 1931 to make way for the new City Square); Neil Gow, the fiddler, was hired by the town council to play at the town's celebration of King George III's coronation; and in spite of the Jacobite leanings of some of the town's élite, throughout the century, in common with many of their counterparts in the other Scottish burghs, the provost and magistrates orchestrated support for the British monarchy through their public celebration of the king's birthday and other royal anniversaries of note, and ordered the ringing of bells and hoisting of flags whenever news arrived of British military or naval successes abroad.

Dundee in the first decades of the nineteenth century still retained many of its medieval features and seemed set to become a prosperous and modestly fashionable Scottish town; the 1825 Improvement Act, for instance, presaged the laying out of Reform Street in 1832, 'the finest neo-classical street to survive

Flanders from which the Dundee Flemish weavers originated. The Scottish surname Bremner apparently comes from the same source.

Becaus of the frequent resorting of wnfrie craftismen of the said vocatioun of Brabanar Craft daylie to the said Hill of Dundee, fra all quarteris about, and without ony licence or tollerance of the said deacon and frie craftismen of the said bruch, vsurpis the libertie and priuilege of the said craft be werking of sindrie wobis of wollin and lynnin to sindrie nichtbouris of the said bruch to the grit preiudice of baith the saidis pairteis.

To add insult to injury, the medieval equivalent of the 'Hulltoon Hunz' frequently ran riot in the city centre as testified by a further entry in the burgh records:

It was ordanit for remeid of the insolent puir youth that hes na uther craft but to steal hedder and to cast stanes, and that fechts and perturbs the burgh mony ways, the maist pairt of them nocht native, but born and coming furth of the Hill and uther landwart places, that the Bailies tak order with the said boys, and that nane of them be sufferit to bear fish in the mercat but they that hes the town's takin and are of age betwix the years of seven and eleven; and quhat boy beis fund braking this act sall be skurgit through the burgh and banishit for ever.

TOKEN/BADGE

By 1600, however, it appears that a compromise was made between the two parties, the beginning of unity between Dundee and the Hilltown.

IMPRIMIS by Contract of the date the eighteen day of Marche the year of God ane thousand and six hundreth yeares it is appointed and agreed betwixt William Crawoord (then deacon of the Brabiners or Weavers of the Toune of Dundee), and the brethren Craftsemen vnder sub-scryband thereintill, on the one part, and the Brabiners residenters in the Hill of Dundee on the other part: It is first there statute and ordained, that the saids Brabiners (or Weavers) of the Hill of Dundee shall be apprentises to the Weavers freemen of the toune of Dundee for all the tyme and space of five yeares immediatelie following the date of the said Contract. 2dlie And by that same Contract these of the Brabiner or Weaver Trade in the Hill of Dundee submittis themselves by solemn oath to the status, ordinances, and lawes that shall happine to be made (in tyme comeing) for the good and benefite of the said craft of Weavers, as hes been made statute and ordained be the masters and freemen of the saids Craft their predecessours. 3^{dlie} And by the above mentioned Contract the saids Brabiners (or Weavers) of the Hill of Dundee are solemnelie engaged and sworne after the expiring of the said five years of apprentiship, to enter themselves free to the toune and craft if they be apt and able.

in Dundee'; and there was the construction in 1834 of the High School, the style of which reflects the contemporary interest in Greek architecture.

During the 1820s, however, a process of dramatic transformation began to take place. Indeed, signs of what was to come had been noted earlier, in 1799, when 'Philetas' in the *Dundee Magazine* had remarked that 'Vice, manufactures and population' seemed to have 'kept a steady jog trot together'. Flax-spinning mills had first appeared in Dundee in 1793, in Chapelshade and Guthrie Street. But the owners of these and other early mills – which had sometimes been powered by the labour of blind men – had had little lasting success. In 1821-2, however, ten new mills were built and by 1834 another fourteen had begun to turn out yarn. Amongst these were A. & D. Edward's 'Coffin' Mill and Baxter's second Dens Mill (the first

Jute merchants, the Jute shelter, c. 1900. *Dundee Art Galleries and Museums*

had been constructed in 1806-7). In 1836 Robert Brough and William Halley completed Wallace Craigie Mill or Works, which is still in use today. With the erection and extension of so many mills, Dundee's hold on the Scottish linen-trade strengthened, with imports of flax to the town rising twenty-fold between 1815 and 1845. It was during this period that troops which had formerly been garrisoned in Perth, were, on the orders of the Secretary of State, transferred to Dundee, on the grounds that they were more likely to be called upon by Dundee's civil authorities which faced the problem of controlling the 'large Manufacturing Population' which was congregating in the town.

Although the industry's growth was periodically checked by slumps, world demand for coarse cloth rose rapidly during the nineteenth century: sailing ships required vast quantities of canvas (Baxter Bros' speciality), tents and tarpaulins were needed – as the American west and Australian gold-mines were opened up, for instance; and as world trade expanded so too did demand for bags and sacking for grain, wool, fertilisers and other bulk commodities.

Linen cloth could be used for all of these purposes. For some of them though, bagging for example, there were alternative, cheaper, raw materials to flax. One was hemp, but even less costly was jute, a much tougher and coarser plant. In the latter 1830s, a ton of machine-spun jute could be bought for as little as £12, whereas the flax equivalent could cost as much as £54. At first, partly for technical reasons, mill spinners showed little interest in jute. However competition, fears about the vulnerability of supplies of Russian flax, and the removal in 1832 of the government bounty on coarse-linen exports, combined to persuade some of them to experiment with jute. An additional factor in favour of jute spinning in Dundee was that the local whale fishery could supply the oil which was required to soften the jute fibres. Ironically, this early advantage was identified in the twentieth century as being positively harmful to Dundee's jute industry, for although many spinners had turned to mineral oil before the end of the Victorian era, in the 1920s complaints were still being received from the United States and Canada about the 'peculiar odour' of Dundee goods, as opposed to the 'sweet and pleasant smell' of Calcutta jute.

The outbreak of the Crimean War in 1854 confirmed the ascendancy of jute in Dundee as demand for gun and wagon covers, nosebags and sandbags, escalated. Depression followed, but further expansion in jute occured during and after the American Civil War, when Lancashire and Glasgow found their supplies of raw cotton cut off. Between 1864 and 1868 several new mills and factories were added in Dundee, and older works extended, some of them gaining extravagant adornments in the form of classical pediments or Italianate bell towers, as at Don

c. 1544 - 55 Years of religious turmoil and plague.

The great Reformer George Wishart had close associations with Dundee and a great affinity for the city. This is from Maxwell's *Old Dundee*:

In 1544 and the following year the plague, that ghastly terror of the Middle Ages, visited Scotland with much severity. A writer in August of the latter year says, 'In this tyme the pest was wonder greit in all borrowstowns of this realm, whair mony peipil deit, with greit skant and want of victuals.' Dundee was stricken early with the malady, and the infliction was very heavy. Knox tells us that when word reached Wishart 'that the plague of pestilence began four days after that he was inhibited preaching, and was so vehement that it past almost credibility to hear how many departed every four-and-twenty hours,' he 'took his leave of Kyle, and that with the regret of many; his reason was, "They are now in trouble and need comfort; perchance this hand of God will make them now to magnify and reverence that word which before, for the fear of men, they set at light price." Coming unto Dundee . . . he delayed no time, but even upon the morrow gave signification that he would preach; and, because the most part were either sick or else were in company with those that were sick, he chused the head of the East Port of the town for his preaching place; and so the whole stood or sat within, the sick and suspected without the port or gate. The text upon the day which his first sermon was made, he took from the Hundred and Seventh Psalm. "He sent his word and healed them," and therewith joined these words, "It is neither herb nor plaister, O Lord, but thy word healeth all;"' and he spoke so earnestly and eloquently thereon that 'he raised up the hearts of all that heard him.'

The sumptuous interior of Dunalistair, a Broughty Ferry Mansion. *Private collection*

Bros, Buist and Co.'s Ward Mills. Standing head and shoulders above them all was Cox's 282-foot (86-metre) campanile chimney, which, though functional, also proudly declared that Camperdown Works was the largest jute enterprise in the world. The Franco-Prussian War brought further prosperity in the early 1870s. These were heady days for Dundee's close-knit fraternity of linen and jute barons such as Baxter Bros, Cox Bros, the Grimonds and Gilroys. Unprecedentedly high profits (levels of which were not as high again until the First World War) were used to construct palatial mansions on the outskirts of the town, in West Ferry and Broughty Ferry, and to purchase country estates further afield. Remarkably little, however, was re-invested in Dundee outside of textiles: instead Dundee capital found its way to England and places further afield, such as South and North America, where it was invested in land, cattle ranching and railways.

The immense wealth of the few was in sharp contrast to the poor conditions of the great mass of the people. More than any other Scottish burgh of its size, Dundee was a working-class town, with only 12 per cent of its resident families living in houses of four or more rooms at the end of the nineteenth century. The fact is that the jute capital of the world was also the home of some of the most impoverished urban workers in Britain. The appalling social consequences of rapid industrial growth which was not accompanied by a proportionate increase in the provision of sanitation and housing was observed as early as 1841 – by the Reverend G. Lewis, who on a journey to the textile towns of Bolton and Manchester, the horrors of which had fuelled Engels's outrage, had 'looked in vain' for evidence of 'deeper physical degradation' than he had met daily in Dundee.

For Dundee's population had been rising and continued to rise rapidly – expanding six-fold in the hundred years to 1901. Dundee's success in textiles was largely dependent upon waves of immigrant labour, mainly drawn at first from the surrounding counties but in the 1840s particularly from Ireland. In 1851, over half of Dundee's resident population had been born elsewhere, more than one-third in rural Irish counties such as Cavan, Monaghan and Fermanagh. Owing to the labour requirements of the textile industry, more than half of the immigrants were females; Dundee was overwhelmingly a 'woman's town', in which, in 1901, a remarkable 54 per cent of females over the age of fifteen worked for a living. An unusually high proportion of Dundee's married women (who were most frequently the wives of unskilled, male, jute workers) went out to work, usually in preparing or spinning, which were considered to be less prestigious tasks than weaving. Adult males in the industry tended either to be in the better-paid, more 'skilled' or super-visory positions, but most males who worked in jute were young,

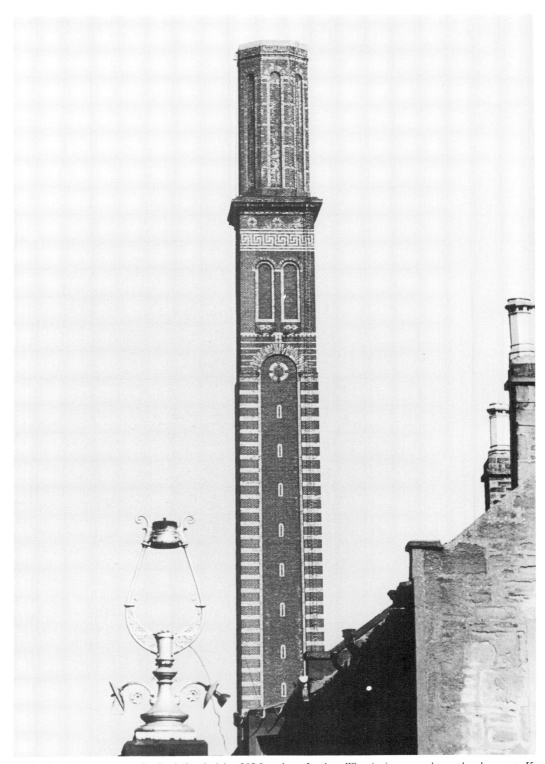

The definitive Jute Barons totem pole, Cox's Stack rising 282 feet above Lochee. The site is now under re-development. *Ken Sharp*

Fish Street. *Dundee District Libraries*

with some 800 of them being 'turned adrift' every year once they reached adulthood, when they would have had to have been paid adult wages.

Low wages and the consequent inability of most textile workers to afford high rents, provided little inspiration for private, speculative house builders. The result was a chronic housing shortage and overcrowding. Between 1841 and 1861 Dundee's population expanded by 30,000; at the same time only 568 additional houses were built. In 1901 a massive 72 per cent of Dundee's population occupied either one- or two-roomed houses. The high cost of living in Dundee and periodic bouts of unemployment added to the city's social problems, one of which was an unenviably high rate of infant mortality. Those who survived the early years of life could fairly readily be identified as Dundonians, at least if they were mill workers, as they were smaller and lighter than average. Premature ageing and scars resulting from accidents at work also marked off the female preparers and spinners from the rest. Dundee's female mill and factory workers worked and played hard, and both within the workplace and on the streets made their presence felt through a robust culture, rich in wry, earthy humour and song, which was totally devoid of deference towards men, be they masters,

overseers, trade-union officials or their own menfolk. Although Dundee had its share of music halls and theatres, and later, numerous cinemas and dance halls, in the heyday of jute, the most popular forms of entertainment in the city were of the informal sort – and cheap – with 'promenading' and 'haein a gossip' the most popular.

Dundonians did, however, work at things other than linen and jute – although the fortunes of most of these other occupations did tend to depend on what was happening in the textile trade. Shipbuilding and engineering were the biggest employers of male labour outside textiles, and generally speaking, paid considerably higher wages. By 1914 though, only one yard in Dundee, the Caledon, was still building ships. It continued to do so until fairly recently. Indeed in the early 1950s the shipbuilding industry in Dundee was second only to Glasgow – although admittedly in terms of tonnage launched it was a long way behind. The Caledon remained open throughout the 1950s and in 1963 and 1964 was busy making box girders for the Tay Road Bridge. Earlier, Dundee had earned a considerable reputation as a whaling port, the biggest in Britain in 1872. Yet the city's lead was short-lived and, paradoxically, the launch of the *Terra Nova*, Dundee's best known whaler, was also the last. In

The innovative Logie Housing Scheme, from the Law

43

The Hilltown, c. 1950

1911 only seven whales were brought back to Dundee, compared with forty-eight in 1881.

Confirmation that the glorious years of jute were over came in the inter-war period, and by the time of the outbreak of the Second World War the numbers employed had fallen by 10,000, to less than 25,000. Even with rearmament and government orders for sandbags, the unemployment rate in Dundee remained well above the Scottish average.

Yet although the period as a whole was a bleak one for Dundee, a process of slow metamorphosis had begun. A handful of young professors at University College, Dundee, founded in 1881, had been shocked into action by the severity of the poverty they saw around them. Reports such as that on industrial and housing conditions in the city, published in 1905 by the Dundee Social Union, brought home to contemporaries something of the nature and severity of the problems which Dundee faced. Plans for the future began to be laid, notably with the work of James Thomson, City Engineer from 1906, and between 1922 and 1924 City Architect and Director of Housing. In 1910 and 1918 Thomson, the 'most underrated figure in the history of Scottish town planning', produced visionary schemes for the

View of town and Second Railway Bridge.
Dundee Art Galleries and Museums

45

redevelopment of Dundee, many of which have now come to fruition. Thomson himself designed the Caird Hall, and pushed through the construction of the Kingsway at a time when motor traffic was in its infancy. The establishment of a municipal house-building programme was central to his plans, and Dundee's Logie council-housing scheme, with central heating and a tree-lined central avenue, was the first – and one of the finest – in Scotland.

Overcrowding, especially in the central parts of the city, was by no means eliminated by 1939. Yet pointers for the future had been laid. After the war, some new industries which had been sited in Dundee during the conflict remained. Others, such as NCR, followed. The jute industry embarked on a process of reorganisation, modernisation and diversification. Poly-propylene extrusion may not have the same ring to it as jute spin-ning but, from the mid-1960s this man-made fibre has been the successor to jute, and Dundee firms currently supply some two-thirds of UK output. That companies whose roots go back deep into Dundee's industrial history – Low & Bonar, Don & Low, and William Halley & Sons, for instance – have survived the demise of jute, and flourished with a new product range, is no mean achievement.

Although several of the mills and factories have been demolished, many remain, but now as light-engineering works, furniture factories, kitchen and bathroom showrooms, pubs, snooker halls and even homes – an ironic twist, given that the linen and jute barons who put up the buildings in the first place rarely provided housing for those who worked inside them. Dundee's past is no longer a burden but can be an attribute. The refurbished mills and warehouses act as a mortar-and-stone reminder to Dundonians that despite the cycle of exploitation and poverty in which they were formerly locked, it was their predecessors who provided the muscle power, sweat and tears upon which the city's worldwide reputation in textiles was built. They stand as clear proof that Dundee is experiencing a metamorphosis. Those mills which have been converted for use by small businesses, in the Blackness Business Development Area for example, are at the heart of this process. Unpretentious and dignified, yet adaptable, uncannily, they somehow reflect the character of the city's people. Dundee is to have an industrial museum but unless somehow its creators, uniquely, manage to present a past which is not sanitised, romanticised and trite, it is as well that the mills should remain, functional and living. They are a much more evocative and apposite symbol of the people's past than any purposely crafted monument, rich in allegory, but except to those in the know, without meaning.

Twenty-four hours after leaving Dundee that first time, I *was* offered the job at Dundee University. The successful cand-idate had been unwilling to leave one of the country's 'ancient'

institutions to come and live and work in Dundee. He probably never got behind the image.

I did and have discovered a vibrant city and in the large chunks of its as yet unwritten history, a lifetime's work. The main features of 'Juteopolis', for example, have been frequently described and interpreted. The reasons why Dundee should have developed as it did, however, have not been seriously explored: 'The Making of Juteopolis' still awaits its author. Of course, it is in the nature of his work, that the historian largely learns of these things through periodic visits to the city's archives in City Square, and the Local History room in the Wellgate Library. Yet acquaintance with the work of the Dundee Oral History Project introduced me to a people whose dry, biting humour told of a hard spirit in adversity not to be found in the documents, and which MacDiarmid may have missed.

There was something else about Dundee though: for the best part of two decades I had stood on the slopes of Firhill Park in Glasgow and watched Partick Thistle's post-1971 slide into First Division obscurity. After a time in Dundee (and having done my duty to Thistle by turning up to see them at grounds such as Glebe Park, Brechin), I discovered Tannadice and Dundee United, Cup finals, European football – and hope founded on more than yesterday's dreams. It's great, and long may it continue. I'm staying anyway.

Stobswell: Wallace and Burns and boys in United colours . . . from scenes like these!
Ken Sharp

Historic Accounts

c. 1644 - 45

The civil and religious wars which swept over Scotland, England and Ireland had disastrous consequences for Dundee. With its strong Presbyterian tradition, its stance against the royalist forces of Montrose brought this rebuke from the great General's biographer: '[Dundee] is a most seditious place, which was a faithful receptacle to the rebels in these parts, [and had] contributed as much as any other town in the kingdom to carry on the rebellion.'

This was used as an excuse for the attack which followed when the defending soldiers had departed.

[Montrose, by ten o'clock] in the morning summoned the townsmen, if they consulted their own safety and that of the town, to surrender; but, if they refused, he threatened them with fire and sword. They spent some time without returning any answer, and at last they put the trumpeter in prison. Montrose, highly provoked with this affront, stormed the town in three different quarters at once. The townsmen endeavoured for some time to oppose them; but the Irishmen and the Highlanders made their assault with such fury, that they quickly drove them from their stations, and, making themselves masters of their cannon, turned them against the town. At the same time some of them broke open the gates, and took possession of the church and the market place, while others set the town on fire in several places; and had not the common men, by an unseasonable greed of plunder and desire of strong liquors, immediately fallen to pillage and drink, this opulent town had undoubtedly been soon burned to the ground.

c. 1651

The attack by Montrose was a precursor and warning of an attack in 1651 by the English Cromwellian forces under General Monk. Sir Robert Sibbald, who was a child residing in the Murraygait at the time, wrote an eye-witness account of the siege.

In the time the Englishes were storming the town there was a battery erected by them from which they fired a canon and muskets into the High Street from the Banet-raw opposite to the Morrow-gate. The townsmen had putt up a sconce of dealls in the middle of the street. My sister Geals, a child then of eight years of age had passed somewhat higher than the sconce, and was exposed to their view. I ran after her to bring her back, and they fyred at us in the returning; the ball missed us, and battered upon the street. I took it up and brought it with me.

Sibbald's family was one of the few fortunate ones, for excepting the massacre of Drogheda in Ireland, there was no more brutal event in Cromwell's history of violence. Monk's attack devastated Dundee. Here is one account of the work of his forces once they had breached the walls on that fateful day.

He commandit all of quhatsumever sex to be put to the edge of the sword . . . there were eight hundred inhabitants and soldiers killed, besides about two hundred women and children. . . the Governor was cruelly killed after quarter was given to him.

Apparently many took refuge in St Mary's Tower, and defended it well. Fire was used to drive them out, the defenders . . . 'smothered out by the burning of wet straw and then they yielded on mercy to one Captain Kelly.' One of the historians of old Dundee, writing in 1891, describes the fate of those who sought mercy.

About seventy years ago, when the houses on the south of the church grounds were removed, many bones were found beside them. At the restoration of the tower, when the scaffold poles were being placed, the skeletons were lying so closely at its base and had such little covering of earth, that it was necessary to remove some of them before the ends of the timbers could be rested. And recently, several heaps of bones were found under the floor of the Steeple Church, behind the site of the old Music School. As the place was never used as a burial ground, we may conclude that all these are relics of Monk's bloody work.

When all had submitted, the plundering began.

It is reported by credible men that the English army had gotten above twa hundred thousand pounds sterling, partly in ready gold, silver and silver wark, jewels, rings, merchandise and merchant wares,

Detail from Edward's map of Angus, late 17th century. *University of Dundee*

and other precious things belonging to the town of Edinburgh, by and beside all that belonged to the town, and other people of the country, wha had sent in their guids for safety to that town. The plunder and buttie they gatt exceeded twa millions and a halffe . . . The soldiers had a very rich booty in this garrison, for it was at this time the richest town in Scotland, and there were sixty sail of ships in the harbour . . .

It was said that every soldier in Monk's army got booty to the value of £50 sterling for his day's work. Monk's biographer, Dr Gumble, confirms the wealth seized, but his conscience perhaps dictates his pleasure at the fate of some of the treasure.

The soldiers plundered the town of all its former and newly deposited wealth, which amounted to vast sums, nothing but plate and money was regarded . . . But see the just judgement of God, most of the wealth being shipped to be transported upon several vessels that were taken in the harbour – there being sixty of all sorts taken – the ships were cast away in sight of the town, and that great wealth perished without any extraordinary storm. Although the laws of war may approve of those outrages and plunderings, yet divine justice does not at all allow, but rather chastise them. Ill got, soon lost.

Richard Franck, who was with the English troops in 1651, revisited the town on more peaceful business in 1656, on an angling tour. His somewhat grandiloquent dialogue records his memory of the events.

Arn. Now our next advance is to the town of Dundee: but give me leave to call it deploarable Dundee, and not to be exprest without a deluge of tears; because storm'd and spoil'd by the rash precipitancy of mercenaries, whose rapinous hands put a fatal period to her stately imbellishments, with the loss of many innocent lives, altogether unconcern'd in that unnatural controversy.

Ah, poor Dundee! torn up by the roots; and thy natives and inhabitants pick'd out at the port-holes. Can honour shine in such bloody sacrifices, to lick up the lives of inhabitants, as if by a studied revenge? Can nothing sweeten the conquerour's sword, but the reeking blood of orphans and

49

innocents? Blush, O heavens, what an age is this! There was wealth enough to answer their ambitions, and probably that as soon as any thing betrayed her. Could nothing satisfy the unsatiable sword, but the life of Dundee to atone as a sacrifice? English men without mercy, are like Christians without Christianity; no moderation nor pity left, but parcelling out the lives of poor penitents in cold blood? Who must answer for this at the bar of heaven, before the judge of all the world? But he that doom'd Dundee to die, is dead himself, and doom'd e're this; and Dundee yet living to survive his cruelty.

Theoph. Is this Dundee! Disconsolate Dundee, where the merciless conquerour stuck down his standard in streams of blood?

Arn. Yes, this is that unfortunate and deplorable Dundee, whose laurels were stript from the brow of her senators, to adorn the conquering tyrant's head. Here it was that every arbour flourished with a fruitful vine; and here every border was beautified with fragrant flowers.

Thomas Tucker was also with the Cromwellian forces, and returned in 1655 to give a detailed report on Scottish ports for the English excise. He had less of a conscience than Franck.

The port of Dundee comes next in view, which is a pretty considerable place, lyeing by the mouth of the river Tay, which, springing out of the mountaynes of Albany, and running through the feilds, at length spreads itself into a lough full of islands, and afterwards contracting itself, taketh in Amund, [a river of Athol] passeth on to Dunkell, and thence by Scoone maketh its way into the German Ocean. The towne of Dundee was sometime a towne of riches and trade, but the many rencontres it hath mett with all in the time of domestick comotions, and her obstinacy and pride of late yeares rendring her a prey to the soldier, have much shaken and abated her former grandeur; and notwithstanding all, shee remaynes still, though not glorious, yett not contemptible.

With such an emotive subject as massacre and sacking, accounts of the events are inevitably coloured by personal feelings, and exaggerated or minimised accordingly. What is certain is that Dundee suffered terribly and if it did ever recover, it certainly took many decades. In many ways, Dundee as Scotland's second city, died at the hands of Monk. Dr William Guild, a contemporary minister summed up the feelings of many when he prayed thus for the revival of Dundee: 'give it beautie for ashes and the oyle of joy for mourning'.

The siege of St Mary's. *Dundee Art Galleries and Museums*

'Dae it wi yer Buits Oan!'

Dundee Doctors

by J. S. G. BLAIR

Dundee for me as a boy was the big town across the water I saw in every kind of weather as I travelled to school there along the south of the Tay on the Tayport train. It was the town where later I studied Clinical Medicine while at St Andrews University in those times of sharing, and later still trained as a young surgeon at Maryfield and Dundee Royal Infirmary. Then, I really began to know Dundee. But it was not until I joined that fine body of men, the Dundee Field Ambulance (the only Territorial Army Medical Unit in the land to have the honour of legally wearing the Tam O'Shanter – usually reserved for the Highland Regiments alone), that I got to know Dundonians so well that I can talk their language and share their deepest feelings. Their friendship is true, sincere, and lasting. So while I now know Dundee as the big city down the river from that other older historic city of Perth, where I have lived and worked hard for a quarter of a century, the affection for these wonderful friends remains. The folk who came to the casualty of Maryfield Hospital, the women who had their babies there, the doctors who 'sent them in' and who understood them, my good friends in the Field Ambulance, were all part of a long tradition of characters you would meet in Dundee and nowhere else.

If we go back to the earliest accounts of Dundee doctors we find that they were characters too. The first recorded was Robert Jonson, barbour, in 1495. Soon after, in the sixteenth century, came Will Fowlair, Will Gray, James Man, Robert Pypar, Patrick Walker and John Kinloch. They were described as barbour, surgeon, or surgeon-barbour. They were often at odds with their fellows – in 1521, for example, James Man was in trouble with the bailies for a breach of the peace after a quarrel with Jhone Butte. He appeared before them soon after for refusing to take up the collection in church!

Robert Pypar's name appears from the date when he was admitted a burgess 'as barbitonsor', 1527, till 1589 when he was succeeded in his practice by his grandson. He had a surgery in the High Street under the old Tolbooth and was important enough to have a close named after him: 'Wm Shippert's Close' at the west end of the High Street was renamed 'Robert Pypar's Close'. His activities feature in the town records – collecting bills, supplying drugs to James Caraill, Surgeon, pursuing Thomas Fetty over '15 doz. of bedes of sybowis for 11s. the

THE TOUN COUNCIL
c. 1550 - 1600 A Steiran Toun

Insights into street life in what was undoubtedly a thrang, steiran, city are given in Dundee's extensive burgh records.

Councillors, then, as now were honest douce guidmen. [Nae guidwifes wes councillors lang syne. Ed.] To make sure their deliberations were completely above board, they were sworn to an oath of secrecy.

> . . . the haill Council were also sworn and gave their aiths for the faithful discharge of their offices in giving true counsel to the common weill, in convening on the ordinary days and uther times quhen they sall be chairgit, and in keeping close and secret that quhilk sall be spoken in Council, as also for assisting the Magistrates at all times convenient – be the haly name of God. [And it was ordained] that gif ony sall reveal or open the secrets quhilk he hears in Council to ony manner of person, then the revealer sall be dischairgit of forder place, and never bruik office in time coming . . .

If someone had the temerity to question the wisdom of the Council or its minions on the 'croun o' the causey', they were gently shown the error of their ways.

> Gif ony person be fundin missaying or blaspheming ony of the Council chosen for the time, or ony *taxters* or *cunniars* of wine or ale, or ony person doing business at the command of the Provost, Bailies, or Council, [that blasphemer] sall pay to the Kirkmaster forty shillings; and gif the person [pay not and] hes not guids strenzeable to be poyndit, then the man [offending shall] lie in the stocks forty-aucht hours, and the woman in the *cuckstule*. Gif ony person be fundin disobeying any one bearing office within the burgh, he sall pay five pounds of money but ony forder process, [and if he pay not] his readiest guids sall be poyndit therefor; and quha beis convictit sall come to the Mercat Croce and upon his knees desire forgiveness of the person quhom he has offendit, and gif he disobey shall tyne his freedom.'

TAX ASSESSORS
TASTERS

STOOL OF REPENTANCE

To make sure the streets were safe for decent Councillors to walk, they had strict laws on beggars, ordaining that

ALLOWED na beggars be *tholit* but they quhilk are born within the burgh, and nane be sufferit to beg except they have the town's seal upon their hat or cloke, and be auld, cruikit, lamit, or debilitated be grite sickness [so that they] may nocht labour nor wirk for their leving; and gif there be ony others within the burgh, [that they] dispatch them off before Sunday nextocum, under the pain of burning upon the cheek. [And also] that na vagabonds that hes na occupation nor masters to serve quhairby they may leve and have sustentation, and na manner of nicht
DICE/CARD PLAYERS walkers, *dysars, cartars*, nor drunkards remain within the burgh; certifying [such] that gif they be found they sall be put in firmance and prison unto the time that inquisition be tane of their guiding and manner of conversation, and gif they be found culpable, shall be banished, and punishit otherways in their persons, according to their demerits; and that na neighbour give
IMMEDIATELY harborie to sic-like persons, but *incontinent* shew them to the officers of Bailies.

A strict social hierarchy was maintained through appropriate dress restrictions for each class. Thus it was ordained that

. . . na men within burgh that live be merchandise, unless they be in dignitie as Bailze, or gude worthie man of the Council, shall wear clathis of silks, nor costly scarlet gowns, nor furrings; and that they make their wifis and dochters
DRESSED in like manner *abulzeit ganeand*, and
APPROPRIATELY corresponding to their estate; on their heads, short curches, with little hudis, as are usit in England . . .

And in 1621, in another Act, that

husbandmen and laborers wear na clothing but grays, quhyit, blue, and self black made in Scotland, and that their wyiffs and children wear the like. That no servants, men or women, wear any clothing except canvas stuffs made in the country, and that they sall have no silk upon their clothes, except silk buttons and button-holes, and silk garters without pearling or roses. . .

There was far too much strong drink, swearing, and sex on the pavies of Dundee, so the unco guid set out to curb the license of the fowk. The treatment of drunkards was laid down:

Forsameikle as we knaw it to be the command of God that there sall nocht be ony

dussone', coming to a deal over the purchase of hides, and having to pay his share to the clerks of two Dundee ships, the *George* and the *James*, in which he ventured some of his money. He clearly combined his medical interests with some wheeling and dealing in business! It is also recorded that on 5 September 1550 Pypar sued Gibbe Saidler 'for the curing of Riche Saidler's heid hurt be ynglismen' apparently in the 1548 invasion. The balance due was about seven shillings. In 1563 he had a dispute with his next-door neighbour about mutual rights to their respective booths and Robert had to take down a wooden erection he had put up which interfered with the booth next door.

The first Dundee doctor to found a medical dynasty was Findlay Duncan. Along with Jo Brown, another surgeon, he was one of 193 burghers tried and acquitted of rioting at the sack of the monasteries in 1543. He had a surgery at the top of Long Wynd, but his dwelling was on the south side of the Overgate just west of Tally Street. In 1550 he was made a burgess. He had patients as far afield as Forfar, and was a medical referee in courts set up by the magistrates to help settle disputes between patients and surgeons. A dispute between Matthew Wedderburn and Patrick Walker, surgeon, 'anent the healing of the said Matthews Thome' was referred to his jurisdiction. In November 1564 the assessment of 'Patrick Walker's labour done upon Gilbert Ramsay' was referred to what we would now call a panel of professional arbitrators, 'Robert Pypar, Findlay Duncan, James Man and Jo Brown, Cherurgeons'. This board must have been made up of practically all the surgeons of the burgh.

Patrick Walker must have had a jealous grudge against his more successful colleagues – something not unusual over the centuries! He was convicted of what was called the 'invasion of Findlay Duncan, Cherurgeon, with ane drawn quhinger [short stabbing sword] yestrene' in the home of another surgeon called Robert Lovell. The magistrates ordered him to 'offer his sword to Finlan [Findlay] and ask his forgiveness'. The same Patrick must have had a short temper – again a not unusual failing of certain surgeons today – and pursued patients fiercely not only for fees but for expenses also. In 1568 he was 'granted a decree for 15s. for healing a straik Fower insche deep in the flank of John Robertson, mariner'.

Findlay Duncan died *c.* 1587–90, and was succeeded in the practice by his son William. Though William was called a surgeon in burgh records, he is referred to on his tomb in The Howff as a physician. In his lifetime he was a town councillor, bailie, and Dean of Guild. He married Katherine, daughter of the first Alexander Wedderburn, the Town Clerk, and thus was brother-in-law of David Wedderburn of the *Compt Buik*. William's son, William Duncan of Seasyde, acquired the estate of Lundie. His direct descendant was Admiral Duncan, the victor of the Battle of Camperdown.

Litigation was not unknown in the Dundee medical practice of those days. In 1614 Margaret Chalmers, wife of Alexander Smith, sued the surgeon John Fordyce through her husband. Fordyce had attended her for nine years, after promising 'under God' to heal her damaged right arm for 'fourtie lib money', a boll of wheat and two of meal. Just as patients are still sometimes referred to Edinburgh for treatment, so was Mrs Smith. Her husband alleged that the Edinburgh surgeons had said that 'John Fordyce had not rytlie understood the hurt' and had done her more harm than good. Dissension amongst doctors is also nothing new. But Margaret eventually lost her case. Perhaps the second medical opinion did not impress the judicial authorities!

The first doctor of real distinction in Dundee was the first to be designated 'physician' in the burgh records. This was Dr David Kinloch. The Kinlochs were an old and distinguished Scottish family. They were from Fife, where they were land-owners from the twelfth century, and their descendants remain in north Fife to the present day. There were four medical Kinlochs in Dundee before David, all surgeons. Dr David inherited Kinloch's Meadow, north of Dundee, from his father. Born in 1559 and matriculated at St Andrews University in 1576, Dr David later went to the Continent, and graduated MD in Paris. There he became known as a distinguished physician and attended the French royal family. Returning home he won the respect of King James VI and was made 'Medicinar to his Majestie' in 1596. The King thought so highly of him that he sent him back to the Continent on diplomatic missions and when in Madrid, trying to secure the betrothal of the Infanta for the future Charles I, he was imprisoned as a heretic and condemned to death. His life was spared after he had cured the Grand Inquisitor who had been dying 'of a strange fever'. According to a story handed down in the Kinloch family, Dr David heard of the strange illness, tied a message to the tail of a black cat with whom he shared his prison fare and sent him through the bars of his cell. Following the best traditions of romantic fiction, the message was received, the doctor's treatment was successful, and he was set free, loaded with honours.

Kinloch returned once again to Scotland, this time to remain longer. He married in 1597. As well as being a doctor, he was a scholar and wrote poems in Latin on medical subjects, which give a fascinating account of the state of medical knowledge of the day. They are to be found, along with others by two of his fellow burghers – a merchant, James Goldman, and James Gleg, the master of the Grammar School (later Dundee High School) – in *Poetae Scotigenae*.

Kinloch died at the age of fifty-eight, in 1617. His monument in The Howff has a Latin euology: 'A most honourable man, of famous learning, and in his life adorned with many singular virtues; a most skilful physician to the Kings of Great Britain

drunkards and blasphemers of his holy name among his people, we therefore ordain that gif ony man be apprehendit in drunkenness, and notit with the same, gif he be responsal and have geir, he sall pay for the first fault five merks unforgiven, for the second, ten merks, and for the third, ten pounds, to be taken up be the deacons and distribute to the puir. And gif he will nocht mend, but continue, then the Bailies sall give him ane *sys* of neighbours; and gif he beis convictit, he sall be banishit for year and day, and sall nocht be receivit without his open repentance. And the person that hes na geir being com-prehendit in the fault, sall be put in the thief's holl the space of twa days and twa nichts, for the next fault, four days, and for the third fault, the whole oulk in the said theif's holl: and the same act to proceed upon drunken women.

COMPENSATION

Drinking houses were made subject to stricter rules:

In consideration that some drunkards within the town, and some quhilk dwell without and repair to the town, use wine and ale taverns out of due time – namely, under nicht, and therethrow provoke drunkenness, huirdom, and *tuilzie*; and siclike, in the morning pass to taverns and ale houses, and draw others with them, in time of preaching and prayers on the Sundays and uther oulk days, to the grite sklander of religion, the peril and prejudice of the virtuous, and to the common misorder; we therefore ordain in respect of the persons that keep house and table to them, that na men nor women quhilk sell wine or ale, ressait or receive ony idle and vain persons, either of this burgh or coming fra land, within their houses, and keep table to them efter nine hours at nicht, nor in the morning until prayers and preaching be done; and likeways on Sunday in time of preaching in efter-noon that the same order be observit.

FIGHTING

And even fornication came under the eye of the Council!

Gif ony man and woman within the burgh sall happen to commit fornication, for the first fault they sall be admonishit be the preachers to forbear, and efter the preachers' counsel sall shaw their open repentance publicly in presence of the haill congregation, and so forbear in times coming. But gif he and she beis [again] apprehendit with the said fault, they sall stand three hours in the gyves, and be thrice doukit in the sea as said is; and gif that punishing serves nocht for amendment, [and they] theirefter continue, they sall be banishit for ever. [Some offenders were, however,] fund obstinat in repenting in presence of the congregation, [and those were ordained] to stand six hours in the branks, and gif they then mend nocht, to be doukit in the sea.

However, the short sharp shock of 'cauld douks' in the Tay or sitting on the 'cuttie stool' proved to have little effect. Three years after the proclamation above, it was admitted that: 'Fornication continues and increases daily in the burgh, and that it ceases nocht for the pain of open repentance.' [Strong drink, swearing and especially sex are still prevalent and show no sign of abating 300 years on. Makes you think. Ed.]

Showing characteristic Dundonian black humour the Council created an early example of job sharing when the Public Hangman was also made responsible for waste disposal.

The Council appointed Michael Mores – now electit common officer for executions within the burgh – to attend upon keeping clean of all the calsays, streets, and the kirkyard; and disponed to him the haill fuilzie that he sall apprehend lying betwix the Burial Wynd and the Burnhead attour twenty-four hours efter the outlaying thereof, and in other parts, lying attour forty-eight hours, with power to him to confiscate the same to his awn use; [for which purpose they agreed] to furnish to him ane wheill barrow upon the town's chairges; [this being the first public outlay for cleansing plant] and forder, they gave full liberty to Michael to slay all the swine that he can apprehend within the burgh, and apply the same to his awn use; and siclike, to attend upon all vagabonds and idle beggars eisane to the burgh wha are not born [therein] and expel and put them furth; and ordained that in case ony persons should mak him impediment in the using of his office, or trouble or inquiet him in ony time coming, either be word or deed, [that they shall] pay six shillings eight pennies, or be wardit for the space of twenty-four hours upon bread and water.

What with the sale of dung, stray pigs and the odd hanging, Michael would have been worth a groat or twa. Interestingly, the work of the scaffie, redding back court middens, went on well into our own century, a fact immortalised in the rhyme recalled by older Dundonians.

My father's a midnight mechanic
He redds aa the middens at night
And when he comes hame in the mornin
his buits are aa coverit wi . . . Sweet
  Violets!

and France, by whose patents and seals the antiquity of his Pedigree and Extract is clearly witnessed and proven.' A recent account of his life, by Dr W. B. Over in the *New York State Journal of Medicine* of 1966, refers to his being 'the first Scottish physician to write about human reproduction'.

These were our earlier Dundee doctors. They were not university men but apprentices to a master, who later became masters themselves. Some of their fees were high – in the late sixteenth century, treatment for a broken leg was £5, £10 for a severe wound of the hand, and £20 for a broken thigh. Sometimes they were paid in kind – by new boots or a new doublet. A drawing of 1590 shows the dress of the typical Dundee burgess, or professional man: a kind of Norfolk jacket, trousers like modern plus-fours, a beret, and a sword at the waist.

The next outstanding medical man in the town flourished in the early eighteenth century. Patrick Blair came from an established local family and was born in 1666. As so often with the young Scot, he went abroad to make his way and earn some money. His first service was as surgeon-apothecary with the army in the Netherlands. Here he gained a great deal of practical knowledge of surgery. Returning to Dundee, he became as much a natural historian and botanist as doctor. In 1707 he prepared and articulated the skeleton of a porter of St Andrews University who had hanged himself on the stairway to the Hebdomader's room. This was used by the newly re-formed Department of Medicine and Anatomy established there in 1722, for student teaching. For this he received 100 marks, and his servant who transported the pieces, a lesser amount 'for drink money'.

Blair's most exciting dissection, however, was done in 1706. A travelling elephant was being taken north by its keepers, and collapsed and died on the Ferry Road. With Provost Yeaman, he hurried to the scene, had the skin 'flea'd off', and proceeded to dissect the body. His main concerns were the size of the crowd looking on, the heat of the day, and the fact it was a Saturday. He dissected as fast as he could before the Sabbath but when he returned on the Monday he found much of the innards dried up, and a whole forefoot stolen as a souvenir by some unsporting Dundonian. This last was recovered, with the provost's help, some six weeks later. The dissection was completed (the smell must have been awful) with the help of other surgeons, and the skeleton and stuffed skin put on exhibition. Patrick Blair went further. He persuaded a number of local professional and businessmen to have built a Natural History Hall, where the elephant was displayed, and also set up a Garden of Physic – with himself as the superintendent.

The scientific account of the dissection was sent to Sir Hans Sloane in London; it was the first dissection of an elephant in Britain. Dr Blair was elected FRS in 1710, and was thus Dundee's first Fellow of the Royal Society. In 1712 he was

graduated MD of Aberdeen University, 'on the recommenda-
tion of the Bishop of Aberdeen and several eminent physicians
in Angus'. He continued scientific investigations, correspondence with other Fellows in London, Oxford and elsewhere, and
seemed on the way to an illustrious career as a natural historian.
But in 1715 he got caught up in the rebellion, was – by his own
account against his will – induced to join the Jacobite Army, and
only just, at the twelfth hour, reprieved from execution in
Newgate jail.

Patrick Blair FRS did not return to Dundee. He practised in
London, and later in Boston in Lincolnshire. Here, in 1720, he
published his *Botanick Essays*, his most famous work and the
first in English to give convincing evidence of sex in plants. He
died in 1728 while working on a dictionary of British plants.

There was also another group of Dundee doctors – the hospital
ones. The first voluntary dispensary was opened in 1735, but
little is known of its early years. In 1782 the growing need for
medical care for the townsfolk was becoming obvious, and
Reverend Robert Small DD and Mr Robert Stewart, Surgeon,
opened a fresh subscription. Reverend Dr Small was a
distinguished churchman – Moderator of the General Assembly
in 1791 – but his literary accomplishments were considerable,
and his concern for the poor real and sincere. In 1794 he published a pamphlet titled *The Importance of the Poor*. Mr Stewart
was also a cultured and widely read man, and an MD of Edinburgh by thesis. With Sir Alexander Douglas and John Willison,
two physicians, they worked hard to make the new hospital a
reality. As Dr H. J. C. Gibson said in his *History of Dundee Royal
Infirmary*: 'Such a beginning is typical of the spirit of the voluntary hospital – the will to give, both on the part of the physician
and surgeon, who generously contribute their skills, and of the
churches and community at large, who have never failed to
ensure the necessary financial support and to furnish able and
enthusiastic directors to carry on the management of the house.'

A site was bought to the north of King Street where Victoria
School stood. The first patient to be admitted was not in fact
from Dundee. William Dove of Monikie came in on 11 March
1798, remained for a fortnight, and was then sent home 'with
necessary medicines'. At the end of the first year 45 patients had
been admitted, 23 cured, 15 relieved, 5 died, and 2 had remained
under care. Medical audit is nothing new.

The diets varied, even in the late eighteenth century. There
was a full diet, starting for breakfast with porridge and ale,
continuing with good broth and flesh meat for dinner, with small
beer, and ending at supper with bread, ale and more porridge.
The lowest diet was made up of porridge or bread and milk for
breakfast, weak broth, boiled bread and milk, rice and milk,
barley and milk, rice or bread pudding, and 'breadberry sowens'.
Supper was the same as breakfast.

Dr David Kinloch. *University of Dundee*

DRI, with Newtyle railway and cemetery in the foreground, c. 1870

Nursing at first was of poor quality. There was no real distinction between nurses and servants – these were known as 'supernumerary nurses'. In this there is a striking similarity to 1990, with shortages increasing the number of untrained orderlies. As well as domestic duties – cleaning the floor of sand by seven in the morning, they attended to medicines and diet and kept the wards aired. They were allowed to apply poultices, blisters and such but they did not dress wounds or go to the operating theatre. They were reminded that 'they must not neglect, insult or quarrel with the patients on any pretext whatever'. Many of these care attendants were unfortunately downtrodden women who could not find employment elsewhere. Mrs Farquharson was appointed the first nurse at six shillings a week with board and lodging. Student dressers were employed to dress wounds and assist the Attending Surgeon. Each had to provide himself with an apron with sleeves and pockets. A box of clean dressings and a basin for the old ones was supplied by the 'house'! Each had to work under the supervision of the Attending Surgeon.

Special care was taken in the construction of the operating theatre, which had roof lights and special doors. Soon it was found necessary to put up a rail 'encompassing the operation table at a proper distance for protecting the operator from being pressed on too closely by the gentlemen who attended to see the operations performed'.

The first Royal Charter was granted by King George III and signed on 8 May 1819. It included in its constitution the 'Dundee Infirmary and Asylum' as a corporation consisting of two independent bodies. For already the directors had seen fit to provide care for the mentally insane, at first in the main Infirmary but by 1812 at a separate site in the north-east of the town.

By 1855 a new Infirmary had been built, between the barracks by Lochee Road and the then railway to Newtyle. It was at the top of what became known as 'Infirmary Brae'. The pressing need of the nineteenth century was for bigger and better facilities, for the town in this century grew enormously in size and population, as it progressed to a status and wealth it would not have again in the twentieth. The population was about 25,000 at the start of the nineteenth century and rose to 80,000 by 1850. The wealth of the mill owners was not matched by a corresponding improvement in conditions of life for the poor. The water was grossly infected, overcrowding in slums was atrocious, and the workers lived short, disease-stricken lives. From this time on poverty was a constant factor in medical care in Dundee.

Infectious disease was such a huge scourge that hospitals built for 'fever' patients became a priority requirement. The first public hospital was built by the local authority in Lochee, probably at the site of the present Wellbourn Home. It was intended for smallpox patients. The larger King's Cross Hospital was opened in 1889. At first it consisted of two wards only but over a quarter of a century increased in size to seven. It became, as it has remained, the best hospital in Dundee, run over the years by a succession of doctors whose names have become part of

Midwife with Baby, Stirling Street, 1922.
Dundee Art Galleries and Museums

Dundee's history – Dr A. M. Anderson, the first Medical Officer of Health, Dr Charles Templeman, Dr W. L. Burgess who was the first Professor of Public Health and Infectious Diseases in St Andrews University, and, in the recent past, Dr Bill Jamieson and Dr Mary Kerr. Dundee women used to say of their children, 'The bairn's no' had a good start in life till he's been in the Kingie,' and really meant it.

Hospital care advanced. The numbers of in-patients treated rose steadily, as did the number of out-patients and surgical operations. In the last quarter of the century a training school for nurses was begun and developed. This new and important enterprise for Dundee Royal Infirmary was fortunate in having Dr Robert Sinclair as Medical Superintendent and Mrs Rebecca Strong as Matron. Mrs Strong had been a pupil of Florence Nightingale herself at St Thomas's Hospital in London, where she had the distinction of being the first nurse ever to take a patient's temperature.

At the end of the century there was a further step forward. The University of St Andrews established a complete University Medical School. From then on Dundee Royal Infirmary was a

J. D. Saggar (standing) with Guru. India,
c. 1919. *Private collection*

teaching hospital, with professorial departments, students, and research. Standards inevitably rose, with women playing an increasingly important role in our own time. St Andrews University appointed Dr Margaret Fairlie as the first woman Professor of Obstetrics and Gynaecology, and Dr Jean Herring was her equal in Obstetrics, while Dundee has a Professor of Microbiology – Professor Heather Dick.

Yet even in the twentieth century poverty in Dundee was such that in some homes a succession of jute workers occupied the same bed in rotation. Some older Dundee people still remember being on 'half-and-half' – half their day at school, half at the mill. Doctors were detailed off to 'do' Poor Law patients, and for the year of their appointment were rushed off their feet by the work they had to do – visits more than surgeries in much of the century. They were paid by the local authority but could see 'ordinary' patients too. If by chance their Poor Law patients became better-off, they would often join the practice as 'payers'.

The twentieth century had as many outstanding characters as the sixteenth. Dr Rodgers of Tay Street was remembered in the 1920s. Always immaculate, with a flower in his buttonhole, he never had a cigarette out of his mouth, even when examining a patient. There was the Buchanan dynasty in Albert Street, in the Maryfield part of the town, the Rankines in King Street and the Rorie dynasty farther down. Not all spent their lives in those streets; 'W. E. A.' Buchanan senior commanded the Dundee Field Ambulance in 1939, and was captured at St Valery in 1940 with the rest of the Highland Division. Derek Buchanan became Scottish Secretary of the BMA in the 1980s.

Dr J. Gordon Clark began his career in the Albert Street block of practice houses – and in 1948 became an NHS consultant. His humour was remembered by two generations of St Andrews students – 'J. G., King of the GPs' he was sometimes called. He did a great deal of life-insurance work. One day a nervous businessman had his medical examination starting at 4.00 p.m. Anxiously he asked 'J. G. C.' how his health was, at the completion of the examination. 'With a bit of luck you'll get hame for your tea,' was the reply.

Number 1 South Tay Street was another famous practice site – Jimmy and Harold Dallas. Their letters of referral to the DRI were famous, and generations of house doctors read them with pleasure. 'Jeemy – or Hughie – could aye get ye into the Infirmary,' boasted their patients. So popular were they that patients queued outside their surgery door, in all weathers, waiting to be seen.

Another similarly famous practice, which also had mainly poor patients, was the Lochee one of the Saggars. These Indians, 'D. R.' (the eye specialist) and 'J. D.' were known to Dundonians as 'the black doctors' and were dearly loved. They were both active members of the Labour Party and served on the town council. 'Saggar Street' commemorates them still. An amusing but apocryphal story credits 'D. R.' with obtaining spectacles on free prescription for each and every one of his patients over the age of thirty, when the National Health Service started in 1948.

W. Fyfe Dorward was yet another great figure. His patients were also mostly poor. They lived in the side streets between Magdalen Yard Road, Perth Road, Hawkhill and Blackness Road and worked mostly in the jute mills or for the railway. Dr Dorward shared their poverty, for money was scarce for him and his family too, especially in his early years. This was partly what gave him the idea of writing – to try and make a little extra cash. In time he became one of the best known 'Docs' in the whole of Scotland, from his *Sunday Post* articles. Later, too, he became Police Surgeon for Dundee, lecturer in Forensic Medicine at the University, and at the time of his death was President of the Police Surgeons' Federation.

The practice at 2 Garland Place had a succession of characters who were also outstanding practitioners. Dr Noel Nelson was one. In the late 1920s, when the Depression was beginning to affect Dundee, he put up his plate. At first he wore striped trousers and a bowler hat. He had few patients. So he would go up Blackness Road, stop his car, go up a back close, have a cigarette, and come out again. He did this, he said, hoping someone would see him and ask for a consultation! As he got older, his health deteriorated. One cold winter morning he was listening to the chest of a young woman, ill in her house: 'Lassie that's a terrible wheeze ye've got.' 'That's no mine, doctor,' she replied, 'That's yours.' Popular and hardworking, his patients loved him, to the extent of sharing their humour: 'Dae it wi' yer buits oan,' said a Dundee wifie to him on hearing his wife's second baby was another daughter.

His junior partners in the early 1950s were David Simpson and John Langlands. 'Jovial John Langlands' as his classmates called him, became one of the best known Dundee doctors over the next forty years. He was a shrewd diagnostician, bubbled with laughter on a happy occasion but was kindness itself when sorrow arrived in a home.

A Royal Physician began our list of physicians, so two complete it. Professor Ian Hill came to Dundee from Edinburgh in 1950 as the last Professor of Medicine in St Andrews University – at least for the present. He developed the new kind of university department which arrived with the National Health Service in 1948, of full-time staff with no private practice. He brought a succession of experts in several fields to Dundee from elsewhere in the country, who brought special expertise with them. He was later knighted and became Physician to HM the Queen in Scotland.

But Dr Kenneth G. Lowe, an Arbroath man and St Andrews graduate, was the power behind Professor Hill. House doctors

Professor Ian Hill, by J. McIntosh Patrick. *University of Dundee*

of the day remembered his arrival in 1952 at Maryfield Hospital from the Hammersmith Hospital in London, where he had been one of the team of three who developed the first successful artificial kidney in Britain. He brought to Dundee his training in the new cardiology, and his quiet kindness, as Professor Hill's assistant and later in a Personal Chair at Dundee University Medical School, was known to two generations of students. He succeeded Sir Ian as Physician to HM the Queen.

Dundee's hospital doctors were never the world-famous names of Edinburgh or Glasgow, but they were none the less men of true distinction. Distinction does not belong to the 'big names' alone and these people – perhaps especially the family doctors – were unforgettable in their lifetimes. All doctors relate to their patients and it is perhaps true to say that Dundee surgeons and physicians over the centuries have been the kind of characters Dundee folk needed to care for their diseases and hurts. Dundee people are quite unique . . . and so are their doctors.

c. 1665 - 1700
A description of Dundee is given by the Reverend Robert Edward, minister of Murroes.

The town is divided into four principal streets, which we may suppose to represent a human body, stretched on its back with its arms towards the west, and its legs towards the east. The steeple represents the head, with an enormous neck, rising upwards of eighteen storeys, into the clouds and surrounded with two battlements or galleries, one in the middle, and another at the top, like a crown adorning the head – whose loud-sounding tongue daily calls the people to worship. The right hand is stretched forth to the poor, for there is a large and well-furnished hospital on that side; but the left hand, because nearer to the heart, is more elevated towards heaven than the right – indicating a devout mind panting after celestial joys. In the inmost recesses of the breast stand the sacred temples of God. On the left breast is a Christian burying-place, richly and piously ornamented, that the pious dead may be long held in veneration and esteem. In the belly is the market-place, at the middle of which is the 'cross', like the navel in the body. Below the loins stand the shambles, which, as they are in a proper place, so are they very neat and convenient, having a hidden stream of fresh water, which (after wandering through the pleasant meadows on the left), runs under them; and which having thus, as it were, scoured the veins and intestines of the town, is afterwards discharged into the river. Here the thighs and legs are separated. The sea approaching the right, invites to the trade and commerce of foreign countries; and the left limb, separated from the thigh a full step, points to home trade, in the northern parts of the country.

And Sir Robert Sibbald, wrote this description of Dundee which accompanies Captain John Slezer's drawing of the city in Theatrium Scoticae. *'It is adorned with excellent buildings of all sorts. It hath two churches, a high steeple, a harbour for ships of burthen, and a considerable traffic with strangers, whence the inhabitants are generally rich, and those who fall into decay have a large hospital provided for them.'*
Sir Robert Sibbald was also the man behind an early 1680s' attempt at a comprehensive survey of Scotland. The account of the Shire of Forfar, from which this description of Dundee is taken, was compiled by John Ochterlony of Guynd.

Dundee hath a great landward parish besyd the towne, which is a large and great towne, very populous, and of a great trade, and hath many good ships. The buildings are large and great, of thrie or four stories high; a large merkat place, with a very fyne tolbuith and cross; two great churches, with a very high steeple well furnished of bells, as is also the tolbuith. They have thrie ministers, whereof the towne presents two, and the Constable of Dundie one; their Magistrates are a Provost, four Bailies, Dean of Gild, and others are shirreffs within their own bounds: they are joyned in nothing to the shyre except the militia, whereunto they furnish 150 foot. It lyeth upon the water of Tay very pleasantlie, and hath good yards and meadowes about it. They have four great fairs yearly, two mercat days everie week, and a great fish mercat dayly. There is a great consumption there of all kynd of victualls; the excyse of malt there being little short of the whole excyse of the shyre and burghs, besyd a great victuall mercat twice a week for service of the towne, besydes great quantities of all kinds of grain, coft by the merchants, and transported, by which returnes they import all kynd

Captain John Slezer's drawing of Dundee from the North, c. 1680. *Dundee District Libraries*

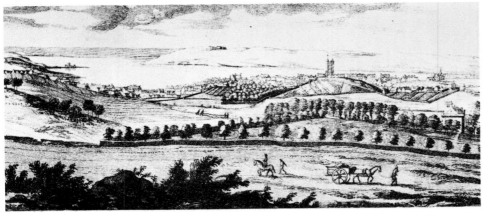

of commoditie from Holland, Norway, Denmark, and the east countrey. They export lykwayes all other our native commodities, and import other things necessary for the service of the countrey, which serves above 20 myles round about their towne. Their trade is very great, as is evident by the books of Custome. They have dependance in many things upon the Constables, who have been of the name of Scrimgeour, heritors of Dudope, and Standard-Bearers of Scotland, ane ancient, loyall, and honorable familie, and of late were made Earls of Dundie; but the estate falling in his Majestie's hands as *ultimus heres*, the Lord Haltoune, now Earl of Lauderdaill, was constitute the King's donator, and has the same privilege and superioritie, with the haill estate of the late Constable and Earle of Dundie.

The toune has a good shore, well built with hewen stone, with a key on both sydes, whereof they load and unload their ships, with a great house on the shore called the Pack-House, where they lay up their merchant goods . . .

The Mercurius Caledonius, *Scotland's first newspaper, published in 1661, contained the following.*

This, our town of Dundee situated on the River Tay, hath ever been famous for the abundance of that little fish termed for its excellence the Cherry of Tay, catched here. It is like (if not a species) to the whyting; but so surpassing it in a delicious taste that hardly it can be so called.

And the Reverend Thomas Morer, an English chaplain to a Scots regiment, gave this description in 1689.

. . . a very pretty town, seated at the bottom of a hill almost at the mouth of the river Tay, which runs up to Perth; 'tis furnish'd with two or three small piers for the conveniency of shipping, and the buildings are such as speak the substance and riches of the place. It is a royal borough, and considerable for its trade, wherein it has supplanted St Andrews on the other side the river, and about seven miles from it. Here we were handsomly treated at the charges of the corporation, who complimented us with burgess-ships.

The final years of the seventeenth century proved disastrous for Dundee and Scotland. The civil and religious strife combined with blighted harvests brought the country to its knees. The nation's hopes for salvation were channelled into an attempt to plant a Scottish colony in Darien, the narrow isthmus in what is now Panama; from there they would control trade between the Atlantic and Pacific oceans. The murderous climate, the shipwreck of supply boats, poor leadership, Spanish aggression and English duplicity all combined to doom the colony to failure. Many historians believe that it was this failure which led inevitably to the Parliamentary Union with England.

The last Scots in Darien at the time of the colony were the sailors of the Margaret of Dundee. *They had been sent out to provision and reinforce the second expedition, but arrived in Caledonia on 16 June 1700, unaware that their countrymen had deserted New Edinburgh two months before. The captain, Patrick Mac-Dowall, leaves us with this final impression of the end of the Scottish dream in the Americas.*

We sent away our boat. By the time we judged our men had got in, we heard two cannons from the fort. We fired one, and they another, we supposed, in return. . . . We then no longer doubted but our countrymen were there. And so set our own boat to tow us in . . . we were big with the fancy of seeing our countrymen in quiet possession of the place and in particular some of us were full of the expectation of seeing our dear friends, comrades and acquaintances – in short there was nothing but a general mirth and jollity among us . . . but it was soon dampt when our boat came aboard giving us the lamentable, sad, dismal account of the Spanish ensigns on our fort. Captain Robertson was for away at once but I told him we could not go so . . . and took four men to row us in to Fort St Andrew. As soon as I thought they could well discern our colours, I hoisted our Scots flag of truce . . . but they had no design to parley. In the fort I saw a great part of our rampart entire towards the look out, and our postern gate. I observed some very good houses, and a fort where Mr McKay's house stood. I saw guns on the point battery and the men in their several liveries. I must say, if I thought my falling in their hands could have been of any advantage to the interests of my country, I should have had verie little regard to what might have occurred myself thereby; but I was cautioned that I might yet live to do us some service . . . and was prevailed upon to come aboard. But afore that I had the flag of truce pulled down and let only the Scots colours fly . . . and in token of defiance, fired two small shot amongst them. And so having no way of staying there and without intelligence of what had become of our friends and ships, we judged it properest to leave this place, which we did with a very sorrowful heart, I believe one and all of us.

Beauty Revealed and Concealed

The City Through Her Architecture

by CHARLES McKEAN

'Dundee's architectural character defeats any attempt to evaluate it by comparison with other Scottish cities.'

Sinclair Gauldie

Do not be diverted by the mills. A peculiarity of the city of Dundee is the perverse way it seeks the myth, legend and imagery of dark satanic mills, at a time when most of the rest of the world is seeking to forget them. They represent only a portion of the history and character of this great city and imply a certain perverse masochism in the Dundonian. It is designed to keep intruders, visitors and tourists at bay (just as those who run Dundee, its businesses and its professions, all went to one of only three schools – Morgan Academy, Harris Academy, and the High School; know each other, belong to the same organisations, and form, in consequence, a very private oligarchy). Like a girl convinced that she is ugly and who therefore keeps a veil over her face, Dundonians have refused to appreciate the qualities of their own city, and as a consequence, seem to prefer to keep strangers at a distance.

Of all major towns in Scotland, Dundee has possibly the finest site. Situated in a shallow bowl protected from the north of the Sidlaws, it gazes south across one of the greatest river estuaries in Europe, (as compared to Edinburgh, Greenock or Inverness, all of which languish on the south side of their estuaries). By nature of its location, it enjoys a peculiar micro-climate more benign than its immediate hinterland, and very often at distinct variance with the rest of Scotland. But for all its advantages, it has disadvantages. The local stone is a poor, soft, brown stone, which erodes easily and always looks as though it needs cleaning. The broad Tay estuary, inviting though it may be, is notoriously uncertain, dangerous, and subject to shifting sand bars. It required heavy engineering works to transform Dundee's port into anything commercially successful.

A marketing analysis of the city, taking account of its strengths and opportunities, might still conclude that its opportunities and strengths should outweigh all other factors. But the weaknesses and threats – a combination of individualism, lack of self-awareness, failure to appreciate the physical advantages of the

The Strathmartine Lodging, an early 18th-century hotel. *McKean from Lamb's Dundee*

63

Old Dundee, from the Steeple of St Mary's

city, and a preference for short-term gain – have had the consequence of missed opportunities and wasted assets.

Dundee was the economic centre for the County of Angus. All roads in southern Angus led to Dundee at its heart, and to the ferry on the principal north-eastern route through Scotland. It gained much from passing trade. The wealth of the fifteenth- to seventeenth-century burgh is evidenced not just in the trading records, but also by the magnificent Old Steeple, a relic of Scotland's largest parish church. The castle figured little in history. It occupied a strong, but perhaps strategically doubtful site, soon overrun by the town. Its rock was eventually levelled. Dundee was a prosperous mercantile centre, with direct connections with the Continent, and substantial colonies in the Baltic. The harbour must have been large enough to contain fifty ships: for that is what General Monk had seized when he sacked this substantial, wealthy, stone-built town in 1651. Although the sacking was disastrous in terms of both human slaughter and damage to the economy, it is clear from the large number of paintings of the ancient burgh by David Small for *Lamb's Dundee* that many buildings survived it. That early Dundee still informs the street pattern: beneath the great satanic mills, therefore, lies that seventeenth-century burgh, third in importance in Scotland.

It leant further east than the town today, centred with its original Tolbooth and a chapel, along the Seagate. From the names of the alleyways we may presume that boats were simply pulled up on to the shore. That Dundee was not primarily a seaport, may be inferred from the original remoteness of the market place from the harbour, on an inland plateau linked to the harbour only by several sloping alleyways, too narrow for carts to pass. By the time Daniel Defoe visited in 1725, a broad, well-paved route planted with lime trees had been constructed to remedy the deficiency. The town was graced with the usual priories and hospitals and a substantial number of lairds' and noblemen's town houses, to which they would return to reside during the winter. The hinterland (now part of Dundee), was unusually fertile of lairds' country seats of the larger sort – Dudhope, Mains, Wester Powrie, Ballumbie, Gagie, Murroes, Affleck, Claypotts, Huntly, House of Gray, Pitkerro and Baldovan.

Dundee prospered in the late eighteenth and nineteenth century as with the rest of Scotland. It was certainly not short of mercantile aspiration. In 1731 it had invited William Adam to design the Town House which, until its unfortunate demise in 1931 (its demolition providing work for the unemployed), was one of the most splendid civic buildings in Scotland. By the late 1770s, the city acquired a grandly titled Town's Architect, Samuel Bell. Bell was responsible for the civic buildings that any self-respecting, bustling market town then required. In 1776 he

designed the pedimented Trades' Hall to close off the eastern end of the Market Place, and in 1783 the English Chapel (later Union Hall) to close off the western end towards Nethergate. His master work, equally a symbol of the new eminence and wealth of the Dundee merchants, is St Andrew's Church, completed in 1772 (so famous that a direct copy was instructed by the Heritors of Banff for erection in the north). Bell's fondness for Venetian windows, the dominant feature of both the Trades' House and the Union Hall, are here visible on the flank. In 1787, Bell built the new Steeple Church on the site of the demolished nave of St Mary's; the imposing house of Lord Provost Alexander Riddoch, 158 Nethergate; a delightfully quirky block of mansion flats – the Morgan Tower, almost opposite, in 1794; and the Theatre Royal in Castle Street in 1809.

The new Trades' Kirk, Trades' House, Theatre, and Chapel for the English were evidence that the burgh was prospering. The smart neo-classical 1828 Coffee House in Shore Terrace by George Smith provided an Assembly Room and Exchange, and Smith's imposing High School in the appropriately named

Exchange Coffee House, Shore Terrace. Now the premises of David Winter's, the building once contained the Merchant's library, reading rooms, assembly rooms, and a coffee house. *Dundee District Libraries*

65

Reform Street. *McKean* Euclid Crescent followed six years later. The classical Sheriff
Court, erected in 1833 by George Angus, and the largest
Customs House in Scotland, by John Taylor in 1842, completed
the status symbols required for this burgeoning burgh. What
they lacked was the cohesion of new streets to unite them
together so evident in rival cities. The reason for that may be
attributed to the attitudes and activities of Lord Provost Alexander Riddoch.

The town under Provost Riddoch had steadfastly set its face
against the building of 'new towns' like Glasgow, Edinburgh,
Aberdeen and Perth for reasons of economy and a distaste for
intervention where none was thought to be needed. As a consequence, the town had forfeited its share of the magnificent early
nineteenth-century Scottish architecture. Isolated developments like King Street, *c.* 1805, and South Tay Street designed
by the Town's Architect David Neave in 1819, reveal what
could have been achieved had Dundonians wanted it; there was

otherwise the narrow douceness of unexceptional Castle, Crichton and Union Streets. The exception is the post-Riddoch Reform Street, designed by George Angus in 1832 to a plan by William Burn, focused axially upon the portico of the High School. The only example of formal planning in Dundee, this major undertaking not only swept away much of the old Market Place, but required the cutting through of a hill to the north.

According to the depositions for Riddoch's removal, laid by Dundee citizens before Parliament in 1819, the government of Dundee 'for the last century has passed from the hands of one dictator to those of another: and at this moment the uncontrolled power is vested in the person of a leader who has held the situation for nearly forty years – generally excluding from the Council the more wealthy, independent and intelligent burgesses of the town'. Supporters of Riddoch pointed out that both Edinburgh and Aberdeen had gone bankrupt with their grand plans, whereas Dundee had lived through the comparable period 'all without imposing a shilling of local taxation on the inhabitants'. But even the outsider Thomas Telford, invited in 1814 to report on the harbour, observed disparagingly 'the past conduct of the Corporation and their *confined* views'; which seems to confirm James Norrie's view that Riddoch's 'management of the town's revenues has been characterised as niggardly rather than judicious'.

Thus, by 1840 and the end of Dundee's second phase of development, the town had a few new streets, some substantial civic buildings, but no grand planning. Its attitude during this period of opportunity had been characterised by 'confined views' rather than strategy, and its reputation had been severely damaged by the parliamentary allegations of corruption against Riddoch. Wealthier burgesses who, in Edinburgh would have occupied new classical terraces had, in Dundee, quit the town for smart new villas in Magdalene Green, designed by David Neave, or for the increasingly fashionable resort of Broughty Ferry. The second suburb, Chapelshade up on the Dudhope Hills, begun in 1833, is evidence of a second-wave exodus of merchants from the city centre. The houses in Constitution Terrace, Union Terrace and Dudhope Terrace vary in character from graceful Elizabethan to stubby classical villas; and offered clean air, peace, status and a view, overlooking the older streets downhill, invaded by factories. Older properties were converted or declined into slums which, at their worse, came to rival the notorious conditions of Glasgow's High Street.

Dundee's transformation, from a reasonably prosperous country town with a small amount of export trade and ferry business from Fife, to a major industrial centre can be dated to the development of the harbour, under the magical hand of Thomas Telford from 1825. From then on, modern Dundee boomed. The economy was focused upon export and import, ferrying and

c. **1725**

Daniel Defoe conducted and wrote about *A Tour Through the Whole Island of Great Britain* between 1724 and 1727. This is his impression of Dundee.

We left Strathern therefore, with the little country of Mentieth, for our return, and went down into Angus, on the northern banks of Tay to Dundee, a pleasant, large, populous city, which well deserves the title of Bonny Dundee, so often given it in discourse, as well as in song (bonny, in Scots, signifying beautiful).

As it stands well for trade, so it is one of the best trading towns in Scotland, and that as well in foreign business as in manufacture and home trade. It has but an indifferent harbour, but the Tay is a large, safe, and good road, and there is deep water and very good anchor-hold almost all over it. It is exceedingly populous, full of stately homes, and large handsome streets; particularly it has four very good streets, with a large market-place in the middle, the largest and fairest in Scotland, except only that of Aberdeen. The inhabitants here appear like gentlemen, as well as men of business, and yet are real merchants too, and make good what we see so eminently in England, that true bred merchants are the best of gentlemen. They have a very good and large correspondence here with England, and ship off a great deal of linen thither, also a great quantity of corn is sent from hence, as well to England as to Holland. They have likewise a good share of the Norway trade; and as they are concerned in the herring-fishery, they consequently have some east country trade, viz. to Dantzick, Koningsberg, Riga, and the neighbouring parts. They send ships also to Sweden, and import iron, copper, tar, pitch, deals, &c. from the several trading ports of that kingdom.

The great church was formerly collegiate, being the cathedral of the place, and was a very large building; but part of it was demolished in the Civil War; the remainder is divided, like as others are at Edinburgh, Glasgow, &c. into three churches for the present use of the citizens. They have also a meeting-house or two for the episcopal worship . . .

1759

Andrew Brice described the Dundee of 1759 in his *Universal Geographical Dictionary*.

The town, which is two miles in compass, is better built than most in Scotland. Its market place, from whence the city runs in four large fine streets inhabited by many merchants is almost as spacious as that of Nottingham, being the largest and finest in Scotland except that of Aberdeen and is adorned with a town-house of freestone which is spacious and convenient but so old that 'tis not reckoned among the ornaments of the city. Here a great church formerly collegiate which is an exact cross, larger than that of St Giles in Edinburgh and a high square building which is a great ornament. . . the steeple has a fine tower like to that at Wrexham, in Wales, and higher than that of the Brill in Holland. The churchyard is without the town and adorned with fine monuments round the walls like the Grey Friars at Edinburgh. . . . The houses are not high, but are well built and chiefly of stone, very beautiful and ornamental and this, together with its fine situation and splendid living, has procured it the name of 'Bonnie Dundee'.

whaling, all conducted through the harbour at the very heart of the city. Dundee was unable to restrict its burgeoning Victorian industry to the periphery, or the East End as happened in Glasgow. Victorian Dundee was dependent upon the success of that harbour (also Scotland's premier whaling port): it was through central Dundee that jute was imported, and through Dundee that jute machinery and jute products were exported. Dundee's historic core thereby lay in the way of Victorian prosperity. Commercial pressures upon the centre became enormous, and, since the wealthy had already distanced themselves, few residual voices made themselves heard in protest. Commerce prevailed.

Much of Victorian Dundee was controlled by family mill-owning dynasties such as the Baxters, the Grimonds, the Coxes and the Gilroys. Mills were complete communities, even employing schoolmasters to teach mill boys and girls when they were not working. The fodder needed for these great mills was largely women; and they occupied the long streets of plain (and not infrequently horrendous) tenements with projecting rear platforms or 'platties', whose forms came to dominate the centre. Dundee had been overtaken by the proletarian imagery of a mill town. The new age and its new machinery were symbolised by the mills, such as the Lower Dens Works, created in 1850 by Peter Carmichael (of Baxter Bros) and Randolph Elliot. These enormous, stone, textile factories were designed to accommodate the most up-to-date machinery, with the kind of nervous competitive energy that now goes into microchip factories. Generally plain, their tall stone walls were permitted extravagance around the entrance gates, at the frequently pedimented roof-line, and in cupolas, bell towers and chimneystacks. The most striking was the Cox's Stack – the patterned brick chimneystack of the Camperdown Works designed by James MacLaren, one of Dundee's greatest architects, in 1865. The city was largely in the hands of those five Jute-baron families. Their power was such that, when a Baxter daughter determined to marry a Russian merchant, her father was able to arrange his election to the House of Commons, even though he could speak no English.

A fitting symbol for mid-century Dundee is David Bryce's superb Royal Exchange, 1854, appropriately designed in imitation of a Flemish Cloth Hall. In typical Dundonian fashion, no suitable spot could be found on which to place it. So it was plonked on a new site, on the northern edge of a marsh into which it began to sink during construction, causing its splendid tower to be sacrificed. Here also was the location of Dundee's other major civic building: the magnificent Albert Institute designed by Sir George Gilbert Scott between 1865 and 1867. Albert Memorials were the rage throughout Britain, but because the city was bankrupt as a result of yet another internal squabble (the 'Water War'), the Albert Institute had to be built by private

The original perspective of the Royal Exchange, now used by the Chamber of Commerce, Albert Square. The Tower was not completed, but the ornate building, based on a Flemish Cloth hall still graces the square. *R.I.A.S.*

c. 1799
R. Heron in *Scotland Delineated*

Dundee is a large and flourifhing town, feated on the north fide of the eftuary of the Tay. There is here an excellent harbour and a great deal of fhipping. The houfes, in general, are neat; and fome public buildings have been lately erected, that are noticed by ftrangers as elegant. Among thefe are the new church and the town-houfe. The lofty Gothic fquare tower in the middle of the town, is part of a fuperb confecrated edifice, in form of a crofs, built in the twelfth century, and dedicated to the Virgin MARY. The chief manufactures of this place are glafs, ofnaburgs or coarfe linen, fail-cloth, cordage, coloured and white thread, and buckrams, tanned leather, fhoes, and hats. Vaft quantities of coarfe linen are annually exported from this feat of induftry: In one year, above four millions of yard, it is faid, have been ftamped at the public office. A fugar-houfe has alfo here been eftablifhed, which carries on a fuccefsful trade. The town is faid to contain about twenty-three thoufand inhabitants.

On the north of Dundee, the rich cornfields and extenfive fheep-walks are fkreened by the *Sidly* or *Sidla Hills*.

Near *Lundie-houfe*, and in other parts of this county, fubterraneous buildings have been difcovered, confifting of various apartments; but their origin and ufe have not been afcertained by antiquaries. The eftate of Lundie is the property of the gallant Admiral Lord DUNCAN, who defeated the Dutch fleet off Camperdown, on 11th October 1797.

capital. The surrounding swamp became Albert Square; but what a Square! Off-centre for the High School, off-centre for the Royal Exchange, and off-centre for Dundee's leading streets; and whatever grandeur this fine building ever had is now ruined by a setting on a traffic roundabout. Were the Square paved, and the public given free and ceremonial access, its civic potential would be enormous. The new money also brought a new club to Albert Square – the now demolished Eastern Club. Great walls of commercial building appeared in Commercial Street, designed in continental mode by William Mackeson in 1871, which would look at home in Milan. Thus new streets, mills, banks, a post office and (towards the end of the century) libraries, constituted the key monuments of mid-Victorian commercial Dundee. The harbourside was also rebuilt, upwards, in buildings less individually distinct than important for the general enclosure and scale which they created.

Religion and education being the two safety valves of working-class Scotland, a prodigious quantity of money was invested in fine church architecture of almost every denomination. Architects were attracted from afar to Dundee: the soaring Episcopal Cathedral, one of the most beautiful Gothic-revival buildings in the country, was by Sir George Gilbert Scott; and fine churches were designed by Sir George Washington Browne, David Bryce, C. M. Cappon, Alexander Ellis, Coe and Goodwin, Reginald Fairlie, J. A. Hansom, Frederick T. Pilkington, and by G. F. Bodley. The interiors appear to have been designed as an oasis from the presumably grim reality of the world outside. A significant number of these churches bear the stump or plinth for an unbuilt spire, indicating how the finances must have leached away preventing completion.

There is a certain brisk relentlessness about the schools, colleges, art galleries and libraries. All share a hard-edged and almost materialistic character. The University College, as in so much else in Dundee, developed pragmatically by occupying some early mercantile villas in Hawkhill. Proposals by Sir Robert Rowand Anderson for a full college were never built, although his 1909 Physics Building facing the Geddes Quadrangle, in a rather beautiful rendering of seventeenth-century Scots, provides some kind of ceremonial heart. The Technical Institute and the Scrymgeour Buildings however, lack Anderson's delicacy and the didactic sculptural panels with which they are embellished serve only to disturb. Frank Thomson's libraries in Blackness, Coldside and, possibly the best, St Roque's, are rather frigid Baroque in character.

The romantic Art Nouveau and Scottish revival phase of the late nineteenth century lighted gently upon Dundee, and, in particular, upon the merchants who had continued to quit the centre for the suburbs. They were quite happy to present parks, but otherwise preferred to take their money out into the countryside

Seymour Lodge. Victorian Gothic Mansion, Perth Road. *Dundee District Libraries*

and enjoy it there. Initially content to construct enormously vulgar jute-palaces in Broughty Ferry, or else invest in country estates, by the end of the nineteenth century their houses tended to be smaller and concentrated in West Ferry. Arts and Crafts and the Scottish revival are evidenced by Sir Robert Lorimer who extended Pitkerro in 1902, and again by C. G. Soutar in the delightful Craigiebarn; and most notably in the villas by Thoms and Wilkie of which Greywalls (1929) is the most distinctive. The enormous houses in large plots identified by stone walls, spread along Perth Road and West Ferry, comprise some of the finest stone-built suburbs in Scotland. The glowing timber work within the houses was not infrequently supplied by shipbuilders. Wavy parapets and cupolas, conjoined with the expressed stair towers, strongly reminiscent of the work of Charles Rennie Mackintosh, were also visible in J. H. Langlands' various schools, of which the most vividly Art Nouveau were St Joseph's Blackness Road (1905), Stobswell and the Dens Road Schools (1908).

71

Two stories exemplify the Dundonian's relentless, energetic and short-sighted eye for the main chance. The first is the curious saga of the Queen's Hotel, Perth Road. Two young architects, Young and Meldrum, obtained information that the new Caledonian station would be situated at Sea Braes, on the shoreline immediately below where the Queen's Hotel now is: upon which information, they built the Queen's Hotel as Dundee's equivalent of Edinburgh's North British. Whoever supplied the information took them for a ride, for the railway company extended the line much closer to the harbour. The Queen's Hotel venture naturally proved to be financially disastrous, and one of the entrepreneurs ended up as an assistant in the family sports shop. The Gothic premises of Robertson and Orchar, 16 Victoria Road, offer the other example. Provost of Broughty Ferry, Orchar, with his partner Robertson, built and fitted out machines for jute works, doing so well out of it that he was able to donate the Orchar Art Gallery to Broughty Ferry. When the demand for the machinery in Dundee had been satiated, Robertson and Orchar then exported the machinery to America, and then to Calcutta. By selling the Indians the weapons the latter needed to process jute themselves, it is arguable that Robertson and Orchar thereby pulled the bung from Dundee's economy.

Dundee's economy was in decline even before the First World War as it lost its share of the world jute market; and afterwards slumped along with the rest of Scotland. Its underlying agricultural economy still survived, however, Professor Alan Lendrum recorded his memory of The Pillars (the arcades in front of the Old Town House) used as the centre of feeing for farm labourers from the surrounding county: so much so, that on market days, the cobbles glistened with the sheen of saliva.

Between the wars the city moved in to its first corporatist incarnation, as the Council determined to tackle its appalling housing legacy. In 1919, the City Architect James Thomson began the housing development of Logie, to a curvilinear layout with rustic names – Ashbank Road, Lime Street, Elm Street and Sycamore Place. Despite its hillside setting, it was the first scheme in Europe to have a district heating scheme; and in cold weather, the pavements steamed like New York (no longer – each house now has its own central heating). Thomson had the clever notion of persuading the Council to build a prototype council house, with all the innovations that modern technology could offer council housing, in Blackness Avenue. Later nicknamed the *Mystery House* it was discovered by a puzzled councillor, a few years later, to be occupied by Thomson himself. To the east, Thomson laid out the Craigie Garden Suburb, to a plan of concentric rings of houses focused upon civic buildings – an imagery lifted directly from Ebenezer Howard's *Garden Cities of Tomorrow*. Small blocks of flats and four-in-a-block were designed to appear as self-contained villas.

Thomson was the first to demand the destruction of historic buildings (along the Seagate) on the grounds that they were an obstruction to the insatiable demands of traffic. Inter-war Dundee also brought the usual crop of garages and many cinemas. The cinema with the tallest advertising tower, and second largest capacity, in Europe, was Green's Playhouse in the Nethergate.

After the Second World War, at one point it looked as though Dundee had been finally denuded of purpose, character and soul. Jute and whaling, on which it had built its wealth and vastly increased population, had declined to almost nothing. The silting of the Tay precluded entry to Dundee's harbour of the new breed of large vessels. The industrial myth persuaded the citizens that Dundee's history was solely one of the exploitation of jute workers; and that it was a past best obliterated. In any case, the buildings were black. Grand plans abounded, and in the desperation to attract new commerce everything went . . . and it very nearly did.

The first to go was one of the oldest streets in Dundee, the Overgate, perhaps because the celebrated town planner, Dr Thomas Sharp, had recommended its entire rebuilding back in 1938. It became what seems to be destined to become a short-lived shopping centre. It was followed by the inner ring road, the Wellgate Shopping Centre, and – most destructive of all – the road network that accompanied the construction of the Tay Bridge. New roads filled in the harbour, as Dundee was stripped of its greatest asset, its riverside. Victorian and Edwardian views of a full harbour backed by stately classical buildings adorned with the occasional jewel had lent Dundee a sense of character and purpose. The magnificent Customs House was now beached, isolated by a major traffic artery and overshadowed by a high-level bridge. The free space provided by filling the harbour gathered a box-like railway station, swimming baths, and hotel, none of which will make Dundee '*vaut un detour*'. The political decision to make the northern landfall of the Tay Bridge in central Dundee, in opposition to the technical plan for a land-fall further east, showed short-term gain prevailing against long-term strategy. That bridge has destroyed Dundee's principal asset in return for a doubtful gain.

Enormous swathes of housing were plonked in formerly mag-nificent landscape along the Dichty Burn to the north of the town: each one marginally more rational and quicker in erection than the last, so that, appropriately, the most recently built – Whitfield, was the first to be demolished. These schemes sucked the life from the centre, but failed to provide any opportunity for it to flourish at the periphery. The inner areas virtually imploded as derelict mills collapsed and the population exported; and the sites of their houses and mills were cleared for car parking.

Of all the developments in this post-war phase of Dundee's history, it is the elevation to university status and consequent

Dundonians and Doos, City Square.
Ken Sharp

73

City Square. *R.I.A.S.*

construction of the University, of its Arts Tower, Belmont Halls of Residence, Students Union, the associated architecture faculty for the Duncan of Jordanstone College of Art, and nearby Ninewells Hospital, which emerge with most credit. They brought a sense of sophistication to western Dundee to complement the European reputation being earned by its faculties.

There is now a new spirit in Dundee. Barely six years ago, it had reached its nadir, its predominant image one of dereliction and decay. The first task was to persuade Dundonians themselves of the inherent quality of their city. The first stone cleaning was undertaken almost twenty years after Glasgow. Desultory attempts have been made both to re-route traffic, and to create more friendly spaces at the centre, such as the City Square (although traffic is still the curse of Dundee). But were the centre to be declared traffic-free on say, Saturdays, its citizens (and tourists for that matter) would appreciate what quality they have in Albert Square, Reform Street, Castle Street and the Nethergate. Since Dundee is devoid of great civic set-pieces, what matters are spaces between buildings; and they are too heavily traffic-dominated to be enjoyed. The ring road still represents an enormous wound in central Dundee. It requires to be closed in and bridged: and the Overgate – a leaking bandage in that wound – requires major treatment.

So what of the future? That magnificent setting remains within the bowl of the Sidlaw Hills; and the award-winning University Botanic Gardens benefits from the micro-climate still. Work has begun on a partial recovery and re-use of the harbour, with the restoration of HMS *Unicorn*, and the return

of the *Discovery*. On the western approaches, some of the buildings and the entire landscape of Dundee Technology Park are outstanding by Scottish standards.

But the city's future will lie in whether or not it manages to understand better than it ever has done in the past, exactly what its character is, and how to cherish it.

Dundee's history is one of determination without direction, of tactics without strategy, and of short-term gain as against long-term benefit. Until it has a full appreciation of its own innate characteristics, of its own latent strengths and its own opportunities and how to capitalise on them; and an awareness of its inherent weaknesses, and the threats posed by them, it is unlikely that the city will be able to exploit its opportunities as it should.

Yet, on a deserted Sunday evening on a warm summer's day, stroll from the Victoria Dock past the Coffee House, up Castle Street, to the High Street; up Reform Street to Albert Square; left to listen to the ghosts dancing in The Howff, then up Ward Road to the lower slopes of Dundee Law. Mutilated, abandoned, near to death, revived and potentially on the threshold of a new incarnation, Dundee can be magnificent. Perhaps it requires an outsider to recognise that.

What might have been: James Thomson's design for a Civic Centre on the Earl Grey Dock. What we have are box-buildings which blight the magnificent setting

Historic Accounts

Crawford's drawing of the town and harbour 1793. *Private collection*

DUNDEE 1746 - 99

In the Dundee Magazine *of 1799, a literary gentleman who signed himself as 'Philetas' wrote a humorous account of the changes he had witnessed in Dundee from the middle to the end of the eighteenth century. The year 1746 was of course that in which the second Jacobite Rebellion came to an end.*

Dundee in 1746

Inhabitants. – The inhabitants, at that period, did not exceed six thousand. The living were warned to bed by the sound of the bagpipe and the toll of the curfew, and the dead were carried to their graves with the tinkling of a hand-bell.

Buildings. – The buildings were generally of wood. – There were not then above half-a-dozen of stone houses in the High Street or market place. Large vacant areas were lying in a state of nastiness and puddle in the most central parts of the town, particularly in the Thorter-row and Burial wynd; and premiums for building had been given by the Magistrates. The town in police, inhabitants, &c., had been above a hundred years stationary! A couple of dirty houses called inns, or public-houses, were situated in two narrow and dreary lanes, and not so good as a modern ale-house. These were comfortable caravanseras for the repose of the weary traveller! and, alas! *Bonny Dundee* had none better.

Vivres. – Vivres (especially vegetables) were scarce, and could only be procured fresh on a Friday, and that only in summer and autumn, there being then no winter feeding. Onions, leeks, carrots, common kail, and cabbage, formed the verdant catalogue. (John Lord Gray was the first who introduced potatoes for sale from the field in 1753.) They were indeed cheap, and about one-fourth of the present price. Beef, one penny halfpenny per pound; a hen, fourpence; and eggs, three halfpence per dozen. Spirits had not then shed their baneful effects, in general, over the constitution and conduct of the lower orders. A draught of malt beverage formed all the debauch of the labourer and mechanic, and this was then so powerful as to send them reeling and happy home. Butchers' carrion (for such things *were*, and perhaps now *are*) was then seized and hung up *in terrorum* at the market cross, and afterwards thrown into the river. Flour was unmixed; and milk was unadultered. A choppen of ale was sold for a halfpenny; a goose for one shilling; a decent roasting pig for eightpence; and a Scotch pint of claret for four or five shillings.

Lodgings. – In those days our predecessors were easily accommodated. No houses fetched above ten pounds of rent, and few half that sum. A lodging indeed of five rooms, low kitchen, garret, shop, a couple of gardens, and pigeon house and stable, in the High Street was let in 1755 at £14 rent only. It was thought very dear, and every wiseacre wondered. The shop alone would now rent at £25 a year. *Withdrawing rooms* were not known, at least not used. The man and wife lived and soaked lovingly in their bedchamber; and the dining-room was reserved as a cold bath for the first unfortunate visitor. The *father parent* of the middling and lower classes was then little known to his children; he breakfasted at the alehouse; they went to school, and returned before he went to dinner; they were in bed and fast asleep before he returned in the evening from his club, his twopenny, and his tobacco. Thus, unless on a Sunday, he saw no more of his children than the man in the moon!

Merchants. – The venerable character of 'merchant' was then in the background. The respectable place they now hold in society was not then filled up. *The toe of the peasant had not then come so near the heel of the courtier as to gall his kibe.* The landed gentry, who, (*like the woodcocks*) did us the honour to pass the winter amongst us, strutted it about on tiptoe, and in sullen *hauteur*. The feudal manners then scorched us, and reigned uncontrolled. Floating wealth had not then balanced her current account with landed insolence; and the simple cottager, drudging tenant, and useful mechanic, were in a total state of poverty, servility, and depression.

Carriages. – One single one-horse chaise supplied the demands and travels of the whole inhabitants. Even *John Barnet*, (the *solitary* saddler), who repaired it daily before a journey, grew pert and sausy, from self-consequence and importance. John scrupled not tauntingly to desire his customers who were displeased to employ his neighbour. John should have had his ears cropt.

Milliners and Mantuamakers. – Of these there were two in all, who, with the aid of Mr Durham, the lank taylor (in the mantuamaking line) did all the millinery and mantuamaking business in Dundee.

Dancing. – Mr Noseman was the only dancing-master. I shall ever remember him. He was a tall German; he wore a small silver-laced hat, diminutive round silver buckles, and cane, and walked upright as an oak; drank brandy, and was a thorough pedant in his profession. The present postmaster and I figured away in our first minuet with him on the same day, and paid each a pound of Bohen to the servant maid, as the accustomed and stated dues, and as the first fruits of our labours *saltant*.

Horse Market and Shambles. – In the centre of the town, and in the narrowest street, was held a horse market twice a year. There horses neighed, galloped, trotted, and kicked; and the aged, the women and children were wholly at their mercy. In that same choice spot did our forefathers, in the exertion of their architective abilities, erect shambles and slaughtering place. Wounded animals escaping from the hands of the butcher, seldom failed to stick their horns into the first unguarded inhabitant that came in their way. Trembling scenes for parents, guardians, and relatives, and (I was going to add, husbands and wives) and a rich harvest for surgeons, undertakers, and gravediggers!!!

Raiment. – The raiment of the ladies was costly. Fashions did not change or vary much. High priced stuffs could not be easily renewed. The grandmother's marriage brocade served the grand-daughter for her wedding garment. A *linsy winsy* clad the middling people. The lower order of the sex were barefooted; except on a Sunday, when in imitation of their betters (for white stockings were rare) they put their limbs into mourning. A full suit of broad cloth was the general wear of gentlemen, and every youngster assumed a round curled wig at his marriage or majority: like barristers, it was

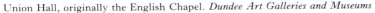

Union Hall, originally the English Chapel. *Dundee Art Galleries and Museums*

77

thought necessary to convey the semblance of wisdom to the wearer. Wig and bonnet makers were then tolerable trades. The first is now sickly, and the last is lost, and in it is a Corporate novelty – there we view a *Corporation without one active constituent!*

Such was the general state of the town (for I am not writing a minute history). Many other matters stood nearly on the same footing as now . . . Little rogues were hanged, great criminals escaped, and captains swore big oaths. Physicians wore large muffs, dangled gold-headed canes, ahemm'd loud, and looked wise; and according to the strength or weakness of the natural constitution, the patient recovered or expired. The rich lorded it over their dependants, and they, in their turn, domineered over theirs. Whig and Tory were the pass-words for broils and bickerings. Sycophants and parasites scraped and bowed, and even gravest men swallowed the enticing bait. The wealthy feasted, and the poor starved. A sceptic in religious matters was a character not then known. Such an animal would have been caged in iron, and shown like a wild beast for sixpence. Toppers swilled, guzzled, and besotted in the tavern; and their ladies in revenge took a cup of spirited or wine comfort at home. Lovers ogled, scoundrels broke vows, and dotards coo'd and bill'd. Servants rode before their masters, and running footmen skipped it before their coaches. Farmers toiled hard, and fed on meal, milk, and water. They now live lustily on beef, pudding and punch. Feasting ruled the roost, gave consequence, led the world, and enlisted table friends and flatterers. Guns and dogs, hawks and hounds, fiddles and flutes, and billiards and cards, made dreadful havoc amongst youth. Fornicators received the benefit of ghostly counsel. The case is now commuted: the Session funds receive the benefit of their cash. Men smacked each other in the forum on the new year's day, and danced *chapeau bas* in the minuet at Christmas. Ladies tripped it in monstrous hoopes, bound themselves up in bone stays and busks, like Egyptian mummies; and footed it to church in gold, silver, lace, scarlet, and short mantles. Cowards blustered, and brave men fought. Official men loom'd large, and taylors and shavers looked little. Ingratitude was healthy, and required no nursing – like fern it flourished in the barrennest soil. Cockfighting was publicly taught and encouraged at school, and (would you believe it, Mr Printer)! the unfortunate combatants were, in imitation of the American savages, slain, boiled, and devoured. To sum up all, the sun rose in the east and set in the west. Lightnings flashed, thunders rolled, and rains poured. Scandal, hypocrisy, and back-biting brought up the rear of this heterogeneal mass; and the world continued to roll like clockwork.

Dundee in 1799

The Town of Dundee, from 1746 to the present era of 1799, hath risen in rapid style to trade, to wealth, and to population. It bears little resemblance to those early times when civilization was hardly in blossom, and refinement not even in abeyance; when our manners were wild, stiff, and formal; when dark ignorance prevailed; when inhabitants and accommodations were confined, limited, and inelegant; and the minds of the inhabitants borne down by poverty and wretchedness.

In extent the buildings of Dundee are now doubled. They stretch to Blackness, Craigie, and to the Hill or Rotten-row; and to the south we have encroached on the river. Some of them approach to elegance. The environs and country are much improved, and we are encircled by water, by gardens, and by villas. Families live in an improved taste, and require more accommodation.

House rents are now from £5 to £40, and even to £50 per annum. Ground for building in the centre of the town hath become extremely valuable, and there is hardly a vacant spot in it. A small area, containing about 300 square feet, was lately sold at a public sale at the amazing price of £300.

In numbers of population we are, since 1750, quadrupled; that is, they may now fairly be taken at 25,000 souls.

In Inns we are completely accommodated. Neither Gordon's nor Morren's would do dishonour to any town in Europe; and it is by rivalship the public can be well served. We have had *enow of John Barnets* in our time already.

The Shipping is wonderfully increased. Foreign tonnage is, at least, quadrupled; vessels are well found and manned, and they voyage without interruption from Christmas to Christmas. The London trade boats sail and arrive every fortnight; and our home tonnage may be reckoned at 8 to 9000 tons.

Piers for the shipping and boats (as yet very imperfect) are greatly extended, and have cost large sums – particularly a shipping one hath been added with arches for the passing tide. The whole staple trade is loaded and unloaded there; and it forms a pleasant and healthy walk to the inhabitants. A ship-building dock is well occupied and employed, and vessels can be built there from 2 to 300 tons. A declivous boat-pier hath been built some years ago, with much judgment, under the management of the late Bailie Myles, at the west-shore, and gives easy access to passengers at all times.

Manufacturers are on a very increasing and enlarged scale. The staple Osnaburgh hath advanced greatly; a single weaver may now earn £50 a year by his daily labour.

78

Buildings have been greatly extended. There are now five churches well occupied and frequented, exclusive of every denomination of sectaries. A *new market place* for *butchery meat*, and a *slaughter place*, have been built. We have an elegant Hall for the Nine Incorporated Trades, a handsome English chapel, and a Glasite octagon; and these give real ornament to all around. The Town-house, a Tolbooth, is a piece of noble architecture; but its present situation can never be viewed to advantage or with justice to the architect. Our forefathers (and even some of the present generation) seem to have looked no farther than their noses when they turned proprietors and builders. Never was a building (if we except the *Mansion-house of London*, and the *Sailors' Hall here* so murdered in situation. It is set down in a hole fitted only for a hog's stye, and what is to be much lamented, it is one of those capital blunders which cannot, without immense expense, be now remedied.

Retail Shops are found in every street and corner, and we are fully supplied with every family article; and (in general) you are well and civilly treated, in return for your money.

Merchants are a respectable, well-educated, and wealthy body. The taverns and ale-houses are deserted for the drawing-room and their friends; and elegance and hospitality preside at their tables. The country squires have, for the present, quitted the town. Like *Cincinnatus*, they have returned to the ploughshares and to their seats, and have thus become *Borough seceders*. They find, that by time, they have acquired very respectable and opulent rivals in the city; that a couple of mansions are not now necessary to spend one *rent roll*, and that *self-consequence* and *importance* are delicate and tender plants that are much more quietly reared and nursed in wilds and heaths, and amongst mountains and forests, than in the bustly circle of mercantile and independent community. We have three Banking-houses. The old banking company established here in 1763, now do business it is thought, to at least sixteen times the extent they did at first setting out.

Gentlemen and Ladies and Servants are well-dressed, and neatly habited. Even our kitchen wenches carry *umbrellas*, and wear *veils*, to protect their pretty persons from the inclemency of the wintry sky, and their beauty and charms from the sun and dews of the summer. The fashion and tone in one article is wholly changed; the ladies alone now wear wigs, and the gentlemen are turned croppies and round-heads.

Vivres of all kinds are confessedly dearer, but are to be had in great abundance at all times. Beef is 6d; a hen, 1s 6d; and eggs, 6d a-dozen; and there is a plenteous and cheap supply of vegetables. We have, in humble imitation of *Covent Garden*, our *melons, cucumbers* and *asparagus*, in the public street. Fish seldom exceed one penny per pound.

Morality and honesty, and some other smaller matters, seem to have made little progress in amendment these sixty years, in despite of schools and establishments.

Vice, manufactures, and population, appear to have kept a steady jog trot together. . . The man who betrays you in the morning, riots merrily with you till midnight. Men and women do not always marry for conveniency: they wed not to be happy, but to be rich, powerful, affluent; that they and their sons and daughters may shine in the drawing-room, and ride in their coaches. Breed and descent, wisdom and madness, tawny or fair, deceased or wealthy, old or young, are alike from the question in modern matches. The elegance of the ancient dancing assemblies is gone! and in its place are introduced card playing! and a warming reel before departure!! Servants pilfer, vagrants steal, and hypocrisy smiles. The dear deceiver, after forfeiting his honour, is received into the favour of every other woman of the sex. Bankruptcy is not the mortal and fatal disease it was. Its virulence, however, decreases by habit; and considering the number of annual patients now-a-days, the recovery is generally wonderful. Skeel tramping is yet in full blaze, and to be seen every lawful day of the week. In urinals we are highly improved; and from the wooden loom and brown jar we have ascended to the fair cream and clouded China-ware. The custom of patching is now happily given up: it had so much of the Jezebel in it, that I congratulate my fair countrywomen on its being deserted. Haggis and *hodge-podge*, sheep and crapped heads, keep their places at the table, in defiance of pork, grisken, and roast beef. Dad gathers it in farthings, and young Hopeful spends it by guineas. The mother toils at the distaff, and the thoughtless and extravagant young Baggage throws it away on gew-gaws. Quakers begin to mingle amongst us, and to groan in spirit. The Jews, as I formerly mentioned, have not, as yet, set up shop here; the stragglers, however, are travelling about the country, with their *faar-keekers*, and so spying the land; whilst the main body are setting out to meet their promised deliverer Bonaparte. Scandal and tale bearing continue to do the honours of the tea-table, and folly and extravagance to hold their rites at the shop of the milliner.

The ladies continue to admire red coats, and to have no objection to the blue. Shortwaists, watering places, and bathing-quarters, are the present general rage; and drowning is now as common in summer as starving was formerly in winter. We tread not now on fairy ground. Spirits and hobgoblins are little known in these days; they flee from society and refinement, and from the busy haunts of men. Those incorporeals are suffered to glide and betake themselves to cloisters, church yards, and dormitories, and to melancholy aisles. As rooks, magpies, and foxes, they nestle and burrow in the deserted and mouldering tower, and ancient chateau; and there they caw and howl to the midnight winds. 'Tis there only they hold their frantic orgies, take their nocturnal rambles, and startle the watchful and lonely sentinel at his post. 'Tis there, mayhap, the ghosts of Malcolm and Claverhouse perambulate a dreary scene, perform their antic rounds – and vanish at the morning air!

Mankind continue to pout and spar, kiss, wrangle, toy, and trifle by turns. Folly, like death, spares neither sex nor age; and the wise heads, the wrong-heads, the blockheads, and the hot-heads, have been precious and prolific families since the days of their father Adam!

Strawberrybank. A quiet Georgian lane in the West End. *Ken Sharp*

CHAPTERS IN THE LIFE OF A DUNDEE FACTORY BOY
c. 1830

The rapid transformation of Dundee into an industrial town is graphically described in the book Chapters in the Life of a Dundee Factory Boy. *Probably written by James Myles, the authorship is uncertain but the conditions described in the mills are corroborated in evidence given to the Factory Commission in 1833. Here, the author describes his mother's departure from rural Angus to the city.*

She then packed up her little property, and consigned it to the carrier who in those days traded between Dundee and Glammis, and with a heavy heart left the spot rendered sacred to her by many endearing associations, and retired to hide her poverty in the busy regions of a great manufacturing town. It was a warm morning in May, when I had scarcely reached my seventh year, that we set out on foot. I asked my mother if we were going to see my father. She gave me no direct answer, but told me we were going where I would see many strange sights, and where I would require to work in a spinning mill to help to keep her living. My young heart bounded with pleasure at the prospect of seeing Dundee, a town that I had heard the country people speak of as very large; and by their conversations I had concluded that there was no place equal to it. As a child thinks *his* father the best and strongest of men, so young people confined to a particular locality, and who know little of geography, think '*the town*' of their district the largest and most important place in the world. I imagined Dundee a vast city, abounding in wealth and grandeur, a kind of Elysium where poverty and suffering were not allowed to enter. Such were my boyish conceptions. Alas! they were juvenile castles in the air that were speedily dissipated by my future experience.

On our arrival in Dundee, my mother's wonted perseverance seemed paralyzed. She knew not what to do. Ultimately she spoke to an old woman, who in those days sold vegetables in the Green Market, and she proved to be a good Samaritan, for she kindly offered us a bed, and tendered my mother many useful hints. After lodging a single night in her house, by her instructions my mother left my little brother and me in her care, and went in the direction of the Bonnethill to seek out a house. In less than two hours she returned and announced to us her success; and on the evening of the same day we found ourselves the tenants of a small room in an old land near the corner of the Bucklemaker Wynd. The entrance was by the first close on the left hand, and the prospect from our window was circumscribed by a dead wall, distant only the breadth of a narrow passage. My new home was indeed a great change for a romping country boy, such as I then was. I had been accustomed to live in the fresh air of creation, to sport by the river that rolled past our secluded cot, to gaze on the green fields and rustling trees which beautified Strathmore, and to listen to the bleating of sheep, the lowing of cows, or the caroling of the skylark warbling his matins at the portals of heaven; but now I was shut up in a narrow close where nothing could be seen but old dirty walls of stone and lime, and the music of the morning which fell on my ear was not the sweet songs of birds, but the harsh guttural roars of coal sellers and fish cadgers.

On the beginning of the fifth week, I got work in a spinning mill at the Dens, which filled our hearts with joy, but so near starvation were we then, that my mother had only 4½d in the world. It was on a Tuesday morning in the month of 'Lady June' that I first entered a spinning mill. The whole circumstances were strange to me. The dust, the din, the work, the hissing and roaring of one person to another, the obscene language uttered, even by the youngest, and the imperious commands harshly given by those 'dressed in a little brief authority', struck my young country heart with awe and astonishment. At that time the Twelve Hours' Factory Act had not come into operation and spinning mills were in the glory as huge instruments of demoralisation and slavery. Mercenary manufacturers, to enable them to beat more upright employers in the markets, kept their machinery and hands active fifteen, and in many cases seventeen hours a day, and when tender children fell asleep under the prolonged infliction of 'work! work! work!' overseers roused them with the rod, or thongs of thick leather burned at the points. The lash of the slave driver was never more unsparingly used in Carolina on the unfortunate slaves than the canes and 'whangs' of mill foremen were then used on helpless factory boys. When I went to a spinning mill I was about seven years of age. I had to get out of bed every morning at five o'clock, commence work at half-past five, drop at nine for breakfast, begin again at half-past nine, work until two, which was the dinner hour, start again at half-past two, and continue until half-past seven at night. Such were the nominal hours; but in reality there were no regular hours: masters and managers did with us as they liked. The clocks at the factories were often put forward in the morning and back at night, and instead of being instruments for the measurement of time, they were used as *cloaks* for cheatery and oppression. Though this was known amongst the hands, all were afraid to speak, and a workman then was afraid to carry a watch, as it was no uncommon event to dismiss any one who presumed to known too much about the science of horology.

It was during this winter that I got the first unmerciful beating from a mill overseer. I was attending a spinning frame. It got too full in the shifting, and I was unable to keep up the ends. The foreman challenged me. I told him I was doing the best I could. He flew into a furious passion, dragged me into the turning shop, cut a strap off a lathe, and lashed me cruelly. He then seized me by the ears and hung me for a few moments over a window three storeys from the ground. In reading of such a ferocious action as this, methinks I hear the reader exclaim, 'Surely that is not true'; but I beg solemnly to state that it is true to the very letter, and there is one old mill foreman in Dundee who can corroborate all I have said.

Employers, excepting a few high-minded and generous men, wallowed in nought but a sea of selfishness and icy indifference. The common sympathies of humanity were crushed by the raging passion for gold, and the pride of wealth alienated their hearts and understandings so much from the sufferings of the young and moral necessities of the poor who toiled for them, that they surely in the whirlwind of competition and avarice, dreamed they were superior mortals born to trample and tyrannize over those whom necessity had placed at their command.

Here are just a few of the testimonies given to the Factory Commissioner in 1833.

4. ELIZA MILL, thirteen years old, solemnly sworn, depones, that she was up before four this morning, which made her fall asleep when the mill was inspected at one to-day by the Factory Commissioners; that she is often so tired at night that she falls asleep before leaving the mill; that her feet generally swell in the evenings; that she got a severe accident to her arm when she was in a mill in Arbroath; that she has worked in mills ever since she was seven years old; that she is often very hoarse from the stour, and has a pain in her breast. Depones that she cannot write.

3. JAMES PATERSON, aged sixty years, solemnly sworn, depones, that he is an overseer in Messrs. James and William Brown's flax spinning-mill in Dundee, and has been in their employment for about seven years; that he was previously at the spinning mill at Glammis for twelve years, and there lost his right hand and arm, caught by the belt of the wheels, in the preparing floor; that medical advice was afforded gratis, but nothing else was done for him; that he got no pension or gratuity whatever for the great loss he had sustained, although he applied for an allowance again and again; that the children are much tired and fairly 'set' at night; that he is in the reeling flat with the women, who are tired and sleepy; one of them at present, Margaret Porter, in bed, merely from standing so long for a fortnight past; that 'it would be God's blessing for everyone to have shorter hours'; that he has been about forty years in spinning-mills, and has seen the young people so lashed with a

Beef Can Close, made famous in the song 'As I cam doun the Overgate'. *Dundee District Libraries*

leathern belt that they could hardly stand; that at Trollick, a mill now given up, he has seen them lashed, skin naked, by the manager James Brown; that at Moniferth he has seen them taken out of bed when they did not get up in time, lashed with horse-whips to their work, carrying their clothes, while yet naked, to the work, in their arms with them.

10. CATHARINE IRONS, eighteen years old, solemnly sworn, depones, that she has worked in the wet spinning-apartment from the beginning; that she stands on a wet floor; that the wet spray of hot water is splashed on her waist, so as always to keep her wet, and that every rove that comes forward she has to put her hand in the hot water; that she is very subject to colds since she worked in that apartment, and that she has hacked and swelled feet and hands; that the workers in that apartment generally complain of their health suffering, and some of them are often absent, seven of them this morning; that all the spinners in that apartment get a thick coarse linen petticoat from the master.

2. JOANNA GREIVE, nine years old, solemnly sworn, depones, that she has worked at these mills for a year and more; that she is whiles tired, and her feet and legs swell, and so ill that she cannot go to school, and the moment she gets home to the fireside falls asleep; that she has often a sair head, and was away with a sair head this morning; that a man comes about and awakes her in the morning; that her mother does not rise so soon as her; that she sometimes gets a lick with a hand when she is in a fault, which makes her 'whiles to greet'; that she can read in the Testament, but cannot write.

5. JOHN ROSS, aged twenty-two, solemnly sworn, depones, that he has some years ago at Mr. Kinmond's mill of which James Malcolm is manager; that he ran away from Mr. Kinmond's to take the play for a day, and Mr. Malcolm, who was on horseback, having found him at Broughty Ferry, forced him to run as fast as the horse went, back to Dundee, whipping him all the way with a long whip.

Worlds away from the poverty of the Dundee closes, the Mudie children and Frances Grant in the country, c. 1897. *Dundee Art Galleries and Museums*

MEMOIRS OF A DUNDEE LADY

THE NINETEENTH CENTURY

In the early decades of the nineteenth century, Dundee still retained its character of wealthy 'county town', with its aristocracy and established merchant families, still residing within the city. Insight into the life of this sphere of Dundee society of the period is provided by the memoirs of Mrs Home Scott, published in *Dundee: Past and Present* at the beginning of our own century. Née Mary Jobson in 1797, this lady belonged to an old family with high social standing: her forefather was a soldier with General Monk in 1651, who like many English soldiers, married a Scot and settled in the area. The family were successful merchants. Her father supported the radicals reform movement at the end of the eighteenth century, was a friend of Palmer and entertained Robert Burns in his home in 1787. Mary Jobson married John Home Scott, writer, in Dundee, in 1827. Here are some of her recollections of that time.

THE ARISTOCRATIC QUARTER OF THE TOWN A CENTURY AGO.

Early in the nineteenth century the town contained about 25,000 inhabitants; and all the genteel families lived in flats, chiefly in the Cowgate, Wellgate, Bain Square, and Meadow Street, which was sometimes called 'Quality Street!' The *first* large self-contained houses were built by my father's brothers and other relations; and were occupied in later years by Mr Patrick Watson, Mr James Keiller, Mr A. D. Grimond (Whiteleys), Mr G. Ll. Alison, and Captain Scott; that occupied by Captain Scott was demolished many years ago.

DARKNESS OF THE TOWN AT NIGHT – ONE CAUSE OF THE DARKNESS.

My father generally went to the Bank in the evenings, and remained there from seven to nine o'clock, sometimes later. There were but few street lamps, and in these oil was burned. Sometimes, when Russian seamen happened to be in the port, it was in vain to look for a burning lamp, for they drank

83

the oil and left the town in total darkness! So ran the tale. Being frequently unlit, the lamps could not be depended on the light, and it was therefore customary for the inhabitants to carry little lanterns, named 'cut-throats.' One of these my father always took with him to the Bank in the winter nights. As I sat at the corner window of our house in Bain's Square watching for my father's return, oh, how miserably anxious I felt for his safety until I saw the little speck of light in his lamp coming in sight at the top of the Murraygate. Then with what delight did I run to meet and welcome him, exclaiming – 'Oh, Papa, has anybody touched you?' We had a very few night watchmen, and two or three town's officers. The town drummer, Daniel McCormack, was a remarkable man. No one seemed to know the history of his early life. He was a first-rate scholar; and his intimate acquaintance with Latin and Greek proved that he must have received a classical education.

WATCHMEN! WHAT OF THE NIGHT!

It was the custom of the few guardians on the streets to proclaim at intervals during the night the state of the weather. These announcements were sometimes long and contradictory. One watchman, famous in this way, would awaken the lieges by bawling – 'It's half-past four o'clock, an' a fine, braw, cauld, dark, weety morning'.' Those who heard him could choose for themselves from his announcement what sort of weather would suit them best.

TEDIOUSNESS OF TRAVELLING.

Travelling seventy or eighty years ago was but seldom undertaken. There were no means by which persons living in Dundee could reach London, except by the mail coach or a small London smack. In going to Edinburgh we had always to stay a night at one place or another on the way; and on one occasion seven hours were occupied in crossing by boat from Kinghorn. During all that time I was sea-sick. The coach required three days, and a post-chaise about a week, to make the journey to Harrogate.

EDUCATION ABOUT NINETY YEARS AGO.

My first and only teacher in reading, spelling, grammar, and recitation, was Daniel Macintosh, and an excellent teacher he was. He did not resort to severity in enforcing discipline in his schools, the tawse being seldom used; he preferred moving the moral feelings of a delinquent or disobedient pupil. A common punishment was inflicted by making the pupil stand in a corner with his face to the wall, while his head was covered with an old dirty grey wig! I daresay many yet remember 'Macintosh's wig.'

Boys and girls stood promiscuously in the same classes. Each class had a monitor, who also helped us to prepare our lessons for the next day, so that we had little learning to do at home. We had also an admirable French teacher in M. Daraux, who was succeeded by M. Legendre. Dancing was taught by Mr Nicholson, who paid great attention to our manners and deportment. Macintosh's examinations were grand occasions. They were attended by almost all the genteel families in the town. Dean Horsley (son of the famed Bishop Horsley) came regularly, and frequently distributed the prizes. The recitations evinced careful training; and scenes such as those between 'Norval and Glenalvon,' 'The King and the Miller of Mansfield,' 'Lady Townly and Lady Grace,' as well as other dialogues, were rendered with spirit and expressiveness.

RECREATION AND AMUSEMENTS.

We were very happy in our school days. Our lessons having been partly prepared in the school on one day for the day following, we were not overburdened with tasks at home, and so had a large part of the evenings to be devoted to amusements or physical exercise. Our favourite place of recreation was Bain Square, where the Baxters (John and William), the Sandemans, the Wises (from Hillbank), and many others, assembled every evening. The pastime of 'Scotch and English Men' was entered into with great enthusiasm, and though the game was generally only for boys, the fun was rendered more hilarious when girls, who had been invited, took part in it. On one occasion, when we were keenly absorbed in the amusement, new domestic servants my mother was expecting arrived on the spot. One of them asked me if I could tell her where Mrs Jobson lived! 'Oh, yes,' I replied, 'I am Mary; but I am playing at 'Scotch and English Men' just now and cannot leave the game to introduce you; there is the entry, the door is open, just go in, you can wash up the teacups, mend the fires, make down the beds, and by that time the game will be over, and I will be in.' They passed into the house, and as they did so I overheard one of them remarking – 'Sic a Mistress! playing at Scotch

The Mudie children, the Hollies, Broughty Ferry, c. 1895. *Dundee Art Galleries and Museums*

Dundee from the Stannergate, 1822. *Dundee District Libraries*

and English Men; I'll no stay lang with that lassie!' Little did they know the future, and how little do we know it! The one who formed such an unfavourable impression of the service she was just entering into proved an excellent and faithful servant, and remained many years in our family, and only left it when she was to be married. The marriage ceremony took place in my father's house, and I had the honour of being 'best maid.' Her husband was an excellent gentleman, and their only son was a respected townsman.

In the winter evenings, when out-of-door sports were impossible, the young people occasionally had tea parties, followed by a variety of games, the last one generally being 'Blind Man's Buff,' or 'Hunt the Slipper,' and the evening's enjoyment was finished off with a Scotch reel.

'Twas here we traced the slipper by its sound,
And turned the blindfold hero round and round;
'Twas here, at eve, we formed our fairy ring,
And fancy fluttered on its wildest wing.

A FULLY EDUCATED GIRL ABOUT 90 YEARS AGO.
But, alas our school days very soon came to an end, for upwards of sixty years ago, a girl was considered fully educated when she was about fourteen years of age. Sometimes those of the better class were sent to a fashionable Boarding School (generally Miss Playfair's in Edinburgh) to be *finished off*. But as my dear father would never be prevailed on to part with me, having experienced very heavy domestic bereavements, I have remained in an *unfinished* state all my life! How very different this is from the education of the young ladies of the present day – many of them going from the classroom to the altar!

SCOTCH SONGS: A PLEA.
We had delightful concerts long ago. When Miss Stephens came she enchanted the audience with the exquisite beauty and power of her voice in rendering some of our lovely Scotch songs. I think it is to be much regretted that our young ladies of the present day do not cultivate our charming

The Executive – a charicature of Dundee Town Council early 19th-century. *Dundee District Libraries*

national music more than they do. Many of our finest airs are associated with words of the tenderest pathos, and possess a charm which is rarely found in modern songs. I remember being present at a very wonderful performance on musical glasses. The tones and vibrations were remarkably sweet, clear, and charming. It is a pity this entertainment is so rare: this may be accounted for by the fact that it is very difficult to attain any degree of excellence in the art.

ASSEMBLIES IN THE TOWN HALL.
Several very delightful balls, called Assemblies, were held during winter. They were very exclusive, those only who had been subscribers to them being admitted, but an exception was made in favour of the officers of any regiment stationed in Dundee at the time, or any gentleman from the country, each being received on paying 10s. These balls were held in the Town Hall; and one of the large rooms adjoining was set apart as a card-room. The game played was not always Whist. When Brag was the game the play was often very high. When, between the dances, any strolled from the Hall into the card-room it was painful for them to witness the excitement of several of the elderly ladies. Their hands were shaking so violently that their fingers could scarcely hold the cards. One lady was observed to be free from this agitation. She sat immovable, and betrayed no indication of having a 'good' or a 'bad' hand. She was very successful; and her success was ascribed to her wonderful composure and self-control.

A BALL'S PRELIMINARY TROUBLES TO LADIES.
The ladies were also slaves to the hairdresser for long after this period. For any special occasion, when perhaps a grand ball was to take place, preparations began to be made early, not the least important of which was the toilette. The operator was then in great demand, the rush of young ladies to him being so great as to render it impossible for him to 'overtake' all their heads in one day; consequently some, to prevent the pain of the disappointment which they would inevitably suffer by their not getting to the ball, wisely adopted the precaution of having their hair dressed on the night before, and then sat up all night in an arm-chair not to disturb the monstrous fabric which had been artistically formed so as to impart greater fascination to their charms!

LADIES' DRESSES.
In those days ladies did not have a variety of dresses as we have now, as but few materials were manufactured then for that purpose. The distinction of the dress, however, was more marked. Every lady of good position brought with her, as part of her marriage 'tocher', a large store of very costly beautiful silks and satins, richly brocaded.

THE MINUET.
I never saw but one minuet danced, or rather walked, in a ballroom. It was the custom for the gentleman who was to take part in this exhibition, to secure the honour of the lady's hand several days before the dance took place. On the occasion to which I refer the ball was opened with a single couple minuet, and I distinctly recollect the dress and appearance of the lady and the gentleman. The gentleman, who had white powdered hair, was dressed in a green coat with clear buttons, pale silk knee-breeches with silver buckles at the knees, flesh coloured silk stockings, shoes with silver buckles, and a large cocked hat! The lady, also with powdered hair, was attired in rich brocaded silk, and carried a very large fan. The gentleman led out his lady partner with great ceremony, and after making a profound bow to her, which she returned with an equally low curtsey, the minuet was commenced. The exhibition was pleasing but unexciting. The company of spectators present sat mutely admiring the elegant attitudes and movements of the couple, who, at the close of their performance, retired to a seat, amidst a gentle hum of applause.

Minuets for long after this period were taught in dancing schools, but they never took place in public. I remember taking part in seven different minuets at a private ball. After this came what may be called:

THE AGE OF DANCING.
Although waltzing and quadrilles were not introduced till some time later. When waltzing was first introduced in this country it was very unpopular, and many of our young ladies refused to waltz with the gentlemen. This declinature, however, was often rendered in compliance with the wishes of the ladies' chaperons, who kept a strict guardianship over the fair ones under their charge. The favourite dances were Scotch reels, country-dances, the Lancers, the Haymakers, and the Boulongie (a dance seldom seen now). Well might it be called the age of dancing! Oh, with what spirit we entered into this delightful recreation! Here, I may remark, many young ladies danced beautifully; and I will say (and I might be excused for doing so) their style of dress was suitable for free and elegant motion, and very different from that of the present day, which is not only ungraceful, but so tight as to prevent freedom of movement, and gives the wearer the appearance of being clad in armour.

CHARITY BALLS – YOUNG LADIES' 'POCKETING'.
As bazaars were quite unknown in this country about 1820, the first attempt at raising money for a charitable purpose was made by getting up what was called a Charity Ball. A Miss Annie Stephens, a well-known and much respected lady, was the originator and promoter of it. The object was to obtain funds for a charitable purpose. When such balls were to be repeated they were always looked forward to by the young people with great pleasure. All classes were admitted, and therefore the room was soon filled to overflowing. The mixed nature of the company, and the great variety of dresses of all colours formed a grand and lively picture. These assemblies were most enjoyable, and very laughable scenes sometimes occurred. One in particular was very funny. The young men were expected to treat their partners to refreshments, which were provided in an adjoining room. After a dance a young gentleman would conduct his partner to this room and entertain her to a 'little' repast. He at first helped her very liberally. But he soon became surprised at the rapidity with which the good things he gave her disappeared. Casting a more particular glance at his partner, after he had provided her with another substantial supplement, his intense surprise may be imagined when he saw her artlessly relegating the dole to keep company with the already large collection of cheese cakes, oranges, and other delicacies she had previously consigned to the depths of a huge tartan pocket! This need not excite any wonder, because 'pocketing' was then very generally practised by ladies at dances. And perhaps it was excusable that they should make the most off a ball, which came to them perhaps once in a life-time!

Long ago ladies wore not only one but a pair of pockets, and when a young lady was getting her wedding trousseau the supply of pockets was never forgotten. I was the possessor of twelve pairs of dimity pockets as part of my marriage outfit! Many of our notable housewives keep up the old fashion of wearing a pocket below the dress, instead of in the dress itself – a very sensible plan, as that pocket formed a more secure receptacle for valuables than one worn outside.

87

A Market Day, the City Churches, 1830

CONCERTS AND THEATRICALS.

Besides our delightful assemblies, we had first-rate concerts and an admirable theatrical company. Madame Cataline, that wonderful woman, condescended to visit Dundee, and she and John Kemble performed every night for a week, his nephew, Henry Siddons, having prevailed on him to come. The leading families secured all the boxes for the entire engagement, and part of the gallery was set apart to supplement the pit accommodation. To those who have not had the privilege of seeing Kemble's acting I need not attempt to convey any idea of it; while to those who had seen him he can never be forgotten. His voice, his face, his figure, his movements (particularly in his Roman characters) were regarded as perfect.

While writing about the theatre I may here mention that I lately came upon an old play-bill, printed in 1810 – now nearly seventy years ago. It stated that performance was to be for the benefit of Signor Belzoni, who afterwards became a great traveller. On that occasion he exhibited feats of strength which, I believe, have never been surpassed. In one exhibition he carried seven full grown men, walking several times along the stage with his huge burden, and waving a flag in each hand.

A DINNER PARTY ABOUT 1810 – UNFAVOURABLE YOUTHFUL IMPRESSIONS!

I must now hasten to give an account of the social habits about 1810, and if my readers will accept an invitation to a dinner party (such as took place at that time) I shall be happy to meet them there. The dinner hour was four or half-past four o'clock. As there were no street conveyances the ladies walked to the party. All the guests assembled in the drawing room, and when dinner was announced all walked into the dining-room, the ladies preceding the gentlemen. For a time the confusion was annoying and perplexing. The host kept calling – 'Now gentlemen, divide the leddies; divide the leddies!' I must say, to do the ladies justice, they did all in their power to 'divide' the gentlemen. Order being at last secured, and all harmoniously seated, the hostess made requests to certain guests, begging Mr A – 'Divide the fowls' (which proved a more arduous undertaking than the dividing of the ''leddies''); Mr S – 'To take the pie;' and Mr M – 'To sit near the ham.' After the soup had been removed the drinking usages were begun, and much had to be done in that way. The host drank wine with every lady at the table, after having first requested the honour to be allowed to do so. This example was followed by all the other gentlemen, who thereafter went through a similar ceremony in drinking wine with each other! The host was particularly careful not to overlook any of his guests. The 'dram' was always an essential tonic after dinner, and the company generally seemed to recognise the good sense of the man

Dundee and a busy River Tay, c. 1836, from a drawing by D. A. Andrews. *Dundee District Libraries*

who only indulged in this way on one of two occasions – namely, when he ate fish at dinner, or when he did not! Porter, strong ale, and port wine were handed round with the cheese, closing the feast.

At this stage all the children of the family, including the baby (where there was one) were sometimes brought in and introduced to the guests. On one occasion, a gentleman, who was far from being prepossessing in appearance, and whose mouth had got the lion's share of his features, begged a pretty little girl to come and speak with him. With a startled look of surprise, she hesitated for a moment, then ran off to her mother and asked – 'Dis he bite? will he bite's?' – which evoked great laughter from the company, in which the gentleman, thus unexpectedly reflected upon, constrainedly joined.

TEAS AND SUPPERS.
Tea for the ladies was served in the drawing-room by the hostess, and immediately afterwards the card tables were set, at which elderly ladies were soon deeply absorbed in the playing of 'quadrille' or whist. When the gentlemen entered the room at a later hour they expressed themselves as being very happy to find the ladies had been so pleasantly engaged during their somewhat long separation. Good and worthy men they were, it must be confessed, for they were disposed to be pleased with everything and with everybody. The elderly gentlemen joined the ladies at the whist tables, while the young people enjoyed a merry and noisy round game of cards. When the night had far advanced, and the hour had come when, as at the present time, carriages would be expected to appear to convey the guests to their homes, there was still a vast deal to be done before 'Good night' could be said. On such occasions supper was late. Looking back on those feasts, it seems, from our present-day experiences, perfectly astonishing how, with the very few servants then in a household, they could have been so well managed. No wonder that the landladies had often *red faces*, the duties that devolved on them being so multifarious and arduous. The supper was not made up of scraps of fragments left over from the dinner table, but was a freshly cooked repast, generally consisting of

89

chickens, ham, tripe, sausages, mince collops, rissoled haddocks, mince pies and other warm dishes. When the time arrived for the company to break up, the elderly ladies were carried home (now do not smile, but allow me to finish my sentence) in Sedan chairs, while the younger ladies walked, the Sedan being too expensive a mode of transit for them, and with the aid of duffel cloaks and pattens (if the night was wet), and lasses, who carried lanterns to show the guests their homeward way, all reached their respective homes in safety.

'OLD DUNDEE' DINNERS.

I think we had more profusion and more dishes at our dinner parties long ago than we have now. But the arrangement was different. At that time nothing was handed round as is now done, every viand was placed on the table. There were two kinds of soup, two kinds of fish, substantial dishes at the head and bottom of the table, as well as side dishes, corner dishes, and dishes along the centre of the table. The first course was followed by a very handsome second, and then by dessert.

NO COUNTRY LODGINGS.

It was not the custom about the beginning of the nineteenth century for families to go to country lodgings as is the case now; indeed there was no inviting place to which we could go. At that time there were few houses in Broughty Ferry excepting a row of fishermen's huts fronting the sea-beach. Newport was reached by crossing the river in a small pinnace, the rough passage in stormy weather being more like a 'sea voyage'. Excepting Lochee, where my father in the summer months, for several years, secured a sweet cottage, there was no other place within a convenient distance from Dundee, where suitable quarters could be obtained.

DEAR LOCHEE!

Oh, how delighted we were when the time came for us to go there. How we used to watch the progress of the hawthorn and the laburnum, hoping they would be in full blossom before the fourth of June to enable us to decorate the horse and cart which were to convey us to Lochee, and also to Douglasfield, when the time came, to spend the King's birthday there. Many of our happiest early days were spent at Lochee. What added greatly to our enjoyment were the pet animals we were allowed to keep. We had poultry of various kinds, and my brothers had a pony which greatly delighted them. But we liked our rabbits best.

MAY DAY AND MAY DEW.

This is the first of May! I have resumed my pen to write a few closing words to this chapter of recollections of old Bonnie Dundee, its scenes, social life, customs and manners. How strange it is that some days cling to the memory for ever, and this day is one of them. Many a merry party was arranged to go to the top of the Law early on the first morning of May, where all would wash their faces with May dew believing it would make them beautiful, not all their lives, as Madam Rachel professed to her victims, but until they might renew the charm the following year! I am not aware whether the practice still continues; I hope it does, for it is a very merry old institution!

The Radical Toun

Dundee Politics

by GRAHAM OGILVY

Unpredictable and tumultuous, Dundee's political life over the last two hundred years, has veered from the radical and revolutionary to the irreverent and maverick. A city of political surprises, Dundee has determinedly gone its own way. From the election of its first MP, Géorge Kinloch, outlawed for his support for democratic rights, Dundee has always had the ability to upset the political applecart. Winston Churchill was elected triumphantly as a Liberal and unceremoniously dumped as a Conservative; the city elected 'Neddy' Scrymgeour, Britain's only Prohibitionist MP; and in the wake of the First World War was represented by E. D. Morel, one of the nation's most 'notorious' pacifists. Gradually evolving as a Labour stronghold, it returned Tom Johnson, Labour's first Scottish Secretary of State and later the Labour intellectual and cabinet minister, John Strachey, and yet, for much of the seventies and eighties, it gave the only urban refuge to the Scottish National Party and its Chairman, Gordon Wilson.

But above all the story of Dundee's political life is a remarkable tale of sacrifice and suffering and of idealism and hope in the battle by ordinary people for economic and democratic rights. Frequently enthusiasm for these causes spilled over into rioting and, at times, plots for insurrection. Whenever revolt looked near in Britain, Dundee was at the forefront – during the French Revolution, Chartist agitation and periods of industrial upheaval, Dundonians could be relied upon to take to the streets in force.

Rapid industrialisation and the influx of rural Scots and Irish played a role in forging Dundee as a radical hotbed, but in that it was no different from other Scottish cities. What really set Dundee apart was its relative geographical isolation and compact size. In a city with a tiny, wealthy élite of mill-owners and employers and a huge mass of poverty-stricken workers, the rich man was firmly in his castle and the poor man resolutely knocked at the gate.

The contrasts of privilege and poverty were obvious to all in a community the size of Dundee and, without a military barracks or significant police force until the middle of the last century, popular frustrations could always spill over. Indeed for almost seventy years, from the 1770s to the 1840s, Dundee's workers periodically held the rich to ransom and engaged in collective

1756

As in the sixteenth century, the Hilltown was still a centre for weavers, specifically bonnetmakers whose craft is commemorated in the name of the 'Bonnethill' district today. A 'private gentleman' wrote:

In 1756 – The Hill, or Rotten-Row, was chiefly bonnetmakers – (there were very few hats then in Dundee, except the Ministers, the Provost and four Bailies, Sir George Stewart and Captain Ramsay). The Hill yards had stocks of kail, and a few syves here and there; but generally crops of oats and barley. There was not a sclate house in the Hill, but one on the east side, near the middle, and the old Tolbooth at the foot of the Hill, on the west side beside the Lady-well. The Lady-well itself, and its fine yard, were then private property, and belonged to a David Cook, who was insane, and lived in a wood land on the south side of the Murraygate port. The well is now public, but the yard is still private property, and contains an excellent spring of water, independent of the public well. The bonnetmakers had all seats at the end of their houses, on the street, where they sat and wrought their bonnets with large wires. The houses in general had the gables to the streets, and were only a ground floor, covered with thatch, but mostly only with divots of earth; and several of the houses with stone and feal: only a few of them had glass windows.

91

Policemen before City Chambers, c. 1900. Because of their height and country origin, Dundonians called them 'oatmeal monuments'. *Dundee District Libraries*

bargaining by riot. From the Tayside Meal Mobs of the 1770s, when starving Dundonians ransacked nearby farms and ships in the harbour, to the unemployed agitation of the hungry thirties when police savagely attacked peaceful demonstrators, hardship was usually the underlying cause of disorder.

The response of the authorities was often savage. Six men were charged with offences arising out of the activities of the Tayside Meal Mobs. Five – three weavers, a porter and a quarry-man, wisely fled and were outlawed. A sixth, a sailor named Robertson, stood trial and was convicted on unsatisfactory evidence. He made a desperate plea for mercy, declaring that he would serve any punishment rather than be separated from his family and announced that he would rather be hanged than transported. But his pleas for leniency were ignored and the unfortunate Robertson was sentenced to be transported to Botany Bay for life, with the first seven years of the sentence to be spent in hard labour. It was a virtual death sentence and Dundee's working class had its first martyr. He was not to be the last.

Riots like those of the Meal Mobs were nothing new, but after the French Revolution disturbances took on a political overtone.

At the same time as the crowds thronged through the streets of Dundee with cries of 'Liberty, Equality and No King!', attacked the homes of political opponents and prevented ships laden with food for export from sailing, aristocratic heads were rolling in Paris. It was a terrifying nightmare for the Scottish ruling class and the beginning of modern politics in Dundee where, by 1792, 5,000 workers were employed in the manufacture of linen. With no rights of any kind, they possessed few qualms about taking to the streets to advance their aims.

Just as frightening to the powerful was the sympathy for democratic ideas of a growing middle class of traders and professionals. In 1790 the well-to-do Whig Club in Dundee sent a message of congratulation to the French National Assembly, on 'The triumph of liberty and reason over despotism, ignorance and superstition.' A year later, the Dundee Revolution Society pledged itself to 'the rights of men, an equal representation of the people, a speedy abolition of the slave trade and the abolition of all religious tests for civil offices.' This resolution reflected the ideas of Thomas Paine in his famous *Rights of Man*. A local iron-monger, James Wright whose house still stands in Dundee's Nethergate, arranged for the publication of a cheap edition of Paine's *Rights of Man* and of his later *Age of Reason*. Wright was in correspondence with Paine himself and with the French revolutionary leader Lafayette and also arranged for the circulation of medals commemorating Paine, which were struck in Dundee.

By 1792, working people were, for the first time in Scottish history, joining political organisations, the forerunners of today's Labour movement. The summer of that year saw protests throughout Scotland and in the autumn the Dundee Friends of Liberty was formed with a weaver, George Mealmaker, as its Secretary. The Friends of Liberty was a working-class organisation but a Unitarian minister, the Reverend Thomas Fysche Palmer became one of its leading lights. He wrote to a friend at this time, 'The Friends go on here with some degree of spirit, they have introduced the practice of reading letters, extracts and small pamphlets, and then enforcing them by argument, which seems likely to produce much good.'

All of this must have been heady stuff for 'a society of low mechanics and weavers'. On Friday, 16 November 1792, a crowd planted a 'tree of liberty' in the High Street and forced Lord Provost Alexander Riddoch to take his hat off and walk round the tree three times shouting 'Liberty and Equality Forever!'. In revenge for this indignity, a group of young 'gentlemen' removed the 'tree of liberty' and precipitated a week of rioting and disorder which only ended with the arrival of troops on 26 November. By that time the crowd had attacked the homes of a local bailie and customs officers who had prevented the unloading of grain at the harbour. The lodgings of one Lieutenant

1792

Robert Small gave a detailed description of the city at the turn of the nineteenth century. Significantly he dwells on the beginning of the physical deterioration of the people through industrialisation, something which would be exacerbated as the workers' conditions deteriorated during the nineteenth century.

The people of Dundee have been for a long time entitled to the reputation of industry, regularity, and economy; and notwithstanding the increase of their wealth and numbers, a just claim to this reputation still continues. As their wealth has been almost entirely the result of great attention and industry, it is preserved by the same virtues, and they are still strangers to extravagant and ruinous luxuries. Economy does by no means exclude cheerful and frequent social intercourse, nor abridge their real comforts and recreations. It does not even banish a liberal hospitality; and instead of lessening their humanity and compassion for the miserable, the people of Dundee are inferior to none in generous exertions and contributions, either for the relief of particular distresses and misfortunes, or for the establishment and maintenance of public beneficient institutions. It would be inconsistent with truth not to mention that prosperity has introduced among some a degree of licentiousness unknown in former times; and one alarming symptom of it ought not to be concealed, that notwithstanding the great accessions made since the year 1788 to the number of inhabitants, the number of annual marriages has hardly received the least addition.

The people of Dundee may be also characterised from their religious habits, and nowhere in Scotland is public worship better, or perhaps so well attended. Their numerous sects indicate their zeal and attachment to religious principles, and perhaps an excess of attention to religious controversies; but they give very little disturbance to the general harmony, and instead of increasing bigotry, they seem to weaken it. Though some sects, not only on their first rise, but even at present, cannot be acquitted of harsh and uncharitable opinions concerning those who do not adopt their sentiments, mutual toleration evidently prevails; and they begin to suspect that their dictates have no better claim to infallibility than those of others.

As to the general size of the inhabitants, it is certainly inferior to that of the people in the south and west parts of Scotland, and even of their neighbours in various parts of Fife; and though the linen manufacture is the great source of their opulence and increase, its influence does not seem so favourable, as might be wished, to health, or friendly to the production of a vigorous and hardy race.

93

George Mealmaker by John
Kay. *By courtesy of Edinburgh
City Libraries*

Fyffe who had threatened to 'break every bone in Thomas
Fysche Palmer's body' were ransacked and church bells were
rung to summon huge crowds which eventually forced Provost
Riddoch to order that a grain ship in the harbour be unloaded.

The next month the Friends of Liberty sent the Reverend Neil
Douglas to represent them at the General Convention of the
Scottish Radical Societies in Edinburgh and issued an anti-war
pamphlet. Around this time a Government spy reported to the
Home Secretary, 'the disposition of the people in Dundee was
very bad, all the lower classes and many of the merchants, being
violent for reform.' But the tide was beginning to turn against
the radicals. Despite their agitation, Britain was drifting
towards war with revolutionary France and when it came, in
1793, a vicious patriotic backlash was coordinated by the
Government.

In that year leading Scottish radicals were tried for sedition
and transported to Australia. Among them was Thomas Fysche
Palmer. He was charged with having written an anti-war leaflet,
but his real crime was having mixed with the 'lower classes'.
Before his trial the Lord Advocate of Scotland wrote to his uncle
Henry Dundas, the Home Secretary, describing Palmer as the
'most determined rebel in Scotland.'

Although evidence was produced at the trial to show that
Mealmaker had written the leaflet concerned and that, in fact,
Palmer had actually toned the contents down, he was found
guilty and sentenced to seven years transportation. He was taken
to the prison hulks in London along with Scottish radical
Thomas Muir who had been sentenced to fourteen years. Sympathetic MPs raised their cases in Parliament but during the
debate, Prime Minister William Pitt ordered the prison ship to
sail. A rescue attempt by the French navy failed and Palmer
served his seven years in New South Wales only to die on his
return voyage home.

Palmer's conviction was the signal for a full scale assault on
the Dundee radicals. The Town Council and Dundee
Presbytery passed resolutions of loyalty to the Government and
armed Government supporters drilled in the High Street. For
the first time, 'blacklists' were drawn up of the names of radicals
who would not be given work.

As more leaders followed Palmer and Muir to Botany Bay,
James Wright took a boat out into the Tay and ditched his com-
memorative medals and his letters and books. He then fled to
America where his daughter, Fanny, became one of the United
States most famous social reformers.

His action was typical. The Reverend Neil Douglas disappeared to the Highlands and even George Mealmaker decided
to lie low in Arbroath after his house was raided. But he was captured by a group of loyalists and along with his friend Robert
Sands was held in jail in Arbroath for three days, without

bedding or water. Mealmaker was then hauled off to Edinburgh Castle where he was held for a month and interrogated about a hare-brained conspiracy to capture the castle. He was released through lack of evidence but now the radicals faced a dilemma. If they openly advocated their views, they were liable to persecution but if they went underground it was more difficult to get their message across and, at the same time, organisers were liable to prosecution for conspiracy.

For a time, the Dundee radicals opted to do both and despite the threat of persecution membership of the radical societies peaked in 1794. In that same year, the Town Council appealed for a barracks to be built in the town and set up an armed loyalist vigilante group to 'prevent and suppress riots, tumults and disorder in the borough'.

But the Council also tried to appease the lower orders and set up a meal committee to ensure the distribution of food when times got hard. In 1795 the town erupted again with ships attacked in the harbour and agitators declaring, 'We ought to have had a revolution long ago and the present is the properest time to have one.' Emboldened by the troubles, the radicals in Dundee published an anti-war pamphlet by Neil Douglas entitled 'Britain's Guilt, Danger and Duty'.

With most of the Scottish leaders in Botany Bay and invasion by France expected any day, the thoughts of many radicals turned to revolution. By 1797, Ireland was on the brink of rebellion; elements in the army had mutinied; and the fleet under the Dundee hero Admiral Lord Duncan of Camperdown had mutinied at the Nore, run up the Red Flag and declared themselves 'a Floating Republic'.

Against this background, and inspired by the United Irishmen, the Scottish radicals set up a new secret organisation to win 'the rights of man' and also a Scottish Parliament. The strength of this revolutionary society lay in the east of Scotland in the counties of Perth, Angus and Fife and its nerve centre was Dundee. The society was called the United Scotsmen and its leader was the young rebel George Mealmaker, by now a veteran campaigner. Lord Cockburn later said of the United Scotsmen, 'They were unquestionably of a criminal and most dangerous character; They acted by secret meetings, affiliated branches, and unlawful oaths. The views of its leaders went far beyond any reform, even universal suffrage.'

Rioting, insurrection and talk of revolution and dividing up the great estates among the peasants spread like wildfire in the east of Scotland. The Government quickly banned the United Scotsman and arrested Mealmaker. He was tried in Perth over three days in January 1798. Spies and rewards had broken the underground organisation. One young member, David Douglas, refused to testify against Mealmaker and was transported for five years, but, nonetheless, the result was a foregone conclusion.

95

A Dundee Riot, c. 1850. *Dundee Art Galleries and Museums*

Mealmaker was accused of being a leader of a banned organisation and of writing and distributing seditious pamphlets. For good measure, he was also accused of plotting a blueprint for rebellion which included the burning down of the houses of prominent Tories and Unionists who, by coincidence, were members of the jury. Mealmaker was found guilty and sentenced to fourteen years transportation – a virtual death sentence. He survived the nightmare voyage to Australia in which a quarter of his fellow convicts perished but died in 1807, only a year after his old friend Robert Sands gathered a petition of 6,000 names, pleading for clemency.

Mealmaker's transportation brought an end to an inspiring first chapter in the modern political history of Dundee. But it was only the end of the beginning. The seeds of socialism and nationalism, the two dominant political ideologies in Dundee today, had been sown. The defeat of the United Scotsmen and the repression that followed drove the Dundee radicals underground and they turned their attention to organising the early trade unions, also illegal under the anti-combination laws.

In 1803 the first engineering union was formed in the city, but it was the flaxdressers or 'hecklers' who emerged as the most militant force. They formed a combination as early as 1794 and made the most of their important position in the process of linen manufacture. In 1809, a local linen merchant, William Brown, described the power of the hecklers,

> In some measure they controlled the trade, dictating as to the rate
> of wages to be paid, number of journeymen and apprentices to

96

be employed, and the stocks of dressed flax to be kept up; also as to drink money in various ways – lighting pints, blowing out pints, new year pints, founding pints for new buildings about the works. . . . All were enforced by combination and strike – not rashly gone into however, but after much discussion among themselves, at meetings held in the evenings.

The hecklers were the founders of modern trade unionism in Dundee and they took an active interest in politics. Dundee engineer James Carmichael noted,

They were great politicians and the 'heckling shop' was frequently the arena of violent harangue and fierce debate. They had an eager desire for news and information and one of their number was usually told off to read while the others worked and listened. This gave them the habit of thinking and acting in concert, for they had a wonderful faculty for combining to enforce their own terms.

In 1822 the hecklers struck to defeat wage cuts and a year later the Lord Provost of Dundee offered rewards for information on a plot by hecklers to attack the owners of spinning mills and burn their homes. In two great strikes, in 1827 when 13,000 struck for thirteen weeks and in 1834 when they held out for four months, the hecklers first demonstrated the kind of gritty determination that the Dundee working class has periodically shown ever since.

The final defeat of Napoleon and the trade depression that followed, emboldened the radicals to once again demand democratic rights and social justice. In 1817 old Neil Douglas was charged with sedition after denouncing the royal family and saying that the British victory at Waterloo was nothing to celebrate. In February of that year George Kinloch spoke at a meeting of 6,000 people at Magdalen Green demanding urgent reform. Agitation continued throughout the country until, on 16 August 1819, troops attacked a crowd in Manchester in the 'Peterloo' massacre. The atmosphere in Dundee was already charged. In April, James Thomson, a local minister who became a Government informer wrote to the Home Secretary asking for £500 to set up a pro-Government newspaper. He warned, 'A few spirits have always existed here since 1792, fond of change and hostile to the happy constitution of our country and the spark of disaffection is kept alive by a weekly paper which owes its origin to democratic faction,' (a reference to the *Dundee Advertiser*).

In November the Dundee radicals organised a rally to protest at the Manchester massacre and demand one man, one vote. Ten thousand marched to Magdalen Green with banners declaring 'The Voice of the People is Irresistible!'. Workers joined the procession from their factories, marching in military formation. Kinloch spoke once again, but this time the authorities had been

1832

One of the many projects which engaged the attention of George Kinloch, Dundee's radical laird, was the creation of a railway service from Dundee to Newtyle. A description of this revolutionary form of transport is preserved in a letter to 'Dear Emily', dated 28 May 1832.

You can't think how delighted I was last week with the ride from Dundee to Newtyle in the Railway Coach. The bustle at taking my seat – by the by, neat ladders should be furnished by which to ascend the coach instead of compelling the ladies to scramble up by long strides and coming off the coach is worse for one's petticoats are entangled, and the inconvenience is so bad as you can't imagine. Well, as I was saying, the bustle, the tolling of the Railway Bell, the sudden movement of sixty human beings by an unseen power upwards like a flock of geese in the air and onwards by a horse at full gallop – the light and shade of the tunnel through the Law – by the by, it's rather dark about the centre; however that depends upon who one happens to be seated beside – the promiscuous mixture of young lassies, young ladies, and crones – dandies, parsons, farmers, merchants, weavers and ploughmen – the varied expression of faces, some merry, some stupid, some sad – the driver Sam lauding his merits of his horse and cracking his whip and his jokes. Dundee and its foul-mouthed chimney stalks fading from our view – flying through a mountainous region, the atmosphere of which is cold as the Arctic regions – the sudden bursting on us of the warm, rich Vale of Strathmore – all contributed to my amusement. After passing through the tunnel, a dandy waved his hand indicating his intention to take a seat – in his hand a fishing rod and in his cheek a cigar. He tript lightly to his seat and, though snug himself, annoyed me with the fumes of his tobacco. A labourer sat behind him with a cutty pipe stuffed with pigtail. The smoke and smell was almost insufferable and I was almost choked. I would complain to Mr. Kinloch but he is such an advocate for the liberty of the subject that I have little hope by his means of putting an end to the filthy practice. Little did the dandy know that, but for the nasty cigar, I could have admired him –

Your cousin Rebecca.

The statue of Kinloch in Albert Square. *Ken Sharp*

pushed too far. Kinloch, the radical laird, was a landowner and a Justice of the Peace and the ruling class felt betrayed. He was denounced in parliament and arrested. No doubt with thoughts of the fates of Fysche, Palmer and Mealmaker in his mind, he wisely fled to France before his trial and was outlawed. The experience ruined Kinloch's health and his finances. Following a pardon he was elected as Dundee's first MP in the reformed parliament of 1832 but his years on the run had taken their toll and he died in 1833.

The Reform Act, after which Dundee named one of its main streets as the town expanded, was designed to take the heat out of the campaign to win the vote. But it failed and within a decade the Chartist movement was demanding universal suffrage, secret ballots and the abolition of property qualifications for MPs. Dundonians flocked to the Chartist banner. When the movement divided over whether to use moral or physical force, Dundee overwhelmingly went for the 'physical force' option. The local press noted that a 'number of infatuated individuals have commenced drilling' and the Dundee Workingmen's Association sought legal advice on the rights of its members to arm themselves.

By then Dundee's working-class leaders had gained a wealth of experience and organising know how. A Democratic Society was formed along with a Dundee Trades Universal Suffrage Association, Dundee Bakers USA, Dundee Shoemakers USA and Dundee Youth's USA. At a time of economic depression, when according to the Chartist leader Abram Duncan 'Two and a half thousand men and women were starving in the streets of Dundee', support for the Chartists increased. In 1840 they were able to collect 20,523 signatures, more than a third of Dundee's population, on a petition to commute the death sentence on John Frost the leader of a rebellion in Wales. In the same year they bought a newspaper, the *Dundee Chronicle*, for £700. They opened a co-operative shop in Lochee and even founded their own church.

In 1841, trade plummeted in Dundee. Mass unemployment brought thousands to the brink of starvation. Half of the mechanics and shipbuilding tradesmen were laid off while three-quarters of the building trade's workers were sacked. Of 160 tailors in the city, only five were in work.

Rioting occurred that year and, then, in 1842, the Democratic Society, appalled at the suffering in the city, made a disastrous miscalculation. On 17 August, delegates from seventeen mills met to discuss tactics after members of the Democratic Society in the mills had voted by 1,705 to 175 for a strike to raise wages to the 1839 levels. A number of delegates argued that only by winning political power could they ensure that wages were kept high, and that the strike should also be a political one. When the strikers convened their mass meeting the following Sunday a quarter of Dundee's population turned out to hear the speakers on Magdalen Green. A heckler, Thomas Anderson, argued 'Now is the time to strike and only the Charter can ensure that wages are kept high.' Despite a few protests, the crowd voted overwhelmingly to strike from the next day and to remain on strike until the 'People's Charter is the law of the land.'

It was an impossible demand and reflected, as much as anything, the geographical isolation of the Dundee radicals. The local magistrates swore in a force of almost five hundred special constables, many of them mill 'gaffers', brought before the Sheriff in the early hours of Monday morning. Two days of clashes followed and then, on Tuesday, after listening to a speech

Both sides of a Reform Banner. The thistles of Scotland. George Kinloch. *Dundee Art Galleries and Museums*

1922

In early November 1922 Clementine Churchill described her Dundee election campaign in a letter to her husband, who was convalescing in the south.

The situation here is an anxious one but I comfort myself by remembering how in past election times when we got pessimistic Sir George Ritchie used to say with confidence that you would be returned . . .

If we win (which I pray & believe we will) we really must put in some time and work here and *re-organise* the whole organisation which was in chaos. Of course I feel the minute you arrive the atmosphere will change and the people will be roused. If you bring Sergeant Thompson, etc. tell him to conceal himself tactfully as it would not do if the populace thought you were afraid of them. The papers are so *vile*, they would misrepresent it . . .

If you feel strong enough, I think besides the Drill Hall Meeting which is pretty sure to be broken up, you should address one or two small open meetings. Every rowdy meeting rouses sympathy and brings votes and will especially as you have been so ill. Even in the rowdiest, foulest place of all the people, tho' abusive, were really good-natured. To shew you the sort of place it was there were placards all round the walls with not as you might guess 'no spitting' or 'no smoking' or 'no swearing' allowed but 'Obscene Language not allowed'! . . .

I find what the people like best is the settlement of the Irish Question. So I trot that one out and also your share in giving the Boers self government. The idea against you seems to be that you are a 'War Monger', but I am exhibiting you as a Cherub Peace Maker with little fluffy wings round your chubby face. I think the line is not so much 'Smash the Socialists' as to try with your great abilities to help in finding a solution of the Capital and Labour problem . . .

My darling, the misery here is appalling. Some of the people look absolutely starving . . .

Your loving
Clemmie

(Quoted in Martin, G., *Winston S. Churchill*, Vol. IV (London, Heinemann, 1975))

by the Chartist leader John Duncan, who described the warm reception extended to him in Forfar, the crowd voted to march to Forfar, with thoughts of capturing the county seat. Twelve hundred Dundee Chartists in groups of twenty, each with a 'captain', set off, raiding 'neep' fields on the way. On their arrival at Forfar they were met by a strong force of yeomanry who allowed the bedraggled marchers to meet their local allies before they trudged home to Dundee.

This attempt at a 'rising' ended in total failure. Four of the ringleaders fled to the United States and a further five were jailed for lengthy periods. The authorities were particularly keen to deal with John Duncan, one of the leading Chartist lights in Scotland. He was held for five months before he was tried for 'inciting a General Strike'. Surprisingly, Duncan was found not guilty. But he was re-arrested on a new warrant and subsequently thrown into an Edinburgh lunatic asylum where he died in 1845.

The failure of the Chartists finally spelt an end to Dundee's fifty-year-long flirtation with insurrection. Now working men and women turned their attention to building respectable trade unions and supporting reforming liberals. Many of the large influx of Irish workers who arrived after the Great Famine were more caught up with the politics of the 'old country' than those of their newly adopted home and this was to prove to be a barrier to the politicising of the textile unions. Other trade unionists were wary of the radicals and their far-fetched ideas. They now confined themselves to pursuing demands like a shorter working week.

The ten-hour day campaign found huge support among all sections of the working class. In 1871, Dundee Trades Council wrote to Karl Marx, then Secretary of the first International Workingmen's Association, asking for details of affiliation. This was in recognition of the role played by the International in the fight for a shorter working week and a few months later a branch was formed in Dundee. The unions were also concerned to get working men on to the local Town Council and after a successful Industrial Exhibition which raised the necessary cash they were able to have two of their number elected. The pair were each paid two guineas a week, allowing Dundonians to brand them the 'two guinea pigs'.

But gradually the unions began to move their support away from paternalistic liberals and to the newly founded Labour Party. In the 1880s a branch of the Marxist Social Democratic Foundation was established in the city. It is likely that James Connolly, the Irish rebel leader, was a member in Dundee during his stay in the town and he probably witnessed the 'Free Speech' fights when the socialists, to the amusement of thousands, ignored a ban on their Sunday Meetings and continued to harangue church-goers. By 1892 the SDF's influence

Winston Churchill, Dundee 1922. *Dundee District Libraries*

in Dundee was such that they were able to secure the Labour nomination for James Macdonald, the Secretary of the London Trades Council and one of the ablest Labour politicians in Britain. A Marxist, Macdonald campaigned for a shorter working week, a Scottish Assembly and electoral reform. He stood in 1892 and again in 1895 when he won 1,313 votes out of a total electorate of 18,000.

Ever since the 1790s Dundee had acquired a reputation for its radicalism and virtually every British radical leader of note visited the city at some time. It was in keeping with that tradition that a young Winston Churchill, then a Liberal and scourge of the Tories, was elected as an MP for Dundee in 1908. His subsequent defeat in the 1922 election was a sensation and one of the most remarkable tales in Dundee's political history. By then a Tory, Churchill's 15,000 majority disappeared and the Conservative Secretary of State for War was branded 'a WC without a seat' by the Dundee crowds.

Ironically, it was two pacifists, E. D. Morel, the Labour candidate who had been jailed during the war and Edwin

The Temperance tradition had deep roots in
the city. An advertisement poster c. 1870.
Dundee Art Galleries and Museums

'Neddy' Scrymgeour, a Prohibitionist who had defended conscientious objectors at military tribunals, who sent Churchill packing into his wilderness years.

Labelled a 'war-monger', Churchill's role in sending hundreds of Dundonian soldiers to their deaths in Antwerp was not forgotten and a weary population sickened by the slaughter of the First World War feared Churchill's hatred of the young Soviet Union would lead to another conflict. In 1918, Churchill had urged Dundonians to oppose 'the hun abroad and the pacifists, bolsheviks and Sinn Feinners at home'. But by 1922 these last three were the most active in Dundee's political life. Black and Tan butchery in Ireland united the Catholic population with left-wingers who detested Churchill's right-wing policies. Churchill later said, 'It was the worst election of my life. . . . I was faced by an audience of lions with communist teeth.' But the Catholic hierarchy of Dundee were equally implacable in their opposition to the man who had sent in the Black and Tans. The influential *Dundee Catholic Herald* declared, 'The correct thing for all Taysiders is to see that this dangerous, double dealing, oily-tongued adventurer is not given the power to do further harm.'

Huge crowds broke up Churchill's meetings with three cheers for Morel, Gallacher the Communist candidate, De Valera and Lenin. Whenever he tried to speak the crowds broke into the 'Soldier's Song' and the 'Red Flag'. In the Irish stronghold of Lochee only a strong police presence prevented the candidate from coming to serious harm. In defeat Churchill wept and vowed never to return to Dundee. It was a promise he kept. When the Town Council offered him the freedom of the city in 1943, he refused.

The years following Churchill's defeat were dark and difficult. The hungry thirties brought renewed rioting and militancy. It was an atmosphere which persuaded many young Dundonians to join the International Brigade and fight fascism in Spain. Sixteen gave their lives in that fight. Hundreds more joined the hunger marches to London. It was the last heroic stand of a solid working-class population who lived physically and spiritually very close to each other. In the virtually post-political society of today the spirit of Dundee politics, popular and defiant, is now enshrined in its trade union and shop stewards' movement. The sit-ins and strikes of the eighties and nineties to protect jobs displayed an idealism and tradition of collective action harking back two hundred years to George Mealmaker and the United Scotsmen. The Timex battle of 1993 should not be seen then as the final nail in the coffin for Dundee's working class. The Timex workers lost their jobs but they retained the two qualities which have seen them through hard times of mass unemployment and outright repression – their dignity and defiance.

102

A LITERARY HAVEN
1814

Between 1812 and 1814, the linen manufacturers, the Baxter family, had Mary Wollstonecraft as a house guest and companion for their daughter, Isobel. Mary was only fifteen at the time, but a year later she would elope with and marry the poet Shelley. When she wrote Frankenstein, she acknowledged her debt to the area around Peep o' Day Lane and Baffin Street.

I lived principally in the country as a girl, and passed a considerable time in Scotland. I made occasional visits to the more picturesque parts; but my habitual residence was on the blank and dreary northern shores of the Tay, near Dundee. Blank and dreary on retrospection I call them; they were not so to me then. They were the eyry of freedom, and the pleasant region where unheeded I could commune with the creatures of my fancy. I wrote then – but in a most common-place style. It was beneath the trees of the grounds belonging to our house, or on the bleak sides of the woodless mountains near, that my true compositions of the airy flights of my imagination, were born and fostered. I did not make myself the heroine of my tales. Life appeared to me too common-place an affair as regarded myself. I could not figure to myself that romantic woes or wonderful events would ever be my lot; but I was not confined to my own identity, and I could people the hours with creations far more interesting to me at that age, than my own sensations.

Another famous English literary figure living in Dundee at this time was Thomas Hood, who later became editor of Punch. *He came for reasons of health, and he had relations in the city. The* Guide to Dundee *he compiled was unfortunately lost, but he has left us with some impressions in his* Memorials. *Here is his arrival in Dundee.*

My first concern was now to look out for some comfortable roof under which 'for a consideration' one would be treated as one of the family. I accordingly entered into a treaty with a respectable widower, who had no sons of his own; but, in spite of the most undeniable references, and a general accordance as to terms, there occurred a mysterious hitch in the arrangement, arising from a whimsical prepossession – which only came afterwards to my knowledge – namely, that an English laddie, instead of supping parritch, would inevitably require a rump steak to his breakfast! My next essay was more successful, and ended in my being reguarly installed in a boarding-house, kept by a Scotchwoman, who was not so sure of my being a beef-eater. She was a sort of widow with a seafaring husband 'as good as dead,' and in her appearance not unlike a personification of *rouge et noir*, with her red eyes, her red face, yellow teeth, and her black velvet cap. The first day of my term happened to be also the first day of the New Year; and on stepping from my bed-room I encountered our hostess – like a witch and her familiar spirit – with a huge bottle of whisky in one hand and a glass in the other. It was impossible to decline the dram she pressed upon me, and very good it proved and undoubtedly strong, seeing that for some time I could only muse its praise in expressive silence, and, indeed, I was only able to speak with '*a small still voice*' for several minutes afterwards. Such was my characteristic introduction to the Land of Cakes, where I was destined to spend the greater part of two years under circumstances likely to materially influence the colouring and filling up of my future life.

Hood also frequented Newport and Ferryport-on-Craig on the other side of the river. He would have been amused when the railway company changed the latter's name to Tayport, because the old name was too big to get on the tickets! Hood loved the Tay.

To these open-air pursuits, sailing was afterwards added, bringing me acquainted with the boatmen and fishermen of the Craig, a hardy race, rough and ready-witted, from whom perchance was first derived my partiality for all marine bipeds and sea-craft, from Flag Admirals down to Jack Junk, the proud first-rate to the humble boatie that 'wins the bairn's bread.' The Tay at Dundee is a broad, noble river, with a racing tide, which, when it differs with a contrary wind, will get up '*jars*' (Anglicé, waves) quite equal to those of a family manufacture. It was at least a good preparatory school for learning the rudiments of boatcraft, whereof I acquired enough to be able at need to take the helm without either going too near the wind or too distant from the port. Not without some boyish pride I occasionally found myself entrusted with the guidance of the coach boat – so called from its carrying the passengers by the Edinburgh mail – particularly in a calm, when the utmost exertions of the crew, four old man-of-war's men, were required at the oars. It not unfrequently happened that the 'laddie' was unceremoniously ousted by the unanimous vote, and sometimes by the united strength, of the ladies, who invariably pitched upon the oldest old gentleman in the vessel to '*Steer* her up and haud her gaun.'

1815

When the great engineer Thomas Telford visited Dundee to begin work on the improvements to the harbour, he was accompanied by the poet Robert Southey, who wrote this impression in his Journal of a Tour in Scotland.

Wednesday, August 25. – Before breakfast I went with Mr T. to the harbour, to look at his works, which are of great magnitude and importance – a huge floating dock, and the finest graving dock I ever saw. The town expends £70,000 upon these improvements, which will be completed in another year. What they take from the excavations serves to raise ground which was formerly covered by the tide, but will now be of the greatest value for wharfs, yards, &c. They proposed to build fifteen piers, but T. assured them that three would be sufficient; and in telling me this he said the creation of fifteen new Scotch Peers was too strong a measure.

The Cathedral, which is the oldest in Scotland, is an extraordinary mass of buildings of all ages; the tower, which is the oldest part, being connected by a modern interpolation to a portion of intermediate date or dates. This remarkable pile contains no fewer than five places of worship. We went into two of them. The pews in both were placed without any apparent order as thick as they could be; nor could we have found our way among them (there being nothing like aisles) if our Cicerone had not lifted up seats and opened doors to give us a passage. The congregation must either observe an extraordinary and almost impossible regularity in taking their seats, or they must be subject to very great inconvenience before they can all get packed up for the service. From the one of these kirks we got into the other; and between both is a sort of vestry, upstairs, with some bookcases round it, but all with closed doors. The man said that all the books were two hundred years old, and that they were chiefly English and Latin, and some Hebrew. The closets might contain from 3 to 400 folios.

A fellow in the streets with a bell in his hand was tempting children to gamble for a sort of lollipop: strange that this should be suffered in Scotland. *New Pye Office* over a door: upon enquiry some person sold pastry there. What a grandiloquous people!

Garden ground lets here at from 10 to 14£ per acre, and Dundee is said to be better supplied with vegetables than any other town in Scotland. Indeed this part of the country is so flourishing that, two years ago, the Town Clerk assured Mr Telford, the agriculturists had half a million of surplus capital in the Bank of Dundee.

We dined here, T. having business with the Provost and other persons touching his great operations – which took up the whole morning. They would fain have given him a dinner, but this would have consumed the remainder of the day, and time was precious. They dress herrings here without roe or milt, throwing both away. The port wine at the Scotch inns has always been good, wherever we have tasted it; and we are told that it is so everywhere. The tumbler glasses here are so thick that it is unpleasant to drink out of them. At half after four we set off for Arbroath, to which less inconvenient word it seems Aberbrothock has been cut down. A good many persons were assembled to see us depart. I suspect it had got abroad from the bookseller that my Poetship was to be seen, and therefore was not sorry when the coach was in motion and we bade adieu to 'bonny Dundee.'

Thomsonville D.C.?

The Dundee Press

by GEORGE ROSIE

In the demonology of the Scottish Left few institutions loom as large as the Dundee firm of D. C. Thomson & Co. To zealous lefties the firm's red sandstone headquarters in Meadowside is the heart of darkness. They see it as the focus of an implacably right-wing publishing empire run by a reactionary family which got rich by grinding the faces of the helpless (i.e. non-unionised) poor. The Thomsons are so right wing, the zealots say, that even Winston Churchill would have nothing to do with them. Yet they are so cunning that they keep Dundee, Scotland and much of Britain in thrall with their huge-selling newspapers, comics and magazines. Until 'something is done' about the Thomsons, they solemnly argue, the proletariat will never break their chains.

That is one way of looking at Scotland's biggest home-grown newspaper publishers. But as explanations go it is not a very good one. For one thing, decent profit not politics is the Thomson imperative. For another, the huge majority of their employees have made it plain they are happy to trade below average wages for above average security (a mind-set not unknown in the civil service unions). And for yet another, the Thomson newspaper monopoly in Dundee has yielded absolutely no political results. For generations the Thomson press has been banging the Tory drum, and for generations their huge readership goes on voting for the Labour Party and the SNP. In fact, the Thomson newspapers are proof, if proof were needed, of the political impotence of the press.

But they remain one of the biggest – and some say the best – employers in Dundee. According to their latest published figures (for the year ending March 1994), the Thomsons employ just over 2,000 people who are paid an average of just over £16,300 a year (below the industry norm). The firm has a turnover of £88.29 million, on which they made a pre-tax profit of £70.9 million (hugely inflated by their one-off sale of shares in Central Independent Television). The real trading profit is probably around £30 million, still well above the media-industry average. Most of the shareholders are members of the extended Thomson family, and the company is owned from addresses which range from Port Alfred in South Africa, through Dundee and Cupar, to Nassau in the Bahamas. All five directors are called Thomson.

And there is more to D. C. Thomson & Co. than publishing. Until recently the firm owned 25 per cent of Southern

The Courier Building, the imposing Headquarters of D. C. Thomson. The architect
visited the Randolph Hearst newspaper
empire in the States, prior to designing the
building. *Dundee District Libraries*

Television (based in the far south of England), 15.5 per cent of
Lifestyle Television Ltd, 15 per cent of Newsfax International
Ltd and 15 per cent of the satellite television firm Starstream
Ltd. They also had a 32.3 per cent share of the high-street
booksellers Waterstone & Co. Ltd (recently sold to WH Smith)
and almost 20 per cent of Central Television Ltd.

But the 'core' of their operation remains publishing, including
the two Dundee dailies the *Courier* and the *Evening Telegraph*.
But while the Dundee press is now firmly in Thomson hands it
was not always so. Press monopolies are very much a twentieth-
century phenomenon. All through the nineteenth century
Dundee (like most Scottish cities) had a remarkably varied range
of magazines and newspapers. They came and went, of course,
and some of them lasted for only a few years. But there were a
lot of them. One of the earliest was the *Dundee Repository of
Political and Miscellaneous Information* (1793-1795). That
title had no sooner sunk, when up bobbed the *Dundee Magazine
and Journal of the Times* (1799–1802, with a reappearance in
1815).

The Piper o' Dundee's humorous illustration on the opening of the first Tay Railway Bridge, 1878. *Dundee District Libraries*

And in the nineteenth century the Dundee press boomed. Titles proliferated. Some were weekly, some were quarterly, some were monthly and a few were daily. Some were religious and sectarian, like the *Dundee Catholic Herald* (1893-1939), the *Dundee Christian Monitor* (1874-1875), the *Dundee Pulpit and Religious Record* (1872), and the resoundingly entitled *Dundee Protestant Guardian: Or, An Attempt to Expose Some of the Principal Errors and Practices of the Romish Church* (1829-1830). Others were short-lived business papers; *Dundee Commercial Gazette and Shipping Register* (1860-1861) and the *Dundee Commercial List* (1839-1841).

Political sheets did well. Many seemed to be of a radical bent. There was the *Independent* (1816), the *Dundee Reformer and Lochee Observer* (1855), and the *Dundee Warder* (1844). Other nineteenth century newspapers included the *Dundee Chronicle* (1830-1841). Nor did the publishers of Dundee neglect the periodical market. There was the *Caledonian Quarterly* (1821), the *Caledonian Magazine and Review* (1822-1823), the *Angus Album* (1834), the *Angus Magazine* (1868-1869), *Bonnie Bits* (1890), the *Wizard of the North* (1896-1916) and the *City Echo* which was swallowed up by the *Piper O' Dundee* (1888-1901).

107

1929

H. V. Morton visited the city in 1929, and wrote this description in his book *In Search of Scotland*.

The Newport-Dundee ferry was packed. I was sandwiched between a van horse of uncertain temper and a young woman, with freckles and hair like a prairie fire whose small two-seater tried, with clumsy affection, to sit on my offside mudguards. All round us were carts, vans, and cars on their way to Dundee.

Ferries are an unfortunate feature of motoring in Scotland. Some of them, notably Queensferry over the Forth and, I am told, the Kyle of Lochalsh ferry to Skye, design their charges on the ancient assumption that all motorists are wealthy. It costs ten shillings to cross the Forth, a business of a few minutes, and fifteen shillings to make an even shorter voyage to Kyleakin. These charges naturally infuriate the Scot, who combines an almost quixotic generosity with a great sense of value for money. Possibly, if London were a little nearer to Edinburgh, there would have been a traffic bridge over the Forth long ago. The Tay, too, deserves something more than a railway bridge.

The Dundee ferry is, however, reasonable – three shillings for a Rolls Royce coupé and three shillings and sixpence for a Ford four-seater. Cars are assessed on their seating accommodation!

Dundee lifted its chimneys in a cloud of smoke. It looked to me as if Sheffield had gone to the seaside. But even as I looked the wild wind that whipped the Tay into white flecks blew the smoke towards the Highlands; and, clear against the hills, I saw the third largest city in Scotland.

There was nothing very 'bonnie' about Dundee from the ferry, except its amazing situation. What a place for a city! Its wharves and docks lie against a two-and-a-quarter-mile wide river, and within sight, almost within sound, of the sea. It is like Liverpool, the Tay its Mersey, and where the river widens is the blue-green line of the ocean.

Dundee was that morning busy with its marmalade, its jute mills, its cakes, its linen. There was a deep Manchester rumble over the stone setts as the jute wagons went by. It is a city that has mysteriously effaced its past. It has a long and exciting history. William Wallace was a grammar-school boy there. In the old days England took it, and Scotland won it back almost as frequently as Berwick. Even if one did not know these things, such names as Nethergate and Seagate are as good as a pedigree stamped and sealed by the College of Heralds; but look where you will, Dundee has replaced the ancient by the modern.

One of the main exports is, of course, journalists. I imagine that Dundee, with

But by far the most important of Dundee's nineteenth century newspapers were the *Dundee Advertiser*, the *People's Journal*, the *People's Friend* and the *Evening Telegraph* all of which were owned by a shrewd Yorkshireman called John (later Sir John) Leng. After a spell as a sub-editor on his local paper the *Hull Advertiser* Leng bought his way into the *Dundee Advertiser* which he built into one of the most successful daily newspapers in Scotland. Even more successful was the *People's Journal* which was launched in 1858 with the promise '. . .not to write *down* but to write *up* to the good sense of the working classes whose interests will be carefully considered'.

Leng was as good as his word. Under the editorship of a brilliant, radically-inclined Fifer called William Latto, it served up a remarkable editorial mix which combined hard news with 'useful knowledge' in a variety of regional editions. In fact, as William Donaldson points out in his excellent book *Popular Literature in Victorian Scotland*, the *People's Journal* can lay claim to being the first 'national' newspaper in Scotland. Within a few years of its launch the paper was selling 50,000 copies a week. By 1875 the figure had shot up to 130,000. By 1914 the circulation had soared to 250,000 copies, the biggest sale of any paper outside of London. The closure of the *People's Journal* in September 1990 was something of a minor publishing tragedy.

The politics of the *People's Journal* (like the politics of all the Leng newspapers) was distinctly left wing. Not only was Latto a card-carrying radical and one-time advocate of 'physical force' Chartism, but John Leng himself became Dundee's Liberal MP in 1888. He stood for universal suffrage, Home Rule for Ireland and Scotland, anti-Imperialism, free education and the nationalisation of land. His politics were reflected in the columns of his newspapers.

In 1869 Leng began the *People's Friend* as a kind of literary 'overspill' from the *People's Journal*, with the intention of providing '. . . literary entertainment which the masses of the people would welcome with eager avidity'. There is a small historical irony here; the *People's Friend* was the title of the political sheet run by the hard-line French revolutionary Jean Paul Marat who studied Medicine at the University of St Andrews. It is entirely possible that Leng, or Latto, knew of Marat's paper. In 1877 Leng added an evening paper, the *Evening Telegraph*, to his stable.

Interestingly, John Leng's elder brother William was at the other end of the political spectrum. After contributing to his brother's Dundee newspapers, he bought over and became editor of the *Sheffield Telegraph* which he made into one of the most fiercely Conservative papers in England. William Leng was an implacable foe of the trade unions, and won a Royal Commission into the 'trade-union terrorism' which he claimed was crippling his newspaper. Both Lengs were knighted for their services to the newspaper industry. William died in 1902 and John

Leng died in California in 1906, on the last of his jaunts to the United States.

At Leng's death his left-wing publishing empire (four flourishing titles and 40,000 square feet of offices and print hall on the north side of Bank Street) fell into the hands of William Thomson and his sons whose politics could hardly have been more inimical to Leng's. The Thomsons were conservative in every sense of the word. And when they bought the Leng interests in 1906 they acquired an almost complete monopoly of the Dundee press which they have held ever since.

The Thomsons' operation began in earnest in 1905 when William Thomson, a flourishing Tayside shipping magnate, decided to regularise the publishing and printing interests he had picked up on the way to making his fortune. Together with his two sons, Frederick Thomson and David Couper Thomson (and their respective wives Clara, Jessie and Margaret), they formed the publishing company of D. C. Thomson & Co. Almost immediately the company began cultivating industrial Scotland's taste for romantic and/or bloodthirsty fables. The classic working-class customer, the hard-working mill girl, was thick on the ground in and around Dundee at the time.

For example, one of the company's first moves was to reconstruct a magazine called *My Weekly* from being a kind of fourth-rate *Spectator* agitated by trading policies and tariff reform, into a romantic weekly. It was a profoundly unlikely conversion job, but it worked. Eighty-five years later *My Weekly* is still around (but, alas, declining) as a competitor to the London-produced *Woman* and *Woman's Own*. Similarly The *People's Friend* was converted from Leng's notion of 'A miscellany of popular and instructive literature' into a successful woman's magazine of renowned genteelness. The transformation of *My Weekly* and The *People's Friend* were early examples of David C. Thomson's adroit editorial touch.

In the space of a very few years the Thomson brothers had established D. C. Thomson & Company, with its two newspapers the *Courier* and *Advertiser* as a force to be reckoned with. And when Frederick Thomson died in 1917, David Thomson found himself with a lot of (local) political muscle which he used sparingly but to some effect. He was man of distinctly conservative (if not reactionary) views, and one of his victims was Winston Churchill, then Liberal MP for Dundee.

Thomson seemed to regard Churchill as a dangerous, hotheaded radical, and launched a sustained press campaign against him which resulted in Churchill losing his seat in 1922. According to one of Churchill's biographers it was '. . . Two years of ceaseless detraction, spiteful, malicious detraction. . .' by a man that Churchill felt to be '. . . narrow, bitter, unreasonable and eaten up with his own conceit and consumed with petty arrogance . . .'. Dundee legend has it that Churchill vowed never

Aberdeen as a close runner-up, has let loose on the forces of error more grim champions in the form of earnest and unbelieving young men than any other city on earth. Blue pencils over the Border!

Dundee has Calcutta in its pocket. There are men now in Calcutta thinking only of retiring on Dundee. To understand the wealth of this city you must go and look at the houses at Broughty Ferry, Carnoustie, and Newport. No city in the world could have been kinder to its rich ones.

But, like all industrial cities subject to the ebb and flow of prosperity, it is a place of fearful inequality; riches and poverty are side by side; opulence and squalor hand in hand. There are hilly streets in Dundee where the children play barefoot in the gutter. It is always washing day there. I heard the Irish brogue, and saw Pat smoking his pipe at the cabin door:

'Out of work?' I asked one man.

'I am.'

The place looked neat and clean. He explained that his wife worked in the mill, while he was nurse, cook, and housemaid! He looked extraordinarily incompetent. This unnatural domestic life is, I believe, a characteristic of Dundee when the shipyards are idle, as it is of Londonderry, which has work for women in the shirt factories, but little, or none, for men.

I asked him how it felt to be dependent on a wife. He appeared unconscious of any humiliation. He said it was a good day's work to look after two children and he would rather do a day's work than wash one baby! But his wife knew how things were. She gave him beer money, and sometimes took him to the pictures!

Dundee should be a thoughtful town. Right in the heart of it is one of the most gloomy and impressive cemeteries in Great Britain. It is called the Howff. Here sleep three centuries of dead Dundonians, mouldering under an army corps of headstones. It is the perfect retreat in moments of sadness. Here you could just gloat over your misfortune and enjoy to the full the art of being miserable. All round the Howff, on the other side of the wall, the busy city goes about its work, unconscious, I think, of that city of the dead. No city could have wiped out evidence of its history more thoroughly; yet, strangely enough, no city could live in more intimate contact with the dead men and women who made that history. . . .

The first among Dundee's treasures is the great hill of Dundee Law. Edinburgh and Stirling both have high places from which their citizens may take a broad view of life; but Dundee snuggles against a perfect tower of rock from which a man can look down the very chimneys of the city.

Here is another great view in Scotland,

different from anything I have seen, and, in its way, as magnificent. Dundee lies below – street piled on street, chimney above chimney, the broad Tay crossed by the astonishing two-and-a-quarter mile bridge. To the left the docks and the open sea; right ahead, over hills and remote in distance, the golden sands and the roofs of St. Andrews. On a sunny day, with the wind blowing over Dundee Law, your blood tingles and you want to shout.

But turn round and look inland. There is that promise that gleamed so far off at Stirling; there are the Highlands of Scotland! The Grampians, still remote and still mysterious, blue and cloud-tipped, lie against the sky.

This is the vision that Dundee men carry with them to the ends of the earth. No wonder that they always go back there some day.

again to set foot in the city, and David Thomson vowed never to mention Churchill by name in any of his newspapers.

Interestingly despite the proprietor's politics, the printers within the firm were one hundred per cent unionised, every man a card-carrying member of the print union NATSOPA. Some veteran Thomson men claim that the firm and the unions rubbed along well enough, although later, David Thomson was to describe the days when the firm was unionised as 'hell'. But when the NATSOPA men walked out in the General Strike of 1926 David Thomson was outraged. He managed to keep the presses turning with an admixture of doormen, editors, commercial managers, accountants, reporters, warehousemen, ledger clerks and tea-boys, but he never forgave the workers who struck in 1926. From that day on, David Thomson and his company became dedicated anti-unionists.

One result of the strike was that the firm's two morning papers the *Courier* and the *Advertiser* were merged. Any worker who wanted his job back after the strike had to agree to conditions which have gone down in the black museum of the Scottish trade-union movement. There were two documents. One was a letter which (among other things) stated: 'I have severed my connection with the NATSOPA and agree that I shall not accept membership of any union so long as I am in your employment.' The letter had to be accompanied by the worker's union-card which the firm then passed on to NATSOPA.

The second document was a declaration which read: '. . . I hereby undertake not to become a member of a trade union whilst in your employment, and that if I wish to become a member of a trade union I will leave your employment before so doing. . . .'

The documents were a pill that many NATSOPA men could not swallow. The more enterprising of them went on to start (or at least resurrect) the *Dundee Free Press*, one of the more interesting radical newspapers published in Scotland this century. From its first issue (Friday, 11 June 1926) the *Dundee Free Press* was bitterly hostile to D. C. Thomson & Co., and waged a bitter little war against the 'newspaper Mussolinis of Dundee' on behalf of the people of Tayside who had '. . . chafed and writhed under a press monopoly'. For their part the Thomson newspapers treated the upstart *Dundee Free Press* with a lofty disdain.

That superiority was dented (slightly) when the Labour Party took over the Dundee Corporation, and promptly voted to switch all municipal advertising from the *Courier & Advertiser* to the *Dundee Free Press*. Without that shot in the arm it is doubtful whether the *Dundee Free Press* would have lasted more than a few months. But it was a very creditable effort. Apart from its relentless campaign against the 'monopolists' of the Thomson family, the paper had a good nose for local scandals, good lines into the Dundee Corporation, and never hesitated to have a go at the ruling Labour Party. 'It is high time the Labour Party and socialist movement locally undertook the cleaning of its Augean Stables. . .'

The *Dundee Free Press* survived for seven years. But the hungry thirties were not the time for marginal newspapers. Advertising was in short supply, and what there was was going to the big-circulation Thomson newspapers. On Friday, 3 March 1933, the *Dundee Free Press* sounded its own death knell. But the paper went out with a flourish. The British civil service was attacked as a 'bureaucratic incubus' which was suffocating the country, and Westminster was described as 'useless to Scotland'. The readers were referred to *Gulliver's Travels* for an accurate view of power politics and 'men of standing' (such as David Thomson) who '. . . When they see movement that threatens to upset life as they view it. . . are outraged beyond belief, and do everything in their powers to hinder and even suppress the new movement.'

But, in fact, the existence of the *Dundee Free Press* did little to dent the progress of D. C. Thomson & Co. Ltd. Throughout the 1930s, under the steady hand and unerring editorial judgement of David Thomson, the company built up its existing titles and added a shoal of new ones. In 1932 they started *Secrets*, in 1933 the *Hotspur* was born, followed in 1943 by *Family Star*. In 1937 and 1938 came the *Dandy* and the *Beano* respectively. This steady growth was interrupted by the war (in which some members of the Thomson family did more than their share), but in the 1950s, when paper became available again, more new Thomson titles began to appear on the market.

At this point the firm had their second confrontation with the trade-union movement. It began in early 1952 in Manchester (where the Printing and Kindred Trades Federation had been recruiting secretly) and spread to Glasgow when a member of NATSOPA was sacked. Richard Briginshaw (later Lord Briginshaw), then General Secretary of NATSOPA, began by calling out all NATSOPA members in D. C. Thomson & Co. – who were startled when seventy-nine men walked out. Then the Scottish Trades Union Congress (STUC) decided to black the firm, a move that was supported by forty-seven unions including the paper workers, railway workers, and the lorry drivers of the Transport and General Workers Union.

Thomson's fought back by making their own transport arrangements (the nucleus of the fleet of grey-painted lorries and vans which still distributes their papers) and finding newsprint wherever they could. It was a nasty, nation-wide dispute, and when paper mills, paper merchants, wholesalers and hundreds of retail newsagents began to squeal, Churchill's Tory government stepped in and ordered a Court of Inquiry. The result was a bit of a stand-off. Both sides were sharply criticised . But the seventy-nine NATSOPA men never got their jobs back, and the

D. C. Thomson. *Dundee Art Galleries and Museums*

firm have fought off every raid by the trade unions ever since. The National Union of Journalists (NUJ) have been particularly persistent, if unsuccessful.

The last attempt to drive a wedge into the Thomson family's monopoly of the Dundee press was in 1979 when the local Labour Party launched the *Dundee Standard*. Like the *Dundee Free Press* it was a creditable attempt, and involved some talented, if abrasive, people. Among them were George Galloway and Brian Wilson (both now Labour MPs), and Ron MacKay, a veteran of the short-lived *Scottish Daily News* which rose out of the ashes of the *Scottish Daily Express*. But the *Dundee Standard* was too blatantly party-political to reach the audience it needed. It never won a place in the market, and ran into the sand before a year was up, leaving the participants reaching for their lawyers.

The 1952 confrontation with the unions was David Couper Thomson's last battle. The legendary publisher died in 1954 at the age of ninety-three, to be succeeded as chairman by his nephew W. H. ('Mr Harold') Thomson, whose boots have since been filled by B. H. ('Mr Brian') Thomson. Editorial flair seems stamped on the Thomson genes. David Thomson's successors proved as successful as the old man himself. All through the 1950s, 1960s and 1970s the company went on adding to their list of titles; *Topper, Beezer, Bunty, Star Love Stories, Romeo, Bimbo, Sparky, Twinkle, Judy, Victor, Hornet, Diana, Mandy, Wizard, Jackie,* and *Annabel* all became familiar sights on the newstands. Their grip on their markets seemed unassailable.

The firm's greatest single asset was probably an unlikely Englishman called Dudley Dexter Watkins. Watkins was the inspired comic artist who drew Desperate Dan, Lord Snooty and His Pals, Mickey the Monkey, The Broons and Oor Wullie. A Nottingham man with strong religious inclinations, Watkins moved to Dundee in the early 1930s and for a few years pushed a pen in the Thomson art department. In 1934 he was given *The Broons* to draw (a comic strip he expected to last a few weeks) and from there he never looked back. Every week, and without fail, a stream of brilliantly-drawn comic characters came out from under his pen. Watkins's 'Illustrated Classics' of *Kidnapped, Robinson Crusoe, Oliver Twist* and *Treasure Island* are now collectors' items.

Although Watkins died (at his desk) in 1969, the characters he created still seem to haunt the imagination of everybody in Britain under the age of about sixty. The Broons and Oor Wullie still trundle through the pages of the *Sunday Post*, and Lord Snooty and his Pals still battle it out with the Bash Street Gang in the *Dandy*. And that comic superstar, Desperate Dan, has leapt from the pages of the *Dandy* and is now lumbering around a line of stationery (notebooks, clip-boards, wallet files, pencil boxes etc.) produced by the Cambridgeshire firm of Copywrite.

When Dennis pushed his way onto The "Beano" cover he became the first human to star on the front page. ("Human? That boy's a MONSTER!" — Dennis's Dad.)

A company spokesman says demand for Dan-embellished products is 'absolutely phenomenal'.

But the marketing of Desperate Dan (and his *Beano* counter-part Dennis the Menace) is probably a sign of commercial unease. For the glory days seem to have gone. The evidence is that the D. C. Thomson operation has gone off the boil. Circulations have been plummeting. The ten years between 1985 and 1994 (inclusive) have been a bruising time for the Dundee-generated newspapers and magazines. According to the last published figures (January–June 1994), the *Sunday Post* is down from 1.5 million to just under a million. The *Weekly News* has collapsed from 913,000 to just over 500,000.

The company's women's magazines show the same trend. The *People's Friend* is down from 635,000 to 481,000, while its stable-mate, *My Weekly*, has sunk from 696,000 to 434,000. Even the 250-year-old *Scots Magazine*, which subsists on a diet of local history, descriptions of hill-walks, industrial archaeology and Scottish characters, is beginning to slip. From a sale of 83,000 in 1985, it is now down to just over 70,000.

The circulation figures for Thomson's Scottish newspapers tell the same story. Since 1985 the *Courier* has dropped from a daily circulation of 129,500 to 108,200. In the same period the *Evening Telegraph* has drifted from a daily sale of 48,400 to 38,500. The multi-edition *People's Journal* has, sadly, gone out of business altogether.

Most alarming of all, perhaps, is the way that D. C. Thomson's semi-legendary comics such as *Beano*, *Dandy* etc. have retreated in the face of ferocious attacks from their rivals in London (Fleetway Publications and Marvel Comics) and Manchester (London Editions). The combined circulation for the *Beano* and *Dandy* (both of which are now well over fifty years old) is now 293,000 against 446,000 ten years ago and almost 1 million in their heyday.

Just why Desperate Dan, Lord Snooty, Minnie the Minx and all their pals are losing their appeal is hard to say. But the new kids on the block – film and TV heroes like Batman, the Ghost-busters, Thundercats, Superman and My Little Pony – seem to be winning the tussle for the hearts and minds of the subteens. 'Thomson's are relying too much on their traditional appeal,' says Mike Butcher who edits two TV-linked comics from Manchester, 'and they're doomed to decline unless they adapt to this new generation of television and video-sophisticated kids. Maybe it's a shame, but that's the way it is.'

So, if the warlocks of Dundee have lost their touch, it could be bad news. For the moment they seem to do well from their non-press investments and subsidiaries. But their 'core' operation remains newspapers and magazines. If that *is* in serious decline, it bodes ill for the city, and for Scotland. As one of the biggest and most stable employers in Dundee, D. C. Thomson

114

Albert Square, Rabbie Burns gazes contemplatively over at the *Courier* building. *Ken Sharp*

& Co. are one of the lynchpins of the Tayside economy. And while the company's politics may sit uneasily with political Scotland, they are the only major home-grown newspaper and magazine house which is controlled by Scots in Scotland. In a media world of indifferent moral values, shifting financial interests, and slippery multi-nationals they are to be valued. Desperate Dan is, after all, a more savoury character than Captain America.

20th-Century Account

JAMES CAMERON

Of all the eminent journalists who started their career in the Thomson organisation, the late James Cameron is the most famous, and deservedly so. The following passages are taken from his autobiography, Point of Departure.

I found myself hired by the Thomson Publications, who were then, and I believe still are, a phenomenon of the editorial industry, built on a principle of idiosyncratic paternalism. That was, even in my day, a survival from the past. The ramifications of their interests seemed unlimited; they produced everything from girls' twopenny weeklies, of a kind apparently unknown today, to schoolboy magazines and children's comics, to reputable newspapers and moralistic reviews, exactly as multiple bakers produce varieties of cakes and buns. I was attached to the Manchester office of the *Weekly News*, and thus did I most diffidently enter the back door of journalism, with the daily function of filling the paste-pots and impaling the other daily newspapers on the files. For this I was to be paid fifteen shillings a week. My father added to this another ten; on this I lived for some time.

Then my employers – perhaps out of consideration for my father more than for me – had me transferred to the headquarters in Dundee. For the first time in my life it occurred to me that there was a possibility of growing roots.

It was a curious context for such a consideration, since the city of Dundee in the early thirties was a place of singular desolation. The whole of industrial Britain in those days was gripped in depression, even despair, and Dundee could have stood as a symbol of a society that had gone sour. It had, for a start, the air of a place that from the beginning of time had reconciled itself to an intrinsic ugliness. This struck me even in my youth as being odd, even anomalous, since of all cities in the kingdom, Dundee had been placed with the greatest potential for grace and charm: it was set on a firth of breadth and grandeur; it was built around the slopes of a mountain, the Law Hill; it backed on to a hinterland of fields and glens – at one time or another Dundee had the makings of a kind of Naples, which, forgetting the punitive nature of its climate, it geographically resembled. Even in those days I had known Naples; I would often look at that bleak Angus shore half-expecting singing fishermen, and hoping for a drift of Vesuvius smoke from the summit of the Law.

Dundee, however, had for generations dedicated itself to a kind of commercial single-mindedness that had come to fruition, in my day, in black and terrible industrial depression. Even then I felt the impact of its brutal melancholy, the façade of unparalleled charmlessness, an absence of grace so total that it was almost a thing of wonder.

It maintained a gruesome derelict cemetery in the very heart of the business section. Its street scenes might have been created by a disillusioned designer of sets for the more embittered works of Chekhov. It accepted all this sardonically, even proudly. The popular picture-postcard of the time was a wide-angle photographic view of the city, a dense and dreadful panorama of reeking factory chimneys: it was called 'Bonnie Dundee'.

But soon that irony became too much even for the Dundonians – because the chimneys smoked no more, the jute mills were empty; it was a community with an insured population of seventy thousand people, with more than forty thousand of them on the dole. The only plentiful thing was paradox: the opulence of the jute-wallahs in Broughty Ferry, the hopeless hovels of Hilltown and Blackscroft. That, and the phenomenon of Dundee, notoriously one of the most alcoholic towns of the nation, year after year returning to Westminster the only Prohibitionist Member of Parliament – the indestructible evangelist Mr Scrymgeour, endlessly voted for by the distracted wives in a hapless effort to keep the dole-money from the pubs.

I settled down gladly enough. My father was now established as a more or less permanent resident of the Royal Hotel in Union Street. I drifted from lodgings to lodgings, until the greatest good fortune led me to a room in Reform Street, in the flat of Mrs Murray, a widow, the sister of Fiddes Watt, an RSA who had been a portraitist of some celebrity. She had three daughters, with the youngest of whom I fell in love. Her name was Elma, she was then sixteen and a student at Gray's School of Arts in Aberdeen. It was the first time I had ever been in love.

My days were spent in the service of the Thomson Publications, then as now a patriarchal firm of significance in its own peculiar sphere, pre-eminent of its kind in the mass-production of an especially marketable type of sub-literature, of a strangely durable but ever-changing variety. Most of this quite considerable empire was divided into two fields, on the one hand Women's and on the other Boys'. The Women's section was presided over by Mr David Donald, the Boys' by Mr Robert Low. Both of them were to become generous and helpful friends, and introduced me to the pastime of Scottish mountaineering that became, and remained for many years, an obsessive occupation. In the office they were both very important men, while any position of less importance than mine had

When the editor recounted this incident in *They Fairly Mak Ye Work*, few people believed it. The destitute and homeless boys of the Mars Training Ship wish you seasons greetings. *Dundee Art Galleries and Museums*

Hawkhill: Death of a living community. *Joseph McKenzie*

yet to be devised. Mr Low had under his wing the great organs of contemporary derring-do, the *Wizard*, the *Rover*, the *Hotspur*, and the like, all differing in fashions immediately perceptible to the initiate but to nobody else. Mr Donald was overlord of the *Weekly Welcome*, the *Red Letter* and the *Red Star Weekly*, each of which specialized – again in nuances not readily to be understood – in serial fiction of a nature which even after all these years I remember as either unbearably sweet and wholesome, or diabolically bloodthirsty. I was attached to the *Red Star Weekly*, which catered for a public of working girls whose tastes must have verged on the sadistic, so heavily were our pages soaked in gore. We had some sort of a lien on that hardy classic of Victorian violence, *Maria Marten, or the Murders in the Red Barn*. It seems to me that we were recounting that piece of durable *angst* for years, and when it stopped the intervals were filled with sequels, or developments, or associated crimes of passion; I am not sure that we did not have a *Son of Maria Marten*. These works were contributed by sundry authors over the country, my father among them, who were paid thirty shillings a thousand words for their not inconsiderable pains.

The memorable quality of these stories was, paradoxically, their purity. The most frightful things were encouraged to happen: stranglings, knifings, shootings, disembowellings, burials alive, hauntings, drownings, suffocations, torments of a rich and varied nature abounded , and each instalment was obliged to end with a suspenseful promise of worse to come, but in no circumstances and at no point was permitted even the hint of sexual impropriety. This was the ark of the covenant and the cornerstone of our editorial principles. No matter what ferocious indignities, disasters and deaths befell our heroines, it might never be even suggested, however obliquely, that there was ever any purpose behind these excesses other than good clean violence. This made much of the carryings-on somewhat inexplicable, but that was incidental and held to be no difficulty.

This curious attitude can be symbolized in the case of the Cover Picture. One of the functions that fell to my lot was the weekly selection of some particularly gripping or galvanic incident in our principal story that could be illustrated in a compelling way and used as the magazine's cover, as an earnest of the savours within. On one occasion we were beginning a serial based on an actual series of especially brutal murders that had much exercised the newspapers of the time, and which had been catalogued in the press as 'The Man With the Glaring Eyes'. No subject was more tailor-made for us, and with eager professional zeal and pride we had commissioned a fictionalised version of this rewarding series of crimes. In the real-life version the trouble had manifestly been caused by some unusually over-stimulated sexual psychopath; no such innuendo, however, was to be found in our version, in which a recurrent number of nubile virgins were vigorously done to death by some antisocial unknown apparently in pursuit of a wholly mysterious hobby.

On this occasion, then, I ordered from the artist what I felt to be an appropriate drawing that would do justice to our promising theme. When the rough appeared I was well satisfied: it portrayed a deeply sinister back-alley by night, lit only by the baleful gleam of an eerie street lamp, whose sickly beam threw into prominence a foreground of damp and lowering paving-stones, on which lay the true purpose of the composition: the body of a young woman, her throat most palpably cut from ear to ear. It was a highly successful realisation; the draughtsman had clearly put his heart into his work, and he had delineated the character of the lady's injury with an almost clinical fidelity; hardly was a torn tendon or a severed blood-vessel out of place, and the blood that streamed into the rainswept gutter had been limned by an enthusiast. It did complete justice, I felt, to 'The Man With the Glaring Eyes'.

I took this along for Mr Donald's approval with a quiet and calm confidence. When he saw it he blenched. He tore it from my hand and studied it aghast, and in speechless outrage. Finally he said: 'You must be mad!'

Accepting that I might possibly on this occasion have overdone it, I murmured: 'It is a bit strong, maybe.'

'Strong, strong,' cried Mr Donald, 'It's no' a question o' strong; it's no' a bad scene. But for God's sake, boy – look at the lassie's skirt; it's awa' above her knees!'

Abashed, I realized what rule I had broken. I took the drawing back and had the hemline lowered a modest inch or two, and in the cover went, slit windpipe and all.

Later, Cameron left Dundee but continued working on the Sunday Post *in Glasgow.*

In those days there was no tangible demarcation line between the functional processes in the editorial department of a provincial newspaper of this kind. Between the sub-editor branch and the reportorial staff no such schism or tribal difference existed as exists today, since everybody on the newspaper

119

was both alternately, or even sometimes simultaneously. Much of my time was occupied in writing articles of a character almost excruciatingly homely and domestic, treating of the more trivial sort of family or social incident in a style, which I soon bitterly found came fairly easily to me, that somehow combined the facetious and the didactic, the worldly-wise and the innocent; an assemblage of recognizably nudging clichés that was defined in our literary terms as 'couthy'. Few essays before or since can have been as deadly, but the technique was not hard to master, and to this day I detect in myself sinister, atavistic regressions into this appalling sly cosiness of style. This work was – in conformance with our editorial policy of refusing any employee the dignity of individuality – not signed, a fact which causes me great relief today; for the purposes of these compositions I would assume the character of A Feckless Housewife, A Henpecked Husband, Wee Wully, The Saftest o' the Family, Always a Wallflower, A Bairn Without a Name, and kindred archetypes of the ridiculous, eccentric, or pathetic. Everything had to be written in paragraphs one sentence long, and as far as possible in what was held to be the homely idiom of the Scottish working class, which is to say a costive coyness larded with apostrophes and Doricisms which bore as much likeness to the demotic speech of the Gorbals, say, as it did to Greek. Considerable value was placed on what were known as 'human stories', which by definition concerned animals. To this end I would be obliged to write under the title of Percy the Poodle, or An Unloved Alley-cat. In this character I authored some work so truly horrible that it met with heartfelt acclaim. From time to time I ghosted in serial for the life-stories of eminent boxers or released murderers or minor domestic functionaries of the Royal Household, all of whom, varied as their activities had presumably been, recounted their Exclusive Stories through me in a style uniformly homely, moving, gripping and couthy. It is true that in this way I came into contact with people and aspects of life that might otherwise have passed me by – for a time I became oddly involved in the activities of the professional boxing industry, in the wild macabre days of Benny Lynch, and a reluctant interest in that sad sport has never quite left me. I acted as journalistic amanuensis to an eerie creep who was contributing a series called 'Secrets of the Mayfair Vice Rings', who conscientiously established his bonafides by attempting to seduce me on the top deck of a green tram. At intervals I would be despatched, at the conclusion of some especially repellent murder trial – and there seem to me to have been in those days about one a month – to call upon some distracted or avaricious mother up a close in Lanark or Motherwell and guide her hand through an article entitled 'Why My Boy Should Not Be Hanged'. Between these endeavours and my consistent *oeuvre* of canny suburban humour a kind of balance was maintained. I learned to do almost anything after a fashion, and nothing well. I was paid six pounds a week.

The great day was Saturday. This, being press day for our Sunday paper, was for me a regular climax of variety, a professional routine that would be quite unimaginable today. It must be remembered that our organisation was not only a non-union shop, but designedly and even militantly so. Only many years later did a fairly close association with my own Union reveal to me the outrages and heresies I had innocently committed long before, against every sacred canon of organised labour. At the time it merely seemed to me that I was somewhat overworked.

The Golden Decade

Dundee Money Abroad

by GEORGE A. STOUT

It was the spring of 1870 and Robert Fleming, a promising twenty-five-year-old confidential clerk with the textile firm of Baxter Brothers, was about to make his first visit to the United States. He came from a modest background. Born at Liff Road, Lochee, Fleming now lived with his family in Brown Street, convenient for his father who was a departmental foreman in the nearby jute factory at Gilroy's Tay Works.

Robert had five brothers and sisters who died when young from diphtheria and only one brother, John, who lived. John was eventually to have his own flourishing timber business in Aberdeen, to become Lord Provost of that city and Liberal Member of Parliament. He was knighted in 1908.

Robert began his education at the local Free Church School and at the age of eleven won a scholarship in mathematics for two years at the Dundee High School. He started work at the age of thirteen and became a book-keeper with the export side of Baxter Bros, in Edward Baxter & Son. Hence from an early age he was exposed to the possibilities of the New World which was taking a large proportion of the company's output of linen fabrics. Edward Baxter's special responsibilities within the organisation were the private financial and other investment interests of the family and he introduced Fleming to the world of finance.

Now Robert was off to the United States to see for himself and for his master what this exciting country had to offer. The nation was rebuilding itself after the Civil War and expanding westwards into the vast emptiness of the plains. And the currency looked cheap with the paper dollar 'Greenbacks' selling at a substantial discount to their nominal value against sterling. A time to buy America at a discount?

The outcome of that visit was the formation of the first of five investment trusts which Fleming was to establish in Dundee from 1873 onwards, and the introduction of a decade of financial investment in overseas territories by Dundee's citizens which was without parallel in amount and intensity for a provincial town. In the next ten years Dundee investors were to put some £5 million into an astonishing range of investments including railroad securities, land mortgages, acquisitions of raw land and cattle ranching, a sum equivalent to £200 million at present day prices.

c. 1750

'Dundee man meets Dundee man off Java.'
The following account is from the book *Dundee Delineated*.

. . . In the year 1750, Captain Crichton, of Dundee, was captured by Angria, the famous East India pirate, who put the following questions to him:-

Angria   – Where do you originally come from?
Crichton – From Dundee, in Scotland.
Angria   – Ay! ay! from Dundee!! Then, pray, where does the Cross of Dundee stand?
Crichton – Near the west end of the large square, opposite the new Townhouse.
Angria   – How many steps are in it?
Crichton – Six steps, and all go round about it.
Angria   – Quite right.'

Having asked some other questions which were answered satisfactorily, the pirate said, 'Well, Captain Crichton, because we are townsmen, I give you your liberty and your ship in a present.'

Dundee from Balgay Hill, c. 1867. From the Illustrated London News. *Dundee District Libraries*

Yet, but for a turn of fate, it might all have been completely different. Immediately after the issue of the First Scottish American Trust, Fleming left for America intending, but failing, to catch the sailing of the *Atlantic* from Liverpool. However, as he himself described it many years later: 'When we reached New York, posters proclaimed the loss of the *Atlantic* with 600 lives off Nova Scotia. Had I sailed on the Thursday instead of the Saturday, it is not likely that I should have since then crossed the Atlantic 128 times.'

Although primarily attracted to the investment possibilities of the USA, the Dundee money found its way into almost any English speaking country – to Canada, Australia and New Zealand and even to remote Hawaii. How had this interest in overseas investment arisen? Where did the knowledge of distant parts come from? And, most important of all, how had Dundee's citizens accumulated so much free capital?

'The Dens Works have been better than a gold mine'

In the 1840s and fifties Dundee had become a bustling, prosperous industrial city, albeit that the prosperity was ill-divided

122

Cowhands of the Dundee owned Matador Ranch, Texas. *Alliance Trust*

among its inhabitants. From a handloom, cottage industry in linen based on local supplies of flax, the textile industry had been in a growth phase since the Napoleonic Wars. The then modest firm of William Baxter and Son had supplied sailcloth for Nelson's *Victory*. After the war Baxters began industrial spinning with 600 employees at Glamis and subsequently opened a similar operation at the Lower Dens Mill in Dundee.

Wars are often a windfall of opportunity to industrialists and the Crimean War in 1854-56 provided an additional market for sailcloth, tarpaulin and tenting. The development of steam-power looms, the availability of cheap flax from the lands of the Baltic and major improvements in harbour facilities accelerated the rate of expansion.

While Baxters dominated the linen industry, across the town in Lochee the four Cox brothers were becoming equally powerful in the manufacture of jute products. Introduced in 1822, jute had initially been a tricky material to spin, but by the 1840s all the problems had been solved and output was expanding fast. The brothers' Camperdown Works built on thirty acres with over 5,000 employees was an object of admiration and wonder.

123

Its weekly consumption of raw jute was greater than the next three largest manufacturers (Gilroys, Malcolm Ogilvie and John Sharp) put together.

As textiles prospered so too did Dundee's other industries – its engineering works with their high reputation in power units for the mills, for ships and for the railways. Dundee's five ship-building yards were fully employed and the whaling industry's oil found a ready market in the jute batching process. The market for the town's products was world-wide and the industrialists were particularly tuned into developments wherever they might arise.

While the Crimea had been a fillip to Dundee, it was nothing to the bonanza which arose from the American Civil War. The textile industry was already experienced in American trade. The coarse linen 'Osnaburg' fabric was standard wear for negro slaves; American ships used Dundee-made sails; the wagons or 'Prairie Schooners' carrying the settlers westward were covered by Dundee tarpaulin; and jute and linen bags were used for bagging sugar and cotton. About half of Dundee's textile exports were already being sent to the USA. To that was now added all the demands of the military on both sides – tenting, tarpaulins, gun covers and sandbags.

The Americans came out of their war sadder, wiser and poorer. Dundee's industrialists, however, emerged with an incalculable knowledge of the new nation, powerful business connections – and very much richer! On a business visit to the United States which included a diversionary day at Niagara Falls, Mr A. B. Gilroy was asked by a proud guide if he had ever seen anything finer. After a pause he replied: 'Yes I have – 10½oz/40 inch hessian coming over Gilroy's calender at five pence a yard.'

None were more powerful and rich than the Baxter and Cox families and they were to play a prime rôle in the financial extravaganza which was to follow in Dundee. As Peter Car-michael, engineer and technical director at Baxter Bros. expressed it – 'The Dens Works have been better than a gold mine.'

Robert Fleming issued a prospectus to raise £150,000 for his First Scottish American Trust in February 1873, with the pro-ceeds to be invested primarily in American railroad bonds. A prestigious board of directors included John Guild (chairman), John Sharp, Tom Cox and Thomas Smith and reflected the remarkable degree of confidence being placed in the twenty-eight-year-old Fleming (which would be improbable in one so young today). Dundee's citizens enthusiastically over-subscribed the issue. With a flair more appropriate to an experienced promoter, Fleming withdrew the prospectus and reissued it to raise £300,000. The Second Scottish-American Trust was formed later in 1873 and raised £400,000, and the

Share Certificates, Hawaii, Texas and Connecticut. *Alliance Trust*

Third Scottish American Trust two years later with a similar sum.

Over the next twenty years Robert Fleming became much sought after as an adviser in the financing of the American railroad network. He was involved in historic projects such as the Atchison, Topeka & Santa Fe, and Denver & Rio Grande Railroads. He was also concerned with the formation of the Cuba Railroad and the Anglo-Persian Oil Company (now British Petroleum). Not the least of his coups was the bringing into Dundee ownership of the Texas-based Matador Land & Cattle Company.

Robert Fleming married a local girl, Kate Hindmarsh, in 1881 when he was thirty-five and she was twenty-three. By 1886 his operations were increasingly London based and he resigned most of his Dundee directorships. The London office which he opened in 1900 is now the prestigious merchant bank of Robert Fleming. Among the offspring spawned from this charismatic figure were his grandchildren – Richard Fleming, a subsequent chairman of the bank, and Richard's brothers: Peter, writer and explorer, and Ian, of 'James Bond' fame.

The Land Mortgage companies

In October 1873 another group of Dundee businessmen (with Tom Cox the common thread) conceived a different way to exploit the American opportunity. William Lowson, a local textile merchant who was already involved with Edinburgh's financial community, was probably the initiator of the Oregon & Washington Trust Investment Co. which was formed to lend money to farming and other commercial projects in the States of Oregon and the adjacent Territory of Washington. His fellow directors included The Earl of Airlie as Chairman, John Leng (proprietor of the *Dundee Advertiser*), Thomas Couper (D. P. & L. Shipping Co.), and the jute industrialists Tom Cox, Thomas Bell and James Neish. The Secretary of the new company was to be William Reid, a local solicitor and US vice-consul in Dundee.

The audacity of this group was breathtaking. None of them had ever been in the United States before, far less in Oregon, but the reputation of that fertile State was already known in Dundee. On a fact-finding visit to the USA in 1876, after which he wrote a book on the subject, Sir John Leng described Oregon's Willamette valley as similar to the valley of Strathmore – 'where drought is unknown and a harvest is never lost'.

William Mackenzie, the successor to William Reid as secretary, was later to write of his personal inadequacies for the task in hand: 'I knew nothing of company law or management; I had never seen a mortgage and had no acquaintance with the

126

lands on which it was based, or any knowledge of the steps necessary to create the very soul of our business and the secret of its
success, viz. a good charge upon good lands properly inspected
and valued.'

The rules of operation of the company were quite strict and
became the standard for subsequent companies which were
started in the following years. A local board was set up in
Portland, Oregon (then a town of about 11,000 inhabitants) with
instructions to lend no more than one third on the appraised
value of any property. The farm land in the Willamette was the
prime target for loans but property was considered in some
townships – all of which were specifically named. No loans
would be granted on wharves, factories or sawmills nor on
timberland. All loans would be serviced by repayment in gold
coin – there was to be no nonsense about accepting paper curren-
cies or silver dollars!

The major attraction of overseas investment was, of course,
the anticipated rate of return. Rates of interest in Britain had
fallen to about 4 per cent as the industrial revolution had run its
course. America, by contrast, was capital hungry after the
destruction of the Civil War and loans to farmers in Oregon
might earn a mouth-watering 12 per cent. The Fleming companies had been organised on the same principle though the
rates of return were a more modest 8 per cent on railroad
securities.

By the spring of 1874 the Oregon & Washington Trust was in
business, having raised £150,000 of Ordinary capital of which
only £25,000 was paid up, and had made its first loan – to a Mr
A. H. Ankenny of Marion County of $12,000 in gold, repayable
in two years at an interest rate of 12 per cent. In the next six years
£700,000 was lent in Oregon, equivalent to £30 million in 1990
terms.

The unique feature of this and other mortgage companies was
that, on the basis of the uncalled liability of the Ordinary capital,
the directors were able to pyramid a large amount of borrowed
money on which they would pay 5 to 6 per cent for five or seven
years fixed term. The surplus earned over its cost then accrued
to the Ordinary shareholders. To a large degree this borrowed
money was obtained from the clients of Dundee solicitors. It was
the real 'widows and orphans' money which supported the
equity ventures of the, mainly rich, Ordinary shareholders. It
should be said, however, that many a jute clerk or shopkeeper
followed his master into what proved to be a most lucrative long-
term investment in the Ordinary shares.

Once the Oregon & Washington Trust was up and running,
William Reid took off for Portland where he became not only the
local agent for the Dundee company but the promoter of
numerous ventures on the west coast and secretary to the
Portland Chamber of Commerce. He was so caught up in the

William 'Dundee' Reid. *Alliance Trust*

local environment that he 'went native' and became a virtually uncontrollable colleague for his Dundee successor as company secretary, William Mackenzie. He frequently exceeded or ignored his lending authority and was involved in several wildly speculative ventures in railroads, shipping and property.

Reid even took part in the formation of a rival company to his own, the Oregon & Washington Savings Bank. This bank, the first in the State, was half owned by local interests and half by Dundee investors, with its headquarters in Dundee as Oregon law did not permit Oregon-owned banks to function. Its directors included another group of Dundee businessmen, with Alexander Gourlay (engineer) as chairman, William Robertson (iron merchant), Alexander Thomson (ship owner) and George Gilroy (jute manufacturer). Typical of William Reid's actions he lent half the bank's funds to one client, the Oregon Navigation Company.

After ten tempestuous years, Reid overstepped the mark once too often and was dismissed by his Dundee bosses. In his retiral address in 1920 William Mackenzie was to expand on 'Dundee Reid' – as he was known in Portland – in an epic understatement: 'In departure from the truth he had a practised facility.' A local politician, Senator Nesmith, is reported to have written that there were three liars in the State of Oregon and William Reid was two of them!

The Oregon & Washington prospered despite Reid's machinations but the limitations of its trading area quickly became apparent. By 1876 the Dundonians were ready for new pastures and the Dundee Mortgage & Trust Investment Co. was formed, with powers to operate throughout the world. It had twice the funds of its predecessor (£300,000) but the principles of investment remained the same. In its first year it made loans of over a million dollars mainly through appointed agents in Chicago, San Francisco and Indianapolis but also including the farm lands of Iowa and Manitoba.

Wherever they went, the Dundee investors would seek out former Dundonians or other Scots to act as local agents or bankers. The companies' inspector of agricultural properties was invariably a Scot from a rural area (one was from Blairgowrie). The network spread into Missouri, Nebraska and Dakota then down the Mississippi to Memphis and Greenville. The next step was Texas.

The carousel of speculation in Dundee was beginning to spin faster and faster. In the words of the editor of the Dundee Year Book, 'The appetite grows on what it feeds on in American investments as in other things.' The next proposal from what was becoming the William Mackenzie stable of companies was the Dundee Land Investment Co. which was launched in 1878.

This company's objective was out-and-out speculation in land, preferably close to a railway or a prospective town, with a view to sub-division of lots and their subsequent sale at a profit. Almost anything was considered. It was incorporated with a capital of £100,000 but only £15,000 of Ordinary capital was paid up and it was topped-up with £75,000 of borrowings. It would have made today's junk-bond specialists ashen-faced with worry!

William Smith, a farmer at Stone of O'Morphie near Montrose, was engaged at a fee of four guineas a day to investigate suitable land for purchase. 'It appeared to the directors a matter of great importance that any purchase should be in districts not only of good character from an agricultural point of view, but likely to prove popular with Scottish settlers, whom the company might, with mutual advantage, aid in acquiring homesteads.'

Among its more spectacular investments was a three-quarter interest in 162,000 acres of timber and grazing land in Tennessee and Kentucky which is now part of the Daniel Boone National Forest; a half-interest in 250,000 acres of an earlier Spanish land grant in New Mexico named the Chavez Grant, part of which was ceded in World War Two to the US government for the Los Alamos atomic-testing ground; and 200,000 acres of Mississippi bayou in Arkansas, intended for lumber operations, which were let rent-free to negroes for five years on condition of their clearing the land. It later became a cattle ranch.

Another of the company's spectacular deals was the Paladuro loan to the famous Goodnight Ranch in Texas. The property involved had been the ancestral home of the Comanche Indians who pillaged the early settlers in the 1870s, though the Indians had been driven from their land before the decade was out. The history of this loan was tortuous and it eventually defaulted. It was not until after World War Two that the Texas States' Parks Authority finally purchased the property back for the heritage of Texas for $120,000. What a coup if it could have been retained!

Housing properties were also bought and given homespun names such as Lowson Terrace and the Mackenzie Villas in Winnipeg, and Dundee Place in Kansas City. There was, and still is, a township of Airlie in the Willamette valley in Oregon and another one in Minnesota was rechristened Kinbrae after the name of Sir John Leng's Newport residence. However, the name Balthayock, which was William Lowson's estate in the Carse of Gowrie, was turned down 'as Americans may not be able to pronounce it correctly' and instead the name Grayback, that of Lowson's town house, was given to a township in Minnesota.

In January 1879, William Smith took the Mackenzie companies into Texas for the first time when he purchased 22,400 acres in Swisher County in north Texas at forty cents an acre, 'guaranteed to be smooth and rich prairie soil'. Smith retained

The Matador Chuckwagon. Cowboys, and with the different bonnet, John Robertson of the Alliance Trust. *Alliance Trust*

half the property for himself and subsequently purchased the entire tract. It had been an extended visit, lasting eighty-five days, for which he received £357 in expenses.

The Texas connection

By the early 1880s competition in rates in the mortgage market was becoming fierce as American insurance and land-mortgage companies built up their resources and the foreign companies were obliged to push south (down the Mississippi) and west. They even ventured into the Indian Territory, the area that would not become Oklahoma for another twenty-five years, but business with the five tribes who had been settled there (the Creek, Choctaw, Cherokee, Seminole and Shawnee) was severely restricted by government decree.

It was the south-west, and Texas in particular, that became the new attraction. In January 1882, Dundee had a visit from W. J. Ballantyne Paterson from San Antonio, Texas who expounded on the opportunities there. At the office of the Dundee Mortgage & Trust and the Dundee Land Investment Co. where 'he was known personally by some of the directors and recommended by Balfour Williamson' he was well received and walked out the door with credits of $25,000 from each company, for investment in the south-west of Texas.

Texas captured the imagination. It was vast – three times the size of Britain. Tales had been told for years of the mighty herds of wild cattle waiting to be rounded up and driven to the markets in the north-east. The Scots had already made their impact at the birth of the new State – Davy Crockett, Jim Bowie and many others had died at the Alamo. And, from the financial point of view it was an empty State – the total deposits of all the Texas banks amounted to less than £400,000. Nor did potential investors have to take the word of visiting Texans. Did not a Parliamentary Commission report that ranching in America could give annual returns of 33 per cent! The mortgage companies were quick off their mark and, within a few years, had agencies operating in Dallas, Fort Worth and Waco in addition to San Antonio.

In May 1880, the first large public company to undertake cattle ranching in Texas was floated in Edinburgh. This was the Prairie Cattle Company. Significantly, the Dundee participation was large with Lord Airlie as chairman, William Lowson a director and Dundee investors subscribing for one-third of the capital. All the usual names were there – Tom Cox, the Gourlay brothers, William Mackenzie – and many small shareholders of more modest means.

Initial success of the Prairie Cattle Company spawned interest in further investments and Dundee became 'a happy hunting

131

The Seal of the Western and Hawaiian
Investment Company. *Alliance Trust*

ground' for Texan cattlemen and their brokers, anxious to sell
a piece of the action to the less discerning. Three companies were
floated locally – the Hansford Cattle Company, the Texas Land
& Cattle Company and the Matador Land & Cattle Company.
In addition, Dundee investors took a considerable stake in the
Powder River Cattle Company and the Arkansas Valley Land &
Cattle Company which were of course located in other ranching
territories.

The largest, and in the end the only successful venture, was
Matador. The company had been established in 1879 but three
years later Robert Fleming organised a syndicate of Dundee
investors to buy out the existing American owners. Situated in
west Texas it was an impressive ranch with grazing rights over
1,500,000 acres – an area equivalent to Tayside Region! Unlike
some of the other promoters, Fleming had done his homework
and employed a proper survey of the properties and a head-count
of the 40,000 stock of cattle and 265 horses.

'Aloha' Hawaii!

No review of this remarkable period is complete without
reference to two companies whose births were associated with
the mainstream of flotations, although they were independent of
it. The first was the Hawaiian Investment & Agency Company.
This was an orthodox land-morgage business established in 1880
to lend money in Hawaii where, according to the prospectus,
'The native inhabitants are a peaceful and industrious race and
life and property are completely protected.' To emphasise the
point, His Majesty King Kalakua of Hawaii was allocated 200
shares! And to embellish the Pacific theme, the company
adopted as its seal the design of the coconut palm tree.

The chairman of the Hawaiian Investment was jute manufacturer George Halley and he was joined on the board by other
local businessmen: Alexander Gilroy, Thomas Bell, Alexander
Thomson and David Littlejohn. The company secretary was
John Shepherd. Their initial proposals were almost beyond
belief – they considered starting a land company in Fiji, and even
an investment in Egypt. The death of General Gordon at Khar-
toum put a stop to the latter! Within three years the geographic
limitations of Hawaii caused a rethink of the lending territory
and the company was reformed as the Western & Hawaiian
Company. From then it conformed increasingly to the policies
of the Mackenzie companies, using many of the same American
agents.

The other curiosity was the Oregonian Railway Company.
This was a William Reid venture to provide a 240-mile railroad
which would link up the southern border of Oregon and California to the Northern Pacific railway, which ran across the

continent and into Oregon. It was a big undertaking and over £400,000 was raised in 1882, predominantly in Dundee. The idea had possibilities, for the only routes from California to Portland at that time were by sea or a forty-hour overland journey in a stagecoach. It was proposed that the line, when completed, would be leased to the Oregon Railway & Navigation Company which had a stranglehold on transport on the Columbia river.

Taking stock

By the end of 1882 it was becoming clear that Dundee investors had just too many eggs in the one basket. The Fleming trusts had raised £1,100,000, the land mortgage companies a similar sum, the Dundee-sponsored ranches £600,000 and the Oregonian £400,000. In addition there were big investments in Edinburgh, Glasgow and Aberdeen companies engaged in investment and mortgage activities. And finally, there were various interests in lumber companies in the USA and Canada as well as the private, direct investment in these countries of individual capitalists. It was estimated at the time that about £5,000,000 had been invested by the people of Dundee in North America – equivalent to £200,000,000 in today's currency! The *Dundee Advertiser* cautioned that the remarkable success of a few companies 'in the early days of their career' should not be taken to indicate that those who followed would be equally successful. It would be almost three more years before the bubble burst.

The end of the party

It all began to go wrong from 1884. Recession struck the jute industry and imports of raw jute fell to 130,000 tons from the 234,000 tons of the previous year. The industry had increased capacity by over 20 per cent in two years and a major potential threat to Dundee's prosperity, Calcutta production, had almost doubled in the same time with a devastating effect on prices.

This was followed by a downturn in the fortunes of the cattle companies. There was a glut of cattle and prices collapsed. Some of the Scottish companies discovered that they did not have as many cattle as they thought and had to write off non-existent stock! Dividends were cut or eliminated altogether. There was a strong smell of burnt fingers. Worse was to follow.

By 1888, three-quarters of the capital in the cattle companies had been lost and four of the eight public companies were bankrupt. The Matador was worth more than all the others put together and was the only healthy outfit. The Oregonian Railroad ran into engineering difficulties and even more disastrous problems with litigation over the lease of the railway

Ladies and Gentlemen promenading in Baxter Park, after its opening in 1863. W. J. Middleton. *Dundee District Libraries*

line. This eventually put the company into liquidation. It was a calamity which cost Dundee investors about 80 per cent of their original investment.

Equally important, many of the financial leaders were departing the Dundee stage. Lord Airlie, who had been chairman of many of the companies and a strong intellectual force behind the American development, died while on a visit to Colorado in 1881. William Reid had been sacked by Mackenzie and his world crumbled with the collapse of the Oregonian. William Lowson was also tarred with the Reid saga and resigned his directorships with the mortgage companies. Many of the leading figures also lost credibililty (and money) with the Oregonian disaster.

Perhaps the most important factor of all was the departure of Robert Fleming for London. In addition to being the key figure at the Scottish-American trusts, since 1882 he had been a director of the Mackenzie companies, in which he was held in high esteem for his knowledge of the American financial scene. His resignation in 1886 because of increasing London commitments, took away the companies' supreme authority on the stock market, particularly in America.

Fleming was the designer and architect of much of what had been created in the Dundee financial community. He had vision, flair and the ability to assess the market mood. After he left Dundee there was no one to carry on his promotional activities and Dundee's days as a financial breeding ground were over.

By comparison, his fellow financier, Mackenzie, who was only one year his junior, was much more of a builder of companies and organisations. While Fleming was whizzing back and forth to New York doing deals, Mackenzie was patiently putting his group together. But he never floated another new venture. In 1888, he combined his companies to form the Alliance Trust, at that time the largest investment trust company, and, towards the end of his working life, he took over the management of the Western & Hawaiian and later renamed it the Second Alliance Trust.

He made only fourteen trips to the USA during his forty-five years in business though these consumed almost five years of his life. An inspection of the agencies was no sinecure – there were fourteen of them: from Winnipeg in the north to San Antonio in the south; from Columbia (South Carolina) in the east to San Francisco in the west. 'I left home on 3 December and returned to the company's office on 8 April, a period of 126 days. During this time I travelled 18,500 miles by rail and steamer, or an average of 145 miles per day,' as Mackenzie said at his retiral in 1920.

The philanthropists

While the 1870s and 1880s witnessed a wild speculative binge by Dundee's citizens, by no means all the available wealth was consumed in the orgy of overseas investment. It was also a time of great philanthropy and benefaction. The Baxter family took little direct involvement in company promotion but were outstanding contributors to the social well-being of the city.

In 1863, on the occasion of his knighthood, Sir David Baxter purchased the Baxter Park for the community at a cost of £35,000. He gave £30,000 to the Convalescent Home, £20,000 to the Technical Institute and £7,000 to the Albert Institute. Outside of Dundee, he founded four scholarships at Edinburgh University and inaugurated the Chair of Engineering. His brother, Edward, is reputed to have given a considerable portion of his income every year to deserving causes and his name featured on almost every committee for benevolent purposes. But the most generous gift of all was the endowment of the University College of Dundee by Sir David's sister, Mary Ann, when, in 1880, she donated the enormous sum of £130,000. To this gift she later added another £10,000 for a chemical laboratory, while her relation, John Boyd Baxter, added a further £10,000 for College purposes. These benefactions would amount to many millions of pounds in today's terms.

Nor were the Coxes to be left out of the running when it came to gifts to the community. The firm presented Lochee Park to the town, and Tom Cox gave £12,000 to endow the Chair of Anatomy at the University. The public library and swimming pond in Lochee were also due to his generosity and the Lochee churches were heavily supported by the family. Tom's oldest brother James was a railway 'buff' and a director of the North British Railway Company. He was a leading protagonist of the Tay rail bridge and, 'pour encourager les autres', the Coxes subscribed £10,000 towards the funding of the bridge. James was chairman of the Tay Bridge Undertaking. He also played his part in local politics and was provost from 1872 to 1875.

This kind of generosity was not confined to the jute barons. William Harris, a successful miller and corn merchant, gifted £20,000 to Dundee High School and a further £10,000 to the local School Board, for the first public secondary school in Dundee, which became the Harris Academy. Robert Fleming contributed funds for the gymnasium at the University and, at a later date, gifted £150,000 for the Fleming Gardens public-housing scheme. The Fleming family have maintained their interest in Dundee and the present company chairman, also Robert Fleming, was influential in the founding of a Chair of Finance at Dundee University only a few years ago.

Was it all in vain?

The question must be asked, whether or not the mania for American investment in the 1870s and 1880s did long-term damage to Dundee's industrial potential. A solemn editorial in the *Edinburgh Courant* as early as 1885 noted that 'Dundee has committed itself to investment more or less speculative and nearly all outside the range of its proper business to the extent of £5,000,000.' The article doubted whether a manufacturing centre should drain itself of such a large quantity of funds, needed to maintain its factories and work force. The amount invested had been between nine and ten times the value of every building and foot of ground the burgh contained. Taking the annual income of the town as £1,500,000 and annual savings as £250,000, the citizens had spent, on 'financial recreation in foreign lands', the equivalent of twenty years' savings.

With the benefit of a hundred years' hindsight, this judgment may have been too harsh. It is unlikely, for example, that the money would have been better spent in the jute industry. The long-term threat from Calcutta was already present in the 1880s, and Dundee was always fighting a losing battle thereafter.

As for the American investments, only the cattle ranches (Matador excepted) and the Oregonian railway were unmitigated disasters. In 1951 the shareholders in Matador were bought out by American interests for almost $20,000,000, a handsome return on their investment. Fleming's investment trust companies, though no longer managed from Dundee and now obscured in their identity by changes of name, have grown to over £400 million and still include many Dundonians among their shareholders.

But pride of place must go to Mackenzie's Alliance and Second Alliance. The patient building of these by their founder has been continued by his several successors with never a faltering step. To some outsiders it may seem unadventurous or even dull – after all in a hundred years the company has only moved its modest offices round Meadowside, from Panmure Street to

Pumping oil. Alliance No. 2 Well, Cormier Plantation, Louisiana, 1932.
Alliance Trust

Reform Street! The total funds, however, have now grown to
£900 million, virtually all internally generated. At a fair guess,
this probably exceeds the value of all Dundee's other industrial
and commercial businesses put together. And, although the
shares in the two companies are now widely held throughout the
United Kingdom, the annual returns in dividends to
shareholders in the Tayside area alone are some £4,000,000.

And what happened to the American dream? It did not die easily.
In the 1930s and 1940s it found expression in Dundee's twenty-
seven cinemas with their 30,000 seats for the city's 180,000
population – the greatest cinema-going public in Britain and one
of the most committed to American films. Now even that has
gone, but the advent of cheaper air travel has allowed many a
Dundonian to realise the dream. The road 'out west' may no
longer be named Route 66, but it still goes through Chicago, St
Louis, Oklahoma City, Amarillo and all the way to Los Angeles.
Robert Fleming and William Mackenzie knew the way and
would have been impressed; but no *more* impressed than with the
quiet and moving presence of the unfurled Cross of St Andrew
at the Alamo, San Antone.

137

The *Balaena* in the ice off Greenland, c. 1900. *Dundee Art Galleries and Museums*

THE WHALING

In the latter part of the nineteenth century, Dundee was Britain's premier whaling port. Arctic whaling was in decline by the 1880s so an Antarctic expedition was organised for the years 1892-3. The artist W. G. Burn Murdoch was on board the Balaena *and the following passages are taken from his book* From Edinburgh to the Antarctic.

Historic Accounts

Once at Dundee, there is no difficulty in finding the whalers. All Dundonians, from the small boys to the big shareholders, take a proud interest in them. I asked a policeman to direct me to the whaling Company's office; fortunately he could speak pure Scotch – the natives use a *patois* of their own – 'Ower yonder, East Whale Lane,' he said, lifting a leg-of-mutton fist in the direction of a blank wall, 'jist gang straicht forrart.' So I went 'straicht forrart,' meditating as I went on the melodious tones of my native Doric. It was a very narrow lane running up from the docks between two high walls, and there was no mistake about its being Whale Lane, the very air was greasy, and the kerbstones were black and oily.

. . . .

The working classes have, perhaps, as little cultivation as their employers; but want of means prevents them showing an unlimited amount of bad taste. Of necessity they are simple, and simplicity is the *sine qua non* of great art. They show some vitality in music, however. It is only the poorest workman who does not possess a harmonium on which his wife or daughter can play him the air of some soothing popular melody, or one of those martial hymns that have made such a noise in the world since the days of Sankey. Concertinas and melodeons are as common as blackberries, and the twilight hours are filled with their melody, poured forth by the enamoured youth at the stair-foot of his senorita's seven-floor tenement.

I shall never forget the excitement and bustle of that afternoon when we left the Camperdown dock. The expedition had been much talked of, so all the Dundee citizens who could leave their factories were down at the dock gates to bid farewell to their friends. The decks were still littered with sacks of coal, ropes, and spars. And the crew, up to summer Plimsoll line with grog, were staggering on board under deck cargoes of mattresses, blankets, and provisions. Some were hauling their sea-chests along, and wives and children were picking their way about the decks, staring round them at the little barque that was to take their men to the Southern Seas. Some of the older women, when they thought they were not observed, put money into the crevices in our rudder head to bring us luck, with who knows what result.

As we warped through the dock gates the last of the crew bade good-bye to their wives and children, hardened their hearts, and tumbled on board, leaving many a kind face wet with tears, but smiling hope and encouragement; then we swung out into the stream, and the men came aft to the taffrail and mizzen-shrouds and shouted a hoarse farewell to the distant crowd on the pierhead, and a faint 'Hoorae, hoorae, hoorae!' came back over the calm, silvery Tay. Then all hands bundled away forward again, shouting and singing, dived down the fo'c's'le-hatch, threw off their shore togs and shore cares, had one last pull at the bottle, and were up on deck in a minute, drunk and glorious, ready to go to the world's end or beyond it – a jolly motley crowd, not two dressed alike, in dungaree suits of every shade of blue and green, in faded jerseys and red handkerchiefs. Men and boys there were of every sailor type: old Arctic whalers, red cheeked and bearded; tanned South Spainers with shaven chins and faces lined with the rough and smooth, quiet men and boys from the East Coast fishing villages, and gentle men from the Shetlands. Fifty men from all over the world; strangers an hour ago, brothers now – in the one spirit of whisky devilment, and adventure.

Burn Murdoch persuaded one of the stowaways to write down his story – note that both boys have Irish names.

3 September 1892

As i was walking down the overgate is met one of my chums who was going to a football match but he was over late so we went round the docks for we heard that the whalers was going to sail on Tueasday 6^{inst} so we made up were mind to stowaway so we came on the day fixed. First we went to *diane* but we didn't like her so we went aboard the *balenea* we went down in foxel to stow ourselves away; but we got separated an as i was looking about me i seen a lot of boys younger than myself into a keg of meal, but i didn't look long for the time was drawing near to sail i espied a place where a lot

139

A whaler prepares the rope of his harpoon. *Dundee Art Galleries and Museums*

of cans full paint and ile, i well get in here, so in i went i wasnt long in when another fellow came looking for place then he came where i was he knocked all the paint and ile on the top of me so i came out for i was in afful mess an then i went to look for another place an these ise seen my chum and i asd if he got a place yet he said no but i espied another place on the top of a lot of barrels i then tried to get in but it was over stiff so i got a shovel for a batering ram an then we got it open so in i went an then i made room for my chum so he got in an then we seen the mate an some looking for stowaways they were looking among the barrals an then they came to where we was then the mate he came to where we were stowed we seen them coming through a hole in door the light shone through i thought they seen my breeks but they went away then we slept then in morning tow of the men who seen us going in gave us a scouse (soup) an some ship biscuits then at night time we came out, for tow hours then we went in again then the men tolds us to come out then their was a squall then in the afternoon we went on deck we met the mate at the top of the hatch he says to us hullo where did you come from but we did not speak he says O well we will have to get a job for you then he gave us some tar to put on twine and then bail it up.

This is since we came on board

William Brannan
&
Terence Mcmachon

In the Antarctic . . .

Captain Davidson of the *Active* discovered that Joinville Land does not continue to Cape Fitzroy, but is separated from the land to the South by a strait through which he navigated the *Active*. Captain

Eskimos going aboard SS *Eclipse. Dundee Art Galleries and Museums*

Davidson called the land Dundee Island, and the strait the Firth of Tay.

We steamed from Erebus and Terror Bay N.E. with a strong current from the N.E., that swung the ice along at four miles an hour. It was jammed together at one time, then drifted out in long streams, whirling past us round bergs, piled piece over piece. We have had thumping and crushing enough to crack the nether millstone, yet the boat were sent out sealing, though the *Balaena* could scarcely make her own way. How the men cursed! Just as one of the boats had managed to come up astern, some ragged snow islands of all sizes swept together and enclosed it. We thought to see her nipped into nothing, but the crew jumped on to the ice and hauled her into a little space between the white teeth before they closed, where the boat was safe, though she could not get out. We left them there, as it was difficult enough to get the ship out of the jam, and by and by the ice opened a little, and the black spot of struggling figures, by dint of much poling and shoving, made its escape and rowed up astern and got hold of a tow-line, and we steamed out of the swirling currents.

Tales of previous voyages were popular:

We had the story of the loss of the *Chieftain*'s men on the way – a grisly tale, that made a stir in the north two years ago. It had a particular and immediate interest to us, as the boat we were rowing in was one of those which had belonged to the Chieftain, and was supposed to be that in which the tragedy took place.

The mist fell one day up in the north, and two of the Chieftain's boats that were out were lost. One was never seen again, but the other was found seventeen days after, off the coast of Iceland, with only one man in it. The other five had drunk sea-water, and had gone mad and jumped overboard. The man that was found in the boat had eaten his hat and the signal-flag and some other trifles.

141

Both his legs were frost-bitten, and had to come off. Now he sits in a little wooden house in Dundee, where he opens a gate on the N.B. Railway. I daresay he will tell his tale to any one who cares to listen. There was a very grim humour about the last chapter of the story. When the poor castaway was landed at Dundee, the wives of his late companions met him, and made pointed inquiries as to their husbands, about the manner of whose decease there were wild rumours. When he lay in bed recovering, the same ladies continued their visits, to his annoyance, till he hit on the plan of talking in his sleep, as if he recalled the time in the boats. 'Noo, Jock,' he would groan, when Mrs Jock was at his bedside, 'it's your turn noo, ma man. No' but that I'm sorry for ye, laddie, but ye maun dee, man – I'm fair faumished.' My informant did not linger over the story. Sailors seem to avoid the horrible in their yarns, perhaps because they know that they themselves may at any time have like experiences.

Almost all our crew, old and young, are married. They apparently marry in Dundee between the ages of fifteen and twenty, on £1 a week and a childlike faith that their bread and butter will be provided daily. At twenty-five they have large families, and at forty they have grandchildren. Whilst we sat there, leaning against the timbers of the ship in the light of a smoky flare-lamp, talking of these matters of high import I drew the engineer, who was on my right hand. It was by way of a funny caricature. I thought he was unmarried from his youth and generally happy-go-lucky air, and I drew an ideal picture of him as he might appear in years to come, walking out with a damsel, a perambulator, and two and a half brace of kids. To my astonishment, he criticised the drawing by finding fault with the number of kids. There ought to have been two more, possibly three, he said.

Dundee, Archangel and Calcutta

from the writing of
EUGENIE FRASER

Dundee and Archangel c. 1904–20

Dundee's trading connections with far flung corners of the globe
are personified in the life of one remarkable woman, Eugenie
Fraser. The port of Archangel shipped Russian flax to Dundee
throughout the nineteenth century. The firm of Luhrs had
offices in both cities, and they sent Gherman Scholts, Eugenie's
father, to Dundee for training in the business. There he met
Nelly Cameron, the beautiful daughter of a successful Dundee
businessman, Augustus Cameron. The Cameron family lived in
Bay House, West Ferry. In *The House by the Dvina*, Eugenie
Fraser beautifully evokes her family history and the life-style
enjoyed in affluent Broughty Ferry in the first two decades of
this century.

In my father, grandfather found a good listener, one who asked
many questions, and was interested in everything that was said.
Scotland was still comparatively new to my father. He wanted to
know everything about her customs, traditions, her way of life,
so that he in turn could feel, absorb and understand everything
and in this way perhaps would be accepted.

The Scoto–Russian Alliance. Eugenie's
parents on their wedding day

Lunch over, all adjourned to the drawing-room. Gherman, not
wishing to overstay his welcome, rose to take his leave, but was
persuaded to remain for tea.

In a house where a strict Presbyterian rule never permitted any
music other than psalms or hymns to be played on a Sunday, the
family were amazed to hear their father asking Nelly to play some
Scottish airs. She obediently sat down to accompany Mary, who
had a fine contralto voice. One by one all gathered round the
piano. My father, who possessed a good voice and was by now
familiar with the well-known songs of Scotland, joined in the
singing. Later Nelly played some of the favourite pieces she knew
by heart. Gherman was surprised and delighted, for she had
never mentioned that she had this accomplishment.

Back in the dining-room they all sat down to a Scottish tea. The
table was laden with home-baked scones, cream cookies and
cakes. A friendly relaxed atmosphere prevailed. Gherman began
to feel as if he had known them all for a long time. After tea, the
girls, along with Stephen and Henry, prepared to set off for the
evening service in the church.

Father bowed and thanked my grandparents for their
hospitality. They in turn invited him to come back again and

143

Nelly Cameron aged twenty-two

The Bridal Group, Bay House, 1905

to treat this house as his second home. 'Haste ye back,' my grand-mother said, dropping her habitual aloofness and reverting to the homely vernacular.

Gherman walked with Nelly behind the others. They said goodbye at the church gate and my father continued on his way back to his lodgings. A fortnight later he approached my grand-father and asked to marry his daughter. Permission was granted. According to the Scottish custom he bought a diamond ring. He and Nelly became officially engaged.

.   .   .   .   .

I have often heard my father say, echoing the sentiment expressed by other foreigners, that Sundays in Scotland could be dull as opposed to those in his own part of the world. There was nowhere to go to except church or to pay calls on friends or relatives. Now it was different. As the days became longer and clearer he enjoyed walking with my mother, exploring for the first time the lovely outskirts of the town, as yet unspoilt by the sprawling buildings of roads and houses. At other times they joined the throng of young people strolling on the promenade or listening to the band in the park.

One Sunday in the early summer they decided to have a small expedition to the opposite side of the river. They took the train to Dundee and from there crossed on the ferry affectionately nicknamed the *Fifie* to Newport. From there it was possible to stroll back along the road on the Fife coast to a point directly opposite Broughty Ferry. From this small port, known as Tayport, they planned to cross on a second ferry, called the *Dolphin* back to Broughty Ferry, thus completing the round trip.

The day was very warm. They strolled leisurely in easy stages, halting to admire the neat and tidy gardens, the flowers and trees in full blossom.

When they eventually reached the pier they found to their dismay that the *Dolphin* had left a few minutes earlier and was now in midstream. There was nothing they could do but wait until it returned. They walked back down to the beach and settled on a grassy bank. By now it was late afternoon. All was peaceful. From the opposite shore a small boat was crossing the river. They watched it idly. The rower appeared to be in a hurry. As the boat drew nearer they were astounded to recognise the stocky figure of my grandfather. They had forgotten that on an afternoon such as this, when there was neither mist nor rain to disturb his vision, Grandpa, glued to his telescope, was having a field day.

He had seen the *Dolphin* leave the pier in Tayport and watched my parents walking down to the shore, sitting on the grass and perhaps, who knows, exchanging a few kisses. That was enough. He had rushed to the beach to the boating shed, housing his yacht and dinghy, dragged the dinghy down the slipway and raced across the river. My parents hurried to the water's edge to meet the approaching dinghy. Grandpa leaped out and dragged the boat on to the shingle. His face was crimson with rage and exertion. All efforts to help were brushed aside. 'Get in that boat', was the short and curt reply when Nelly, for once defiant and

144

indignant, had enquired what he thought they had done. Gherman was ordered to follow suit.

Later, perhaps realising that he had gone too far, my grandfather explained his action by pointing out that by bringing them back direct to the beach so near the house they were spared the long walk from Broughty Ferry. If so, why did he display such anger? It was difficult to understand the workings of such an eccentric mind. Much easier to accept his belated explanations and ignore the rest.

.　　.　　.　　.

As the wedding date drew nearer, there was great interest in Broughty Ferry in this Scottish-Russian union. Of special attraction was the wedding cake displayed in the window of the bakers in Broughty Ferry renowned for their artistry and quality. Instead of the usual floral decorations on the top tier, the cake had two silver and gold-fringed flags. Against the royal blue brocade, embroidered in silver, was the double-headed eagle of Russia and beside it the gold and scarlet of the Lion Rampant.

The marriage service took place in the parish church of St Stephen's in Broughty Ferry. There was even a faint touch of spring in the clear sky. Serene, completely composed and lovely, Nelly, her long train and veil trailing behind her, walked down the aisle, her hand resting lightly on her father's arm. Her three sisters walked behind her. To her surprise she noticed her father was strangely agitated. His arm trembled visibly as he handed his daughter to the bridegroom. The church was packed and there was a big crowd of onlookers outside. Among them there stood a lady who by some strange quirk of fate was to become my mother-in-law.

The reception was held in the house and the numerous guests spilled over all the rooms downstairs. A glimmer of pale sunlight allowed a family photograph to be taken on the porch outside.

The young couple arrive in Archangel in deep winter.

My parents walked over to their sledge. Gherman embraced the old coachman fondly and introduced him to his young wife. The old man glanced at Nelly, smiled broadly and said something that appeared to please my father. Tucking the bearskin round them while addressing my father by the familiar 'thou' and first name, he fussed for a little and clambered on to his seat. He raised the knout and off went the horses. Behind them on her sledge, perched high on top of all the luggage, sat Tanya, her black draperies flapping behind like the wings of a gigantic bird.

Faster and faster flew the horses. They had now turned into Olonetskaya Street. As they ran through the gates the high turret of the summer house dominating the garden caught Nelly's eyes. 'Look,' she suddenly said to my father and pointed to the sky. There fluttering high against the arctic sky, welcoming the Scottish bride, was the gold and scarlet of the Lion Rampant. She always told me that as she gazed up at this proud symbol of Scotland she knew that this was something that was her very own, something that was part of her being, and it seemed to be saying, 'You must never be afraid, for I shall always be with you.'

Ships travelled regularly between Archangel and Britain, so the family spent many holidays in Broughty Ferry.

For the next few years we shuttled to and fro between Russia and Scotland, either round the coast of Norway or through Finland and St Petersburg, but after my fifth birthday there was a break of some nine years and Scotland became a distant memory. Only the best was remembered. It never rained in Scotland and there were always roses in the garden, apples on the trees and blackbirds hopping around the lawn. The grass on the Grassy Beach was lush and very green, the waters were warm when we went bathing. On Sundays my cousins and their parents came to lunch. Bertie and May, my Uncle Andrew's children, were a bit older than us, but Uncle Stephen's chubby little daughter, Helen, was closer to my own age and I enjoyed playing with her. These were happy gatherings and, looking back, I am inclined to think that my grandparents were rather tolerant with all their grandchildren.

On a hot summer day tea was served in the garden. There were hot, home-baked scones and cream cookies. Jocky was brought out of the kitchen and sat in his cage beside us. Jocky loved the sun and showed his appreciation by stretching out his wings, dancing on one foot and chattering more than usual.

There is one bright scene that seems to stand out, of my brother and I still in our nightgowns, sitting on the lawn one early morning in May and our pretty mother, all in white, gathering the dew on a little sponge and laughingly wiping our faces. 'It will make you pretty,' she said. Later, still sitting on the lawn, we supped porridge and cream out of little bowls.

Nelly and her sisters, Bay House, West Ferry, 1904

Eugenie writes about Augustus Cameron's retreat in Bay House:

This room was known as 'Grandpa's Boudoir'. It was a long narrow room divided by a heavy velvet curtain. Behind the curtain stood a large bath fashioned out of real or imitation marble. Against the wall was a painted glass panel depicting reclining damsels whose voluptuous forms, partially hidden by crimson draperies, exposed magnificent plump breasts and arms. At their feet were flasks of wine and bowls of luscious fruit. White doves fluttered here and there. The same exotic scenes were repeated in the windows of the bathroom.

In the front half, where the tall windows formed a circle flooding the room with sunshine, stood a small table and a basket chair. On the table were invariably a dish of bananas and a decanter of whisky. It was grandpa's custom whenever he arrived from the office to retreat to his room and sit beside the table reading his newspaper or admiring the view while sipping his whisky and eating bananas.

Below his window was a rose bed. On to this bed from the window were thrown all the banana skins. Under no condition was the gardener or anyone else allowed to remove them. It was Grandpa's firm belief that nothing was as good for his roses as banana skins and the roses upheld his view by rewarding him with unusually large blooms.

The most intriguing part of 'Grandpa's Boudoir' was the row of pictures running the whole length of the west wall. All represented the female form in various degrees of partial nudity – perhaps more titillating than stark nakedness.

There was one exception in the midst of this luscious gallery. It was an enlargement of my grandfather. He is taken standing alone surrounded by a great expanse of moorland. Below his proud countenance gazing sternly ahead, can be read the quotation: 'I am Monarch of all I survey.' This somehow never failed to arouse unseemly mirth in my cousin and me when we were so bold as to venture into the sacred precincts if no one was about. We were not encouraged to enter. Grandma preferred to be alone with her letters and Grandpa with his whisky and bananas.

Eugenie Fraser in Russian costume aged two

When the Russian Revolution took place, merchant families like Eugenie's faced hardship and personal danger as the Bolsheviks attempted to gain control. There was some respite in 1919 when, after an epic journey, they succeeded in reaching Scotland.

It was late evening when the Inverness train steamed into Dundee. A kindly taxi driver arranged our trunks. Thankfully we climbed inside. Ghermosha was still clinging to his fish, which had somehow survived its ordeal on the ship.

The taxi took us through the brightly lit streets of the town where people in groups were standing on the corners holding conversations with each other – a novel and curious sight for us. After a short and pleasant drive in the soft darkness of a warm autumn night we arrived, hungry and exhausted, on the steps of our grandparents' house.

Our grandparents, not expecting us to arrive that night, were just going off to their bedroom when we surprised them. In the morning they had read a brief notice in the paper saying that a ship carrying refugees from the north of Russia had gone aground, but somehow didn't connect us with it. We were warmly and emotionally welcomed. My youngest aunt, Vicky, came rushing out of her bedroom in her dressing-gown, followed by her sleepy six-year-old son, Charles. As my aunt's husband was with the army of occupation in Germany she was living with her parents.

In the morning I leaped out of bed and hurried to the window. The sun was up. The garden was ablaze with masses of roses and chrysanthemums. Blackbirds were cheerfully plundering the apple trees. Across the silver waters of the Tay, flowing serenely past the house, I saw again the green and brown hills of the shores of Fife.

147

An early postcard home from Archangel.
'Anything like Dundee fish market!'

Far back in Archangel there would be rain and cold winds blowing. The darkening river was preparing herself for the final battle against the relentless frost, a battle which she was doomed to lose. Here in this late September the sun continued to shine warmly and Jocky's cage was being carried out into the garden.

To us, arriving from a land of grim austerity, of shuttered doors and windows of the shops, empty shelves, of people wearing shabby clothing, Scotland presented a scene of unbelievable abundance.

What a delight it was to walk along the smooth pavements of Broughty Ferry and step inside the 'sweetie shop'. Our eyes were dazzled by the jewel brightness of the sweets in glass containers, chocolate bars laid out in tempting rows, coloured boxes tied with satin ribbons. Further along was a renowned baker's shop where the appetising smell of freshly baked bread, cream-filled cookies, biscuits and cakes met us at the entrance.

Fascinating too was the little shop, named 'The Buttercup, which specialised in dairy products. There, rosy-cheeked girls in spotless aprons patted neat rounds of butter on a marble counter. Somehow the name, the great mounds of butter, milk and cream invariably conjured up green meadows, buttercups galore, and plump docile cows bursting with goodness.

Exciting were the trips to town, by train or tramcar, when along with Mother we accompanied Granny for her weekly shopping. The shop I enjoyed visiting more than any other was the famous, fashionable 'Draffens', where clothing of distinctive elegance was offered to discerning buyers. In the days of plenty, my father used to order articles of clothing, which were sent by cargo ships to our town and delivered to the house in perfect order. Now, to climb the luxuriously carpeted staircase and stroll from one department to another, where ladies dressed in black, stylish dresses tempted us with frocks, coats, hats in the latest fashion, was a source of wonderment not seen since the early days in St Petersburg, now only a vague memory.

Owing to the uncertainty of our position, Mother could not indulge in a wholesale shopping spree, but she did buy me several dresses, shoes and stockings. Granny also added to my stock of clothing, which I welcomed. Mother herself could not resist a large picture hat, trimmed with osprey feathers. Sad to say, that same hat was fated to be lost in a way Mother could never have envisaged.

It was usual to finish off the day by visiting D. M. Brown's, another well-known shop, where on the top floor we listened to a small orchestra while demolishing platefuls of the renowned hot muffins, oozing with butter and jam. On seeing all the well-stocked shops, the cheerfulness of the people, their pleasant orderly way of life, one might have imagined that the war had never touched Scotland, but on looking closer one saw the deep scars of the heavy price paid by such a small country, where there was hardly a family that hadn't lost a son, a husband or a brother.

The family returned to Archangel, however, to rejoin their father. A young teenage girl, Eugenie returned from a concert

148

to discover her house occupied by hostile Bolshevik soldiers. It was a time when members of their social class were being killed.

Soldiers guarding the gates and back entrance allowed me to pass. Upstairs in the hall were more men guarding the door leading to the nursery. I was ordered to go inside where all the members of the family were congregated as well as Katinka and Sashenka. Only Mother was missing. She, it transpired, was going round the house with the men, unlocking presses and drawers, and was now in the garret.

No one knew what the men wanted, but suspected they were looking for arms. Yura's gun, which he used for shooting game, was hidden somewhere, but only he knew where it was.

In a few minutes came the footsteps of the men stamping down the stairs from the garret. We were shepherded into the dining-room. The soldiers carried in a large wicker basket containing a bundle of flags. They were big flags which in days gone by were hung outside the gates during celebrations of royal birthdays. There were also flags of our allies which had been flown on special occasions during the war.

The basket was turned out, the flags spread on the table. The leader of the group, in his sheepskin jacket, sat down and after careful scrutiny of each flag laboriously marked something on a sheet of paper. We stood around wondering idly what was the strange purpose behind this confiscation. There they were. The old Imperial Russian flag, French, British, Belgian, Italian and finally one with the faded Lion Rampant. The man stared curiously at it.

Fifteen years ago on a bright winter's morning that flag had fluttered its welcome to a happy Scottish bride driving through the gates to begin a new life in a strange country. And now here it was again spread out before her. This royal flag of Scotland – her Scotland.

She moved closer to the table. 'This flag,' she began, calmly placing her hand on it, 'is the flag of Scotland. It is the flag of my country – you cannot have it.' There was no reply. The man raised his head and stared. He saw no sign of fear in the eyes gazing serenely back – no trembling of the hand. In the oppressive silence, even his men were tensely watching.

He was the first to drop his eyes. Bursting into loud laughter he turned to his men. 'Here's a wench for you, lads,' he called, and, pushing the flag towards Mother, added in a tone that was insolent and yet admiring, 'You can keep your flag.' She did keep it. Many years later I found it amongst the few things she treasured.

The basket was carried down the staircase. I ran to the window and watched the soldiers in the moonlight dragging it through the snow on the river front.

Later, when we were sitting around the samovar, I heard Babushka say, 'Nelly, you were foolish.' And I who had always leant heavily on the Russian side, for once was on my Mother's. Foolish perhaps – but how magnificent!

149

Dundee and Calcutta 1937–65

When she eventually escaped from Russia, Eugenie Fraser settled in Broughty Ferry and worked in Dundee. She met her husband Ron there, and set off with him to another major port – one which traded with Dundee – Calcutta. She describes the life of the 'jute-wallah' in *A Home by the Hooghly*.

Jute wallah, Calcutta. *Dundee Art Galleries and Museums*

During the First World War Uncle Henry had been an officer in what was known as the Calcutta Scottish Regiment. While on manoeuvres up-country he contracted a serious illness and died a few months later.

My cousin Mae, the daughter of my mother's brother, Andrew, had also gone to join her husband in Calcutta some years before my arrival. She wrote descriptive letters of her life there and my husband, too, in his correspondence with me used to portray a very clear picture of Calcutta and the mofussil.*

Now, driving in one of the American saloons which served as taxis in the mofussil, with Ron pointing out the various landmarks, the racecourse, the Cathedral, the Victoria memorial on the maidan,† I had the feeling that although everything was new and exciting it was also not wholly strange to me.

Earlier, when we left the ship, Ron had suggested that we should stop at Firpo's for some refreshment. Firpo's, the meeting place for jute wallahs, tea planters, burra sahibs and even at times Maharajas, was renowned throughout the East for its perfect cuisine and service. Inside the restaurant the Edwardian decor, crystal chandeliers, snow-white tablecloths and orchestra, presented an atmosphere of gracious living. In the adjoining veranda we found a corner overlooking the maidan. There, on a wide open parkland in the fading twilight, were seen groups of people walking about or standing talking together. The bearer served us with tea, sandwiches and delightful waffles with maple syrup. We would have liked to linger for a while, but before us there was a journey of twenty miles. Already the short twilight had vanished, Calcutta's sultry night was closing in.

Back on the road we passed Belvedere, the imposing residence of the Viceroy when visiting Calcutta, during which time could be seen handsome Bengal Lancers on horseback guarding the gates. Then we carried on through the fashionable suburb of Alipore, home of many affluent Indian and European members of society. Soon we were on the Budge-Budge Road – a country road flanked by fields, strips of jungle, and villages with groups of men sitting in the tea-houses. At times, caught in the beam of the headlights, a shadowy white figure would dart across the road and vanish into the jungle.

Some three miles beyond the Oil Depot of Budge-Budge lay the Albion jute mill in the compound of which lived my cousin Mae. It was too late for visiting. The launch to carry us across

*Mofussil: In India, all outside the capital or large towns, i.e. provincial, rural.
†Maidan: A wide open expanse of grass and trees in front of Chowringhee Road.

the Hooghly lay at the Albion jetty. The *serang* (boatman), a dignified man, helped us into the launch.

I remember well that first crossing. The stillness of the night, the starlight sky, the wide expanse of the dark river, lights twinkling on the opposite shore. No one said very much, but when we were almost halfway across there came drifting over the water the sound of male voices singing, 'far frae my hame I wander, but still my heart returns'. 'That,' Ron explained, 'is a party the bachelors and grass-widowers are holding.' The singing continued to accompany our crossing, but gradually died away as the launch approached Lawrence. It was a low tide. The jetty stood high above the water. With some trepidation I climbed on to the pontoon and up the sloping gangway to the main jetty.

.   .   .   .

Ron and I returned for lunch and later retired for the customary lie-back. Not being used to sleeping in the afternoon, I got up and wandered about the house from room to room scrutinising everything that may have escaped my notice. Some voices outside our back entrance attracted my attention.

On going out I was presented by an astonishing spectacle. It transpired that Derek was having a rather wild party. There were a few men of different ages from the mess khootie as well as the manager and Tom the salesman. Some of the men wore bathing trunks and were diving in and out of the pool. Derek, in bathing trunks, was prancing around the edge of the pool while holding an umbrella over his head and emulating a tightrope dancer. There were also two young ladies in swimming suits, who had arrived with some men-friends from Calcutta. One of the girls was swimming about while her friend, who had long tresses down to her waist, was dancing on the edge and, at the same time, coyly professing a certain fear of the water. In the middle of the pool one of our stalwart men from Angus, fully dressed in white drill trousers and jacket, was standing up to his waist in the water and calling out encouragement to the girl: 'Jump, lassie, jump. Dinna be faird – I'll kape you – you'll no fa' on yer airse . . .'

Later when describing to Ron the fun at the pool and suggesting that perhaps we also could join the party, I was reminded that this was a bachelors' party to which none of the married couples was invited.

In the evening we crossed the river again to Albion to visit my cousin Mae and her husband, Jim Dakers, who was a salesman with Andrew Yule & Company. Both Mae and I, having no sisters, had always been close from the time when I arrived in Scotland from Russia as a young girl. It was a strange and happy coincidence that I should have landed in a compound directly opposite her own. We were overjoyed to meet each other after an absence of almost two years when she was on leave in Scotland and when, prior to her return to India, she had had to leave behind her little daughter, Patricia, to be educated in Scotland.

Mae was suffering from insomnia. Although she kept assuring me that she was well and happy I realised that deep down she was missing her daughter and suffering the same grief and anxiety

151

Eugenie's twins, a friend and their ayah.
Calcutta, 1940

that is the lot of all the mothers who have to part with their child when it reaches school age and has to leave India to receive an education in Britain. Mae was eager to hear the latest detailed news from Scotland. Monday was a working day. It wasn't usual for people to stay up late. At five o'clock in the morning, the bearer knocked on our bedroom door. Soon after, Ron left for the office. There he continued working with breaks for meals and a lie-back. At seven in the evening the working day was over. All the sahibs were to be seen, tired, hot and often drenched in sweat, wending their way back to their respective homes.

Ronald was a kerani. The kerani is the man in charge of the mill office and all the clerical staff. He was responsible for the safe, all the large sums of money delivered every week for the wages of the workers and the salaries of the European and Indian staff. The keranis of all the mills, up and down the river, were young men recruited from Dundee and its district. Most of them had a grammar school background and had served their apprentice-ship in the offices of jute mills and brokers. They also had attended the Dundee Technical College and were, in short, qualified to embark for India. Usually after a certain time working as keranis in the mill offices they were promoted as sales-men in the various head offices, situated mostly in that promised land of Clive Street, Calcutta. The other men, the overseers, in different departments in the mill had held similar positions in the mills in Angus and also attended the Technical College. In addition there were engineers with sea-going experience, prior to taking up a post in India.

In Lawrence there were some twelve Europeans, including the manager and salesman who travelled every day to the head office in Calcutta. Some five thousand workers were employed inside and outside the mill. Each mill had a dispensary with a qualified Indian doctor in charge.

.   .   .   .   .

During my whole sojourn in India I went inside the mill only once when it was working. My first reaction was to rush quickly through and out the opposite door, but some inner voice told me not to hurry. Amidst the haze of heat and dust I saw women in damp grey saris, wisps of jute sticking to their hair, poor worn faces clammy with sweat, yet smiling to me in a friendly manner. Men were standing at their looms and the sahibs walking up and down, with shirts clinging to their bodies, gave me a cheerful wave as I went by as if they were strolling about in some park on a pleasant day. To me, the deafening roar of the machinery, unbearable heat, the pervading smell of jute all conspired to create a special hell – a hell I took great care never to enter again.

When Eugenie's twins are born, they are looked after by a Scottish doctor.

In the adjoining rooms were four mothers, three of whom were the wives of tea-planters from Assam. Further along was a young mother, still only in her teens, from Gujerat. It was considered to be rather unusual for a Gujerati mother to have her child born in a European nursing home and engage a European specialist to attend to her. It so happened that the baby was the only male child to be born in the family, all the others being girls, who, sadly, were never so welcome as boys. Every night the happy father, uncles and grandfather, stood waiting to express their gratitude and respect to Colonel Gow making his rounds. The child, unfortunately, was rather difficult and cried a lot. The nurse, who looked after me and the Gujerati mother, explained that this was owing to the young mother not wanting to be bothered nursing the baby for any length of time. The food also, on account of her caste, had to be brought from outside and being highly spiced disagreed with the baby.

Dundee High School F.P.'s reunion, Peliti's Restaurant, Calcutta, 1928

The twins, although healthy, were not strong enough to deal with me and usually after a prolonged struggle fell asleep, which left them hungry and didn't relieve my own suffering. This kind of misery reminded me of how, during the time of the Russian Revolution, cows, lowing pitifully, with their udders swollen to bursting point, were found in the deserted village. I now knew how the poor beasts felt.

One evening when Colonel Gow was paying his usual visit, the matron brought my problem to his notice. After studying me for a few moments he turned to the matron. 'What she needs', he said, 'is a strong hungry child to start her off.'

'Well,' the matron hesitated, 'there is the hungry little Gujerati.' She glanced at me uncertainly.

'Bring him to me, bring him,' I interrupted. The Gujerati baby was duly brought to me. He was dressed in a bright, emerald-green knitted waistcoat with tiny boots to match. His small features were finely etched, the eyes like black cherries, the hair on his little round head dark and as soft as silk. He attacked me with the strength and vigour of a tiger cub. The relief was wonderful beyond all words and with the twins following him everything worked smoothly. The nurses were especially delighted. 'Bless you,' they said, 'there is peace now in the nursery.'

The little Gujerati was brought to me twice daily, the twins five, but the young mother also had to have her baby for a short while which worked out very nicely.

One day the nurse, after taking the baby to his mother, returned saying that she had found the young mother rather puzzled 'Why he sleep?' she had inquired. 'Before he cry, cry – now he sleep.' 'I could have told her,' the nurse concluded, 'little do you know he's got a drop of Scotch in him.'

The whole exercise had to be kept secret. There would have been a great furore if the Gujerati family had discovered that a European woman had wet-nursed their child.

     ·   ·   ·   ·

With the exception of tea planters who had a pleasant outdoor life in the tea gardens, the other Europeans involved in cotton, paper and jute led a different style of life in the plains. Dundee being the centre of the jute trade in Britain, practically all the Europeans connected with jute in Calcutta, or in the mills, came

153

from Angus or Fife. They came from various backgrounds and, although the magic of India beckoned, all had the realistic down-to-earth approach – simply to improve their lot and make some money.

At one time India offered the opportunity to reap a rich harvest. The mansions in West Ferry and district of the nabobs from India testify to the truth of my statement, 'but these times were long since past and the same mansions by the end of the Second World War were divided and subdivided. It was still possible for some to acquire riches – my late Uncle Henry, a broker in Calcutta, was doing quite well for himself until in his early thirties death overtook him in the year of 1919 – but it was not as easy as it used to be and became more difficult as the income tax rate increased to a high level.

As long as the Raj remained, young men continued flocking to India eager to take up their places in the ICS, army, offices and mills, but no matter what position they held there was a pattern common to them all. No one, with few exceptions, remained in India until overtaken by old age. Old men and women were rarely seen in the European community. Men usually retired when in their fifties and lived out the remaining years in the land of their birth. The companies in any case did not encourage anyone to stay beyond the age laid down by the firm when they could claim their provident fund.

I remember one of the ladies once saying to me, 'I like India but would not care to die here. All I want after we retire is to have a little bungalow and spend the rest of our days at home.' She did not ask for much, poor girl, but died before they were due to retire, and her husband married again.

And that was another aspect of life in India. In spite of up-to-date medicines in the treatment of diseases which in the past filled the cemeteries around Calcutta, there were still cases of unexpected deaths taking place – particularly tragic when they occurred close to the date of retirement.

Nothing was permanent in India – certainly not our homes, carpets or furniture. We were moved from one compound to another and, as each leave came round, commuted between Bengal and Scotland like birds of passage. There were always some kind of vague plans and hopes especially amongst the ladies that after we retired something permanent would be found at home. That little word 'after' kept lurking at the back of our minds.

Dundee Women

by ELLIE McDONALD

In the closes, on the stairs, hanging out windows, jostling each other as they skailed from the jute mills and factories. Dundee women. Vociferous, sure and dominant. Qualities which were more than a match for the petty sneerings of society. Qualities which are echoed in the women's movement today. This was the world I was born into, in a city of grey smoke and grey tenements where the clackety-clack of the looms seemed the only rhythm and poverty its natural accompaniment.

A bairn's world is its own space capsule from which we some-times glimpse a strange and alien world. One summer I found a neat pile of doll's clothes lying on a park bench. Could any wee girl really just have forgotten them? Never having owned a doll, the idea seemed impossible, so I invented a fantastical story to explain away the mystery.

I knew there were other bairns behind the high walls of the big houses who played in gardens, wore new clothes and could believe in Santa Claus. They belonged to the burgeoning middle classes who reaped the benefits of the jute trade. They were light years away from the streets, closes and back-greens where we fought our wars. There, the sound of a woman's voice roaring 'Eh'll tell yer mither on ye' was the voice of supreme authority which carried beyond the happenings of childhood. For us it was a symbol of the natural order.

Unlike other Scottish industrial cities, Dundee's major industry relied on a predominantly female work-force. This unprecedented role-reversal earned Dundee men the nickname 'kettle-bilers' and the further indignity of seeing a woman, often triumphantly, fling her wage packet down on the kitchen table. Given this earning power, women gained the freedom to act in a way which often ignored convention. The sight of a woman on a Saturday night being as 'roarin' fou' as a man was commonplace enough and was added entertainment for street-wise bairns.

One night when I was about eight, we were stopped outside a chip-shop by a drunk woman. 'Geh is a fish supper an' bring it tae meh hoose,' she demanded. After handing us the money she staggered off down the street. We stood gazing firstly at her re-treating back and then at our new-found wealth. Divided by four we could all have a poke of chips. However, my sister, being the eldest, decided that as the money wasn't ours the only thing to do was drop it down the cundie. This she did, much to my disgust.

My sister's first foray into situation ethics was probably inspired by Sunday School, which most bairns attended. There we were taught about Mary Slessor, the Dundee missionary who

155

Dundee women. *Joseph McKenzie*

proved how a jute-mill worker could gain not only eternal life but, what seemed more important, respectability. One rather eccentric teacher taught us a rhyme about the original Wishart Church which Mary Slessor attended. (Curiously, the church was above a pub called 'The John o' Groats' in the Cowgate.)

There's spirits above and spirits below,
The spirits of love and the spirits of woe.
The spirits above are the spirits divine,
The spirits below are the spirits of wine.

The need to emphasise the dangers of alcohol even to bairns was more understandable in Dundee than elsewhere. The women in the jute trade, having been given the role of wage-earner, responded quickly to the altered circumstances by adopting the common male postures of loudness, coarseness and drunkenness. Such behaviour in the male labour force of Clydeside, for example, was not the subject of outright ridicule and contempt. There, young men grew up with a natural awareness of their importance to and position in society. In Dundee, faced with a female-dominated labour force, society retreated behind its fixed ideas of what constituted male and female behaviour. This laid the foundations for the scurrilous fallacies which surround the unique breed of women which evolved from the hardship and poverty of life in the mills and factories.

In other societies, women may wield a great deal of power within certain strict parameters. The cult of the Mother Goddess which was assimilated into our own Christian society still survives as the idealistic vision of womanhood. But a harsh environment strips the human being to its essential self and the stance taken by Dundee women was far removed from any semblance of meek submission. Their role model was more reminiscent of Brecht's Mother Courage.

A friend of mine whose whole family occupied the attics of a tenement near the West Port accepted quite naturally that the working members, including those who were married, handed over their wage-packets to her grandmother each week. Her right to demand this was never questioned by any of them. Abuse of power there may have been, but the response of Dundee women to that power follows a familiar pattern; most revolutions perpetuate the faults of the previous system – bureaucracy is alive and well in both France and Russia.

Given little control over external circumstances, it is essential for the survival of any group that it construct acceptable standards of behaviour. In conditions of poor housing, cleanliness was in the minds of Dundee women as one of the first signals of a person's standards. I once had the temerity to ask an aunt for a drink of water when she had just scrubbed and dried the wooden bunker of her kitchen sink. 'Aa richt,' she yelled, 'but if ye skell ony eh'll paste ye.'

157

Hilltown Child, 1969. *Joseph McKenzie*

Behind that outburst was the age-long need to send the correct signals, to make a clear statement of belonging. But what was unique to the Dundee situation was that from the poverty of the common life on a common 'stair' came a defiant sisterhood, a mass movement of women ready to stake their claim to equality. And it is here, perhaps, that we can find the source of the fallacies. For Dundee women had come of age long before the world was ready to accept that women had a right to equality, and from outside Dundee and from within, society reacted against the uncomfortable reality of women threatening the male power base. Finding itself in an unprecedented position and unable to construct a reasoned argument, society resorted to ridicule and contempt as a means of channelling its unconscious fears.

Today that same society still finds opportunities to defend the indefensible. The common epithets of irresponsible, militant and uncontrollable were heaped upon the female workers in the jute trade. They were echoed years later by male trade-union officials at the Timex factory when faced with women who, as one official put it, did not merely shift the goalposts in any dispute but removed them altogether.

The attitudes we carry from our childhood are acquired unknowingly. For any woman brought up in the Dundee tradition there should be no straining for equality, no need for a new consciousness of the power of women. We have inherited a freedom which seems unnecessary to verbalise. We are just waiting for the world to catch up.

Mrs Wallace's Pie Shop, Hawkhill. *Joseph McKenzie*

'You went out the door of your house, into your home . . . your home was the street.' Joe Austen's depiction of a Dundee Childhood.

Piper Laidlaw winning the V.C. at Loos. *Dundee Art Galleries and Museums*

After Neuve Chapelle by Joseph Gray. (Sidney Steven is third from left, Lietenant Colonel H. Walker is reading). *Dundee Art Galleries and Museums*

Dundee's Flodden

by BRUCE PANDRICH

On 25 September every year, a beacon light shines out over Dundee from the War Memorial on the Law to commemorate those who died in the Battle of Loos on that day in 1915. The poignant atmosphere in the flickering light of the flame contrasts with the sights and sounds of the late twentieth century below. For many, the battle which it commemorates is forgotten and yet its aftermath tore the heart out of the city.

The story of what happened began long before 1915, in the territorial battalions of the Black Watch and a tradition of service for King and Country. The Fourth Battalion was special, however, for it represented a city at war and captured the imagination and hearts of the people of Dundee. 'Dundee's Ain', as it was known, consisted of fathers, sons, brothers, uncles, friends, employers and employees from Dundee and its environs. It touched nearly every family in the city. The officers were drawn from Dundee's relatively small middle class and the men came from the jute and jam factories of the city. Journalism, the third 'J', was well represented and these men provided a regular flow of reports on the fortunes of the Battalion. When war came and the Battalion went to France it took with it all those relationships and intimate links with the city. The fortunes of the Fourth Battalion were the fortunes of the war for the people of Dundee.

When the Battalion left for France on 23 February 1915 the reports in the local papers reflected the mood of the time and the city:

> It was a well-set-up gritty battalion upon which the citizens of Dundee last night showered thunderous cheers, as they marched from Dudhope Castle to the West Station. . .
>
> (The *Courier and Argus*, 24 February 1915)

> . . . women clung hysterically to their menfolk. . . When the station was reached the men had practically to fight their way in, so dense was the throng. . .
>
> The excitement and enthusiasm reached fever heat when the third and last detachment marched out of the Castle. . . to the rousing strains of 'Bonnie Dundee' the men made quick time to the station. At Tally Street the tune was changed to 'Scotland the Brave' while as the men marched into the station the wild but rhythmic 'Pibroch of Donnil Dhu' rang out. . .
>
> (The *Dundee Advertiser* 24 February 1915)

163

Led by one of the city's most distinguished local businessmen, Lieutenant-Colonel Harry Walker, the Battalion received their 'baptism of fire' in the Battle of Neuve Chapelle. One of the young officers of the Battalion, Lt Sidney Steven, the son of Robert Steven, a local solicitor, described the experiences of the Battalion in his letters home:

> We have honestly had a terrible time out here since we arrived. The sights in those trenches will haunt me to my dying day. I think we have lost 140 men . . .

Sidney Steven. *Private collection*

Like so many others, Lt Steven protected his family from some of the horrors of war. Soon, however, there was a need to describe experiences in an attempt to come to terms with war. He recorded the scene after the battle:

> The rain has been pouring down for 24 hours. The company paraded in the darkness and after a long tramp we reached an open field where we bivouacked until dawn. It was a quagmire and we lay in about six inches of water.
> The Colonel passed among us and said . . . 'You'll just have to make the best of it boys.' So we did.

Often Lt Steven's letters, while giving an account of his men, illustrate the special composition of the Battalion and its intimate links with the city of Dundee.

Harvey Steven. *Private collection*

> Lance Corporal Mills, whose father lives at 42 Ure Street. . . was wounded in the head with a splinter from a shrapnel shell. I saw him before he was carried out. He is not badly hurt and will soon revive. Private A. Fraser is another and a very nice fellow. His father lives at 9 St Salvador Street. He was hit in the great battle but I understand is not too badly hurt. Private T. Scott's mother lives at 399 Clepington Road. He was an excellent fellow and was beside me the whole time and was a great help when we were trying to take . . . the trench. He was shot dead just in front of me and fell without a murmur . . .

> Just a short note to ask you if you would kindly visit John Housie, 50 Ferry Road. He is the father of one of my chaps killed in action on the 10th . . . Housie was an excellent fellow and one whom I always respected and looked to for an example of a good soldier.

He also described the changed condition of the men after the Battle of Neuve Chapelle – a vivid contrast to their send-off:

> When we arrived here we looked like a regiment of tramps! But respectable tramps would have turned up their noses at us, we were so dirty and unkempt. Some of the boys had lost their puttees and they limped along barelegged and nearly every kilt had been caught and torn on the barbed wire entanglements.

We had to scrape the mud off ourselves. Our jackets were stained yellow and green with the fumes of Lyddite.

Lt Steven brought great honour to the city when he was awarded the military cross for his distinguished conduct at Neuve Chapelle, a battle about which he wrote:

I shall never forget the sights I saw on that walk towards the battlefield nor on the field after battle. The sight of those German trenches still haunts me. Standing on dead bodies all covered in blood is not much good. . . it was awful.

After Neuve Chapelle came Aubers Ridge where the Battalion suffered heavy casualties. Steven openly expresses his horror at the carnage and compared this with the peaceful routines in Dundee:

. . . you must have been out for your afternoon stroll or lying down for an afternoon nap when we were having it so hot! I never realised at the time it was Sunday. If I had, I think that given the chance I would have gone twice to church without a grumble instead of being out here! . . . Men were being knocked out right and left . . . I can't describe it. No one can have any conception of what it is like unless they have been through it . . . One man had his head blown off and another was screaming for a bandage. It is all too terrible to describe. . . I can't try. All I can say is that our Company lost between 60 and 70 men. . . I have no sergeants now. My other one was shot through the head when he was standing beside me.

And so the Battalion fought and died through 1915. But in all of this some sense of the world outside the war continued:

I had a walk yesterday morning down the now famous La Bassée road with Norman. We walked as far as Croix Basseé. It is a very pretty road and shaded with beautiful green trees. It is only on the way back that one notices that something is very far wrong for just as the road nears Neuve Chapelle the trees are all dead and broken.

An incident which illustrates the closeness between members of the Battalion was the death of Sergeant MacDonald, recorded by Lt Steven in this letter home:

On Saturday morning (8th May) I got a terrible shock. When I was coming out of my billet. . . one of my sergeants came running towards me and told me that Sergeant MacDonald, my platoon sergeant who won the DCM only a few days ago, was black in the face. I rushed along to him but when I got there I found that he was dead. I went off at once and arranged his funeral. I cycled into Vielle Chapelle and saw the Padre there and went round with

165

him to the little cemetery where we have graves always ready. I went back to the billet and got his body in an ambulance car and took the whole platoon with me and we marched into Vielle Chapelle and buried him there. We spread the Union Jack over his body and he was carried to the grave by his brother and his particular friends in the Battalion. With the pipes playing 'The Flowers of the Forest' and followed by his platoon, we took him into the cemetery. The Padre gave a short prayer and then we laid poor MacDonald in his grave. The pipers played 'Lochaber No More' and platoon fixed bayonets and presented arms. Afterwards we all marched back, a very sorrowful party.

From 28 May the Battalion received some respite and prepared for Loos. Steven wrote of the preparation for the momentous battle:

> To tell you the truth I think we are going to be in for a very hot time of it very shortly. The Battalion is to be in an attack on the German front line one day very soon and I think there is going to be some very severe fighting.

Shortly before the battle, Lt Sidney Steven heard that his brother would be joining the Battalion at the front. In fact Harvey Steven arrived in time to inform his family that his brother Sidney had been killed in the Battle of Loos along with many other officers from the Battalion. Twenty out of twenty-one officers involved in the fighting were killed or wounded, and out of 423 men 235 were killed or wounded. Harvey Steven was himself killed by a shell on 7 October.

The story of Harvey and Sidney was repeated throughout the city with whole families lost in the battle and the city plunged into a state of mourning. The psychological effect of the war on the men at the front is perhaps more obvious than the anguish and suffering endured by those left behind. The uncertainty and confusion of war is well illustrated by the story of a member of my own family who was in the Fourth. Reported killed at Neuve Chapelle he was in fact only slightly wounded. Later, however, he was listed amongst the wounded at Loos when he had been killed. The city suffered as the men fought and died. The local papers were filled with stirring and shocking reports. One private in the Fourth gave a vivid account of the battle:

> There will be many wonderful battles before the war is finished . . . but there will never be anything to equal the advance of last week. We had to pay a terrible price but, by heaven, it was worth it! . . . The whole German Empire was out for blood . . . To my last moments I will never forget the faces I saw . . . I have never seen anything to compare with the slaughter inflicted . . . The artillery had been pounding away for hours, during which our nerves went through it properly. At last the word to go 'Forward' rang out. 'Come on Marmalade' shouted a Dundonian . . . Their

machine guns poured a terrific fire on us . . . You won't mind if I say a word about our officers. They were marvellous chaps to a man. Young and old showed their mettle and I hope they will be honoured for all time.

In his three weeks at the front, Harvey Steven recorded the horror of the battle and its aftermath; the pathetic scenes of destruction and suffering. By an irony of war, he took command of his brother's company and was for a while in charge of the Battalion. But the Fourth was destroyed in the Battle of Loos. There were no officers to lead the men and few men to be led. With the Commanding Officer dead and so many others killed or wounded the Fourth, unable to continue as a fighting unit, was amalgamated with the Fifth Battalion.

In Dundee, the impact of the battle was so great that it overcame any optimistic interpretation of its success or achievements. Mr J. B. Taylor, President of the Chamber of Commerce said the city was 'living under perhaps the blackest cloud we have ever experienced'. The effect spread beyond Dundee itself:

> Last night was to Newport the saddest since the shadows of war fell. East and West the news spread, casting gloom and sorrow, and sympathy formed the burden of all conversation. Under many roofs in the place there were relatives stricken by the news.

On 6 October, at the memorial service for those killed in the battle, the Reverend A. W. Fergusson expressed the feelings of the city:

> . . . we have come to God's house this afternoon in our common sorrow – such a sorrow as has never befallen on this city in our day and generation.

The loss to Dundee and to the Battalion was a very personal one. A member of the Fourth wrote home about the death of the Battalion's Colonel Walker with almost religious reverence:

> I am writing this in a rest billet and in the quiet of things one realises the terrible blow sustained in the loss of our officers. We are like a house without a father, for the Colonel was a fatherly man, ever interested in the welfare of his men.

The burial of Colonel Walker and another member of the Battalion, Major Tosh, was movingly described in a letter to the *Courier and Argus*:

> They were laid to rest in a pretty little orchard within range of the guns. What a difference today around the ranks of the dishevelled, war-worn, sad men compared to the boisterous

OOR GALLANT FOURTH

Lads o' valour, lads o' grit,
Lads wha's frames are strongly knit,
Lads wha strike hard whom they hit,
    Are in the Fourth.

The 'Great Push' found them tae the fore,
Like their sires in days of yore.
'Marmalade!' Eh, what a roar!
    Cam' frae the Fourth.

They cared not for the rifles' spit,
They were oot tae dae their bit,
They've proved that they are lads o' grit,
    Oor gallant Fourth.

'On the ba', Dundee', they cried
They as steel in fire were tried,
Nobly lived and nobly died,
    Lads o' the Fourth.

When o' wordly cares I'm free,
And I've crossed the 'sullen sea',
Weel tae the fore I ken I'll see
    Lads o' the Fourth.

The *People's Journal*, 16 October 1915

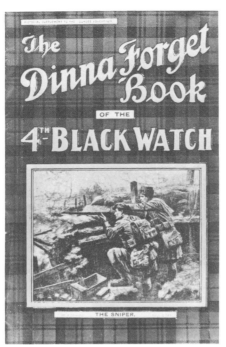

A commemorative supplement published by the Dundee Advertiser.

enthusiasm of the 1,100 who paraded in Dudhope Square that afternoon in February when we marched off to the front. I remember yet the pride in the Colonel's eye that day when he addressed us from the steps of the castle and the cheery smile of the Major as he led the half battalion off the square. How strangely different today! There we stood in the little orchard with our Colonel and Major lying side by side at our feet. It was their last parade. The service was the short simple service of the Presbyterian Church, and the bodies were lowered into the grave by the senior non-commissioned officers and the deceased officers' servants.

Many of the sermons and speeches of the time repeated the message that the men should not die in vain and the fight must go on. But the city was daily reminded of the cost of war. The casualty list increased and no matter how enthusiastic the claims for the battle, the naïvety was gone and the city grew old in the ways of war. In a city with a tradition for high recruitment rates, recruitment fell and those in authority struggled to restore faith.

Apart from the Fourth Battalion, many other Scottish regiments were represented at Loos and the losses from those regiments added to the effects of the destruction of the Fourth. As a symbol and measure of the war, the destruction of the Fourth was a loss of innocence for Dundee. A whole generation perished. The youngest, the fittest, the brightest died. Dundee's future was lost on that day, for those who would have taken the city forward into its next stage of development were annihilated in one blow. We cannot tell what would have happened had these men survived, but the loss of any part is a loss to the whole and both the impact of the tragedy at the time and its later consequences had a profound and lasting effect on the city.

'None Can Compare'

From the Oral History
of a Community

by GRAHAM R. SMITH

Introduction

If Scotland's past, as one historian has written, is an unknown country, then Dundee is probably its most obscure of cities; it has been described as 'the Atlantis of the North'. In an attempt to change this, a group of local unemployed began meeting weekly, in 1984, with the aim of finding ways of exploring Dundee's recent past. The Dundee History Workshop, as we called our group, drew inspiration from the oral-history method developing across Europe. Oral history is based upon the idea that all older people have a story to tell. Most of the history we knew concentrated upon the rich, powerful and privileged; we felt that the past lives of people like us had been neglected. We believed that any serious investigation of our city should reveal that the story of Dundee's past was dominated by the large pro- portion of working people who lived and laboured in the city.

After many discussions the Workshop members concluded that such an investigation should be undertaken in a professional way. We therefore designed, and campaigned for funding for, the Dundee Oral History Project. We explicitly stated that this Project would employ the unemployed in order to undertake quality historical research in an organised manner.

From the very beginning it was obvious that oral history would provide a valuable means of fulfilling our aim of uncover- ing our common past, which was so hidden from traditional history. We were committed to redressing the balance of history, but we also wanted to show that today's unemployed, so often portrayed as useless, or worse, could make an important con- tribution to our community.

Such a principled stance was not a luxury, rather it was a necessity. Older people have a strong sense of when someone is playing them false; in Dundee that sense is even sharper than elsewhere. Dundee, Scotland's biggest village, is a close com- munity, where chancers can be spotted at fifty yards. Principles were also necessary. They inspired previously long-term- unemployed workers with the idea that the Project was of importance.

The very quality and innovative nature of the Project was

Men on mountain of jute, after a mill fire, c. 1900. *Dundee District Libraries*

169

The High Street

rooted in the respect it generated amongst the unemployed, older people and the community at large. The Project employed two interviewers, or fieldworkers, and six people to transcribe the one hundred recorded interviews. Every tape was fully transcribed in dialect. This meant that our interviews could be made accessible to the community.

At the same time we wanted to give something back to older people, who had given us their memories. So the Project's reminiscence team, basing their initial approach upon the transcribed interviews, designed a fifteen-week course of reminiscence sessions for the mentally alert and for use in psycho-geriatric situations. Based upon the life-story approach, the structured reminiscence courses were popular. The power of structured reminiscence can only be fully appreciated by those who have seen the dramatic changes in morale, memory and sociability of older people who have participated in the sessions.

The History Workshop group had also identified the need for the interviews to be used in schools, in order to show youth the value of older people, their contribution to our world, and the importance of their recollections. To this end the Project developed learning-packs and began experimenting with cross-generational work, involving older people and youth in discussion groups.

The Project gained support from all over the world through its publications, with staff speaking at national and international conferences. Requests for advice were received from as far away as India and Australia. Although the Project closed in 1989, as a result of the government cutting the Community Programme, visitors continue to come to Dundee to meet with former Project workers. Recently oral historians from the USA and New Zealand travelled to the city in order to learn from those who were once employed on the Project.

It has been a privilege to have been associated with the Dundee Oral History Project. When I first raised the idea, in the days before Dundee History Workshop, most 'professional' people poured scorn on the idea: 'It would never take off in Dundee.' However, with the help of Iain Flett, Dundee City Archivist, the idea found support amongst the jobless and elderly of the city. I have never lost my faith in the ability of the majority of Dundonians to struggle for progress. The campaign to re-establish the world's best community-history project will go on.

The extracts which follow are taken from the Project's *100 Archive*. This is a tiny selection of the recorded and transcribed life-stories which can be found in Dundee's Central Library.† Reading through the transcripts it struck me that interviewers and interviewees had enjoyed the experience. In many ways all

†Copies of the taped interviews and transcripts are held by Dundee Central Library, Wellgate Centre, Dundee.

those involved in the Project became historians of their own lives, the lives of their families and the lives of our community. We have a common past which is as rich as it is varied. The stories selected here are not intended as a social history of Dundee, rather they are a taste of the variety of human life contained in the city. They are chosen above all else, because I like them.

Childhood

Minnie Way was born in 1895 and is a great storyteller. She recalls her childhood in detail.

> Ah wis at St Salvador's School, so long ago, when the Inspector used to come roond and examine you, ye always got the half day off the school. So the teacher told us all to come nice an' dressed tomorrow mornin' as the Inspector's comin'. Mah mother dressed me nice an' Ah got a lovely hat, oh it wis a beautiful hat. After the Inspector went away the teachers said, 'Now ye all go home.' Now Ah wis told by meh mother to come straight home an' take off meh nice clothes, but the girl that sits aside me in my class, her mother was in the wash house, so she says, 'I have to go to the wash house,' she says, 'Come up with me, and let mi mother see yer nice hat.'
>
> Eh went up wi' this girl ti the wash house an' the mother wasn't quite ready to come home, she said, 'Don't go away, jist play in the wash house.' So we put our hankies through the mangle, we put wir gloves through, an' to this day I will never know what possessed me, Ah put mah new hat through the mangle (laughing), four times or five. Believe me it wis sittin' on meh head like a soup plate (laughing). When I went into the door meh mother says what's the matter wi' yer hat, when Eh told her she nearly killed me, oh Ah got a lickin' . . . Ah couldna sit for quite a while after it (laughing).

Another story she tells involves a trip to the dentist.

> Well you had to pay if your mother took you to her own private dentist, but there was one in Tay Street where you could get done for nothing. I minded telling a wee girl in my class that I was going to get my teeth out on Saturday when my granny got her pay.

Minnie's pal persuades her to go to the free dentist in Tay Street.

> The dentist put a lance in yer mouth and he took away the gum from yer teeth. And it wis bleedin' and he said, 'Now spit there.' And Ah spit. Ah says, 'Oh is ma teeth out?' He says, 'No, but it'll no be long 'till it comes out.' And then he puts the pliars in. They didnae give ye nothing. Well there was a man who always went sweepin' the floors, so he used t' come and stand behind yer

Minnie Way, Fintry, 1990. *Ken Sharp*

171

back and hold yer shoulders down. He was holdin' me down, Eh had a handfull o' the plush out the chair, and screamin'. And out come ma teeth – at last.

Ah went into the school, and Ah wis cryin', and the girl that wis wi' me she wis wiping ma face. There wis blood runnin' . . . Ah must have been like a Red Indian. The teacher says, 'Away you go home and don't come back until tomorrow.' So Ah went home. Ma granny thought Ah had fell or had an accident. She said, 'What's to do?' And I told her, Eh said, 'Ah wis goin' tae save ye money.' 'Oh well,' she says, 'Away ye go to yer bed.'

That frightened me, I wouldn't go back to the dentist's for years and years after that.

Worklife

Working and unemployment take up a major part of the life-stories in the *Archive*. Many Dundonians seem to have worked in numerous jobs, and job security was a luxury many Dundee workers simply did not have between the two world wars. The textile industry dominated employment and the jute lords would employ women and children rather than men. Children and women's labour were, after all, cheaper than that of adult men. Childhood was a short period of life for the older generation, compared to childhoods today.

Jobs, especially for men, were not only insecure but in a number of cases dependent upon good weather. Mrs Christine Laing's* father was one of those whose work as a quarrier involved seasonal lay-offs. Christine's story is typical of thousands of Dundee's youth who could find work much more easily than could their parents. Her father 'wouldn't go to the parish, he wouldn't want charity'. Christine's mother 'went intae work and it helped tae keep things going a bit'. Christine, herself, began work at the tender age of eleven and a half years, at the beginning of the seven-week school holidays.

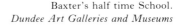
Baxter's half time School.
Dundee Art Galleries and Museums

BAXTER'S OLD HALF-TIME SCHOOL AND SCHOOL-MASTER.

If you had false lines [somebody else's birth certificate] proving that ye wis over fourteen, you got intae work. Eh worked all the seven weeks on false lines, that wis from six in the morning 'till six at night. That went on 'till Eh wis aboot twelve or twelve an' a half.

At the age of twelve and a half her mother applied to the school board for an exemption for Christine, and she was allowed to officially leave school a year and a half before she was fourteen

*Indicates that informant stated that they wanted their name changed to an archive name in any publication or use of tape or transcript. Interview extracts from interviews by Gary Buick, Scott Clark, Harvey Duke, Eliz Feeney, Jack McRae, Carla Ritchie and Graham R. Smith.

172

years old. Like the rest of her family she joined the Jute and Flax Workers Union.

A City Garden by J. McIntosh Patrick.
Dundee Art Galleries and Museums

> It wis ten days holiday at that time, but there wis never no wages. It wis like a lock-out. There wis no work and no money, and people in them days they couldnae save, 'cause nearly everybody had big families, and they all depended on the work.
>
> I remember when they went on strike, they went on strike for a sixpence rise, six pennies at that time, they were on strike for about six weeks. The rest of the family they were on strike as well as us. But the union kept ye going wi' a wee bit.

Others recall the pressure of family circumstance leading to work in the mills at an early age. Alex Simpson* was born in 1893 in Dundee. In 1905 he began work as a shifter in a jute mill. By the age of seventeen years he was finished with working in textiles and became a rigger in the shipyards.

173

Weaving flat – Baxter's Dens Works c. 1908.
Dundee Art Galleries and Museums

When I wis twelve years old Eh got half-time exemption. Eh went tae work in Baxter's 'n' Eh went tae the Baxter's School then. You worked half day, you worked in the morning, then went to the school in the afternoon. Then the next week you went tae the school in the forenoon and you worked in the mill in the afternoon.

Then when I wis thirteen I got a full-time exemption, Eh started to work full-time in the mill, and Eh went to St Andrew's School then. You worked in the mill from six in the morning tae six at night, then you had tae go tae the school for three nights of the week efter that. That wis some going in thay days [laughs]. Oh it wis no that hard but it wis steady work. As soon as one frame of rovins wis full well ye shifted them, took off the full box, roves, 'n' put on the empty roves. Then there wis another frame ready to go. It wis continous from one frame to the other, ye never got a break fae when ye started tae ye came out. Eh didna like it tae start wi', but Ah got used to it in the end, made up ma mind tae like it, ye had tae [laughs], that wis a' there wis to it.

Martha Stevenson* as a child suffered from a heart condition, but even with a severe childhood illness, which meant that she spent only three years at school, she felt it necessary to bring in a wage to her family. Martha was interviewed in 1985, aged seventy-seven years.

174

My mother always worked in the mill, as a matter of fact she was a cops winder, and there was a letter sent from the jute industries one year to say that Rubina McGrachle, meh mother's name, had been consistently the best winder in Dundee. Now this is in a town of experts, at that time there was mills at every corner.

But my mother had had a few miscarriages, and, the week that I turned fourteen, she was in bed again, she lost the baby again, so she was quite ill. And my father was idle – the shipyards were off a long time, aboot thirteen weeks or something.

Eh went out with another lass and went to Malcolm's in Dura Street, it wis a big mill then. Eh got a job. The winders did all the work an' they hid cards or discs and Eh'd take them to the office, back and forth, messages an' that. The gaffer then said, 'You've got to learn the windin' in your spare time.' So there was a woman who looked rather like my mother there, so I asked her, would she teach me the windin'. Eh felt frightened of the machinery, but anyhow it was sixteen shillings a week, well it was a help to my mother then. I wanted to teach ye know, but there was no hope of that for me. So I stayed there until I lifted something one day and I took a bad heart-attack. Anyhow I wasn't supposed to go back to the mill, but I did, a case of necessity, when my father died suddenly. He was killed in an accident at the shipyard the day that he started back at work.

Some of the youngsters graduated beyond shifting. Jean Small* was another who began in the mills aged fourteen, in 1930, she describes herself as 'jist a spinner'.

Eh worked in Sharp's in Edward Street, but we called it Sharpy's. They were good bosses, if there's any good bosses.

It wis child labour, 'cause yer only fourteen an' ye worked on Saturdays as well, half day Saturday. An' when ye think on it, there wis mansions in the [Broughty] Ferry, an' mansions in the West End belangin' to the mill owners. They got that through under payin' [wages], an' big profits, an' child labour. That's what it wis, because at fourteen ye kin imagine what size Eh wis, and ye'd reach up, och Eh dinna ken the height o' it, an' pit big, big roves they called them. It nearly killed ye, but they bosses never thought that ye were over worked.

An' yet in the works Eh worked in it wis a happy work, 'cause a lot o' people are happy in the mill. Eh wis never happy in it, therefore mibee Eh did meh work wi' a grudge. Eh didna look forward t' goin' in but an' awfy lot o' lassies sang, an' were really happy. . . .

There wis wee shifters, all fourteen, an' thir wis a shiftin' wifie, an' she was an old crab, nae metter wha she wis, they were a' crabs. They'd get thay six wee lassies up your pass [space between the frames] and she'd put aff yer machine, an' they would empty it, and if they didna hurry up, an' this is true, 'cause Eh wis a shifter afore Eh wis a spinner, she put on the machine an' yer fingers went roond the spindles. The gaffers in them days ye could never answer them back, because ye would get yer books.

Baxter's Mill skailing.
Dundee Art Galleries and Museums

175

We made faces at them, bit ye never ever ever said t' them what ye thought, or ye'd a got jist put oot the door.

Weavers often saw themselves as the better-off of the textile workforce. As one spinner said:

Well the weavers aye said they were better than the spinners, 'cause they made their ain pay, and we only had a set pay, but we used tae say we were better workers than them.

Margaret Frews* was a weaver:

The weavers were the toffs. There wis some o' the weavers, right up 'till the time the works closed, who still wore their hats and gloves going tae their work, as if they were going tae a party.

Bella Keyser, born in 1922, also worked as a weaver.

Eh hated it, Eh never stayed long in any job. Eh think Eh wis round every jute factory in Dundee tae see if any the other looms wis better than the last ain, because at the weavin' ye seemed tae get everybody's bad work. If the cops wirnae bad, it wis the weft that wisnae good, and, if, the weft wis good, the bloody dressin' wis wrang. Ye got everybody's trouble, 'cause it wis piece work, and if ye didn't make a penny, ye didn't get a penny.

We were very isolated stuck on these looms, ye couldnae speak tae anybody, ye couldnae carry on a conversation, it had tae be all done beh signs o' the mouth and even at times the shakin o' the hands. As tae what time it was: three fingers up, two fingers up, half past two; two pinkies crossed, two; two thumbs fir twelve o'clock. Ye never could carry on a conversation wi' people. And Eh saw thit there wir a lot of spinsters, Eh suppose jist for the simple reason that they never come in contact wi' anybody.

Eh thought it wis a very isolated job, white faces, same thing, day in, day out, clackity-clack, no easy noise, a' the clackin' o' the shuttles wis in yer ears. Ye know ye went tae sleep wi' this clackity-clack in yer ears. And Eh thought, 'Christ, Eh'm gonna go batty here, this is not goin' to do me, Eh've got tae get out of here.' But ye see the bairn in itsell it wis a saviour tae me, because wi' having' a child Eh was exempt [from essential war work].

Margaret Frews*, born in 1919, worked as a weaver for twenty-seven years before becoming a full-time trade-union official in 1961.

I liked the weaving, Eh did like the weaving though. I would've stopped being a full-time trade-union officer, if Eh could've went back tae the weaving, if any boss would've had me.

Margaret always believed that the mill workers' conditions and pay lagged behind that of the weavers. It was a belief she carried through to her trade-union work.

Men and locomotives, c. 1970. *Joseph McKenzie*

In the auld days, oh meh God, they used tae come out o' the mill jist hanging wi' the dust. The mill wis never as well paid as the weaving side, never ever. The batching wis a dirty job. At one time you couldnae put yer cup o' tea doon, if Eh had done that, wi' a cup o' tea, before Eh got meh hand awa' it would be covered wi' dust, thick dust.

The first thing Eh said Eh would dae was tae get that sorted oot, because when Eh saw how hard they mill workers had tae work, there wis nae reason why they should be lower paid, nae reason at a'. One o' the first things Eh set out tae dae was tae get the mill wages up, so that the people will hae something tae work for.

Eh mind when we were trying tae recruit tae the mills, Eh says, 'How do ye no go up tae the Five Ways?' (the auld people's place). Eh says, 'Invite a gang o' them doon tae hae a look at the jute works now.' Because the youngsters wis still influenced by their grans [grandmothers] sayin', 'Dinna go in there an' work, it'll kill ye.' So they did take twa or three bunches o' the auld folk [to the works]. An' the auld folk could not honestly believe the difference that there wis in the jobs that they used tae dae. Eh wis glad tae think that Eh had something tae dae wi' the change, thank God.

Outside of the jute firms, one of the most influential companies in Dundee was D. C. Thomson's. Thomson's not only controlled the local newspapers, but were also responsible for institutions such as the *Sunday Post*, and a large range of nationally famous comics. W. Sydney Scroggie began his working life with the firm in 1935, aged sixteen years.

I was on the boys' papers, *Wizard, Hotspur* etc., and we enormously enjoyed ourselves there. It was more fun than work and we didn't get much pay but really we used to spend most of our time playing ourselves and I used to come back in the evening and do the work we should have done during the day [laughs], but as long as the paper went to press it didn't matter how you did it.

I was always on the editorial side, I was what was called the junior third editor on the *Hotspur*. A load of papers would be shoved in front of you and [you'd be] told, 'Correct these.' And then they shoved a typescript at me and said, 'Right, we want five hundred words cut out of that, but don't spoil the sense of it.' So you just read it through, and cut it, and made various adjustments and alterations. Then they said, 'Right, we want an idea for an illustration.' So you would submit ideas for the illustration, based on the story. 'We want a top line. We want a tail piece. We want chapter headings. We want a caption for the picture.' And that's the kind of work we were doing, what!

It was purely school stuff all the stories in the *Hotspur*, and a school twist to them. And, of course, in those days they were all written text you see, they weren't picture stories – a written text with, maybe if it was a long story, a couple of illustrations done on the premises by the artists, or a shorter one, one illustration and an illustrated heading or title spread as well, you see that was the way they worked it.

178

Watch repairer, West Port, c. 1965. *Joseph McKenzie*

They were good publications, the boys' papers of those days. They weren't rubbish. They certainly represented the Empire as being an important, if not perhaps the most important thing, that's ever occurred in world history, and I am not so sure that I don't agree with them.

They certainly weren't left-wing I can tell you that, because it was as much as your job was worthwhile to you in the 1930s.

Valentine's was another major company and one of the leading Scottish firms, producing commercial view-prints from Victorian times to the present day. Valentine's built a business which grew to include greeting cards. Central to the company's products were the women who reproduced the picture postcards and hand-coloured greeting cards. One of these women was Diane Wood* who joined the firm in 1932.

Eh worked in Valentine's when Eh was fourteen as a hand colourist. And now, at that time, it was just a wee brush, just a long thing like paint-brush. And it was great hand colouring, like great big roses, things like that, but ye had tae learn how. Ye hid tae go on training for this, just 'till ye actually got the knack. Everything was done by hand.

Then you went on to a spraying machine, it was just a little thing wi' gas pressure. And you filled this up and ye got yer stencil, ye used tae put it across on yer card. Mibee ye wid get the blue, somebody wid get the green. And then when ye yist to be lucky, even wi' the hand colouring, the easiest colour wis lemon, yellow.

When ye hand coloured the yellow everything was done and ye coloured everything that wis white. So the yellow wisnae any problem, but the other colours wis difficult tae dae, plus the fact we had a terrible supervisor, she wis a terrible woman.

This woman would never allow ye tae make anything, because when ye yist tae go back and say Eh've finished meh job, she used tae say tae ye, 'Go back and look over all yer job.' Well ye were on piece work. Well ye'd tae go back and [re-do] any fuzzy edges ye know.

Ye'd tae clean. Yer hands wid be blistered, ye'd tae parazone the back [of yer hands] tae dreh thim.

We used tae do the Blackpool Illuminations. Eh used tae wonder aboot that place, I used tae think it wis like Las Vegas, often think it wis a country. Where on earth wis this great place wi' a' this fun? Eh thought it wis a rich man's paradise.

Ye went on tae the spray department, ye come tae the aulder girls, well at this time yer full o' nonsense, ye wir going to the dancin', ye yist tae get yer hair set, and in these days there wis nae washhand-basins or anything like that. So the result wis when you wanted yer hair set ye just pulled the [toilet] plug and ye got the water. Somebody wid set yer hair, that's true, that's really true. There's nothing wrang wi' meh hair the day, it's not white. But anyway the aulder girls they wid go to the Pally, they yist tae learn ye between times how tae go aboot this. Then there'd be

180

lovely ribbon in the store. Mibee ye'd get a lump o' ribbon fir yer shoes, ye yist tae pit it on yer shoes fir the dancin'.

Eh yist tae run hame fir meh dinner. Eh yist tae run up from Valentine's, up Millar's Wynd, and alang Ure Street, doon Forest Park, up the City Road, imagine that. Must have been like the Hawkhill Harriers. Meh granny would mibee hae five o' us at dinner. Then ye thingied up yer hair [laughs], 'cause ye wir always dressed in Valies, ye yist tae hear, 'Valies Dallies; it must be six o' clock.' Valies Dallies that's what folk called us.

Eh got an exchange tae the dispatch department. . . . It wis puttin' snaps in albums and we used tae get homework there, ye could take homework home. Eh yist tae huv meh father doin' thim, meh sister doin' thim, at that time yid huv a big box o' cards. Thir wis twelve in the album. Eh yis tae make this money, and it wis great. Eh mind o' that time it wis when the old King died, well ye went on tae the mourning cards a' this grievin' cards, well ye wir always busy in Valentine's really and truly.

Eh wis married 1939, well ye hid tae leave yer job at that time. Eh hid tae leave Valentine's, 'cause meh husband wisnae in the army at that time. See in Valentine's ye hid tae leave. The married wimen wir put out. Valentine's always had that ruling when ye wir married: ye left; that wis it.

With the Second World War, Valentine's became a part of the war industry.

Eh wis actually called up for munitions, away back tae Valentine's again on the shells [laughs]. Eh went straight over tae munitions, tracer bullets and shells. Eh wis on the inspection at that time, engineering wis strange, but it wis good how wimen were able tae adapt thimselves. Ye yist tae get put on the machines, great big machines, sometimes ye wir scared stiff, frightened. Eh got a braw, a rare job goin' roond sellin' the dinner tickets [laughs]. Thir wir two shifts, well in between there'd be a concert party on, for the twelve-hour shift, they made the tracer bullets.

Keiller's Works – the jujube making room.
Dundee District Libraries

Another important source of employment were the docks and shipyards. It wasn't unusual for sons, fathers, uncles and grand-fathers to work in shipbuilding. John McHardy recalls that his mother's family were all in the shipyards, travelling to find work around the Clyde, Forth and Tay yards. It was a childhood dream to follow the men of the family into shipbuilding. He left school aged fourteen years.

I wanted to go to the yard, doon at the Caledon shipyard in Dundee, 1938, when I left the Stobbie [Stobswell School].
  'You're no going to the bloody yard, bide at the school!'
  I thought I was gonna supplement the family income and get a job, and I went to the yard and got my arse kicked oot the door repeatedly [by my father], and tane by the ear and, 'Get out and stay out!'

181

Finally he managed to convince his parents that he was serious and became a plater's boy. He was forty-six years in shipbuilding.

> Although I got threw oot now and again for my politics and my attitude, they were aye glad to get us back. They thrown you oot on the street and you'd go to the labour exchange and maybe make an application for a job some other place, because they were gonna be looking for platers maybe in a couple o' months, they would tell the burroo no to gie you the job, so you'd be hinging on a hook for them, but I sorted that oot too [laughs].

Jobs in the steel works in Scunthorpe and on the railway in Dundee kept him busy when the shipyards laid him off, but there was always a way back.

> Jimmy Brownlie was the lodge-keeper at that time, he was the Dundee United manager at one time, and Scottish goalkeeper, and he says to me, 'Well big yin what are you wanting here?' And I says, 'I'm looking for a job Jimmy.' So I was there fae 1953 till 1961.

After a number of jobs including 'doing vents for the Clyde tunnel and making tattie-crisp machines for the Soviet Union', he returned to his first love – the shipyard. In 1983 he finally had to retire after a stroke at work.

War

Work played a central role in the lives of the majority of those interviewed by the Oral History Project: however, war also played an important part in these lives. Apart from the steady stream of youth into the regular army during peacetime, tens of thousands of Dundonians fought in the two world wars. Dundonians served in almost every theatre of conflict. The Project collected dozens of war stories, far too many to include here. Some of those interviewed live with the effects of warfare to this day, like W. Sydney Scroggie, who left D. C. Thomson's to serve as an army officer in the Apennines mountain range in Italy.

> We were doing patrols, keeping in touch with the retreating Gerries, what! And it was on one of these patrols that I stood on a shoe mine. Boom! And that was me.
> You were unlucky to lose your life standing on a shoe mine. Either the shock would kill you, or you have some inner impulse to live (which is very powerful). A few guys lost their foot on a shoe mine and just died, when really we couldn't see any particular reason why they should have, you know. I was unlucky that I happened to be staring at the ground, naturally I'm always staring at the ground looking for signs of mines. When the thing

went off I got the explosion right in my eyes, which is rather hard lines, that didn't normally happen.

Very interesting experience really to be badly wounded, you're never really quite the same person, not that it damages you, but in that you have got knowledge about life and about yourself, that people who haven't been badly smashed up don't acquire, you know what I mean?

The fact that I was blind right from that moment did not really seem to bother me all that much and it never has. I know that I am blind, I have only got one eye and the other eye is a wreck. There's not just one thing wrong with it, there's no pupil, there's no lens, it's lost tension, the retina's dropped off its hook. Nobody could do anything with that eye, what!

On the home front, Dundee never suffered from the extensive bombing campaigns experienced by other British cities. However most older people in the city recall the time in World War Two when the bombs did fall. Norman Robertson* recalls:

They dropped the bomb on the power-station in Forest Park Road, ye seen a big blue flash ye know. Eh didn't know Rosefield Street got it, bit sticks o' bombs were comin' ye see.

Apart from that single incident the city suffered no more bombing. The home front in both wars tended to be quiet, however there were important changes in the lives of women workers. Bella Keyser found work in the shipyards in World War Two after working for about a year as a welder for Bonar Long.

Eh went down tae this shipyard. And the ideal image o' the ship-yard wis this big tough riveters ye know, and sweary beasts, so, yer young, yer easy influenced, ye go in there wi' a sweary beast attitude, 'Eh'll be as tough as the bloody rest o' thim, Eh'll show them whaur tae "F" off!'

It wis great buildin' boats. This rusty piece of metal was goin up, 'n' ye wir weldin', and when it wis finished it wis a' painted and polished. The difference when it wis finished ye know, the ships were beautiful, ye see it goin' intae the water, 'n' low 'n' behold it floated, what an end product! It wis fulfilment, it did great for yer ego and great fir yer sense o' achievement, it took away the drudgery out o' the word work. It wis fantastic, ye could see the work developin' in front of yer eyes. It suited meh person-ality, it suited meh physique.

The older men wir very kind tae ye, the younger men wir very abrasive tae ye, they accepted ye because you wir no danger to thim, ye weren't taken on their job, ye wir mibee doin' a man's job, but ye wir only there for the war.

After the war she spent ten years in factory jobs with growing feelings of dissatisfaction and frustration about worklife.

183

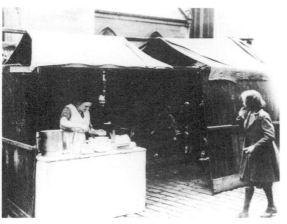

Buster Stall in Mid Kirk Style. *Dundee District Libraries*

Eh hid tae have a lower standard o' livin', because Eh wasn't allowed tae use the skill that they had given me. It suited thim in wartime, it didn't suit thim in peacetime. So Eh marched up to the shipyard and Eh put in this request fir work.

Bella was told to come back and take a welding test.

So Eh goes down the next week. Eh could see the wee laddies running here, and the wee laddies runnin' there, 'There's the woman!' Ye see they're all expecting this young dolly bird t' come doon, an doon comes this fat grey haired wifie [laughing]. And a voice went up and says, 'Och it's Bell, it's Big Bell.' So the two shop-stewards came along tae see that Eh got a fair crack o' the whip, and Eh done the test, Eh wis full o' nerves.

It was very excitin', the old ones that Eh had served meh time with come across and say, 'Hi Bella, Eh hivne seen ye fir years.' It gave me a boost. Eh passed this test, and Ah marched along tae see the personnel officer with the foreman.

She was asked to start in a fortnight.

On that first mornin' thit Eh started Eh wis on the shipyard bus wi' all these men, and comin' down the brae Eh'm quite sure some o' thim wir sayin' tae thir sel', 'What the hell is that woman coming down this brae for?' And Eh stopped half way and thought, 'Christ will Eh turn back or . . . oh no, what the hell eh'm Eh doin' here', and then Eh pulled mehself up and Eh said, 'Eh'm here to prove women can do it'. Eh didn't have to prove mehself, Eh hid proved mehself durin' the war. Eh am now here tae reap the benefit of meh war experiences. So in Eh marched.

Bella was one of the few women who managed to return to their wartime trade. Others, whose lives were just as deeply affected by war, tended to accept the reinstatement of social conformity.

Leisure

Dundonians found a multitude of pursuits to follow when they weren't working. Long hours, poor wages, and even periods of unemployment did not prevent the people of the city from finding some degree of enjoyment.

Inside the home, music was one way in which families made their own entertainment, and many families could boast at least one musician. There was also a wide variety of other pastimes and hobbies, and most cost very little.

One thing I do remember wis an alarm clock that broke down, she [mother] took it all down to bits and the little wheels they made lovely what we called peeries in these days, you would call them tops nowadays.

184

An' then the like of a Sunday, for long enough the standard tea wis a rabbit, an' we used to get the back bone an' mother would scrub it clean, an' we would play with that. Not very often we had a melon, mother always scrubbed the seeds, we made necklaces and bangles with them, mother was awfully good.

Outside of the home there was entertainment: the pub, very much a male preserve until the Second World War; variety, with Harry Lauder amongst the best remembered acts; and a host of other amusements including dancing.

Yist tae git in fir fowerpence. Ye yist tae git in fir tick, fae Jeamie Bell. Ye yist tae run doon and jist say tae him, 'Eh've no got any money, can Eh give ye it on Saturday?' But the bigger dances . . . well we yist tae go tae Robertson's, that wis a wee bit classy, ye learnt there.

Then we yist tae go tae the Pally. Ye hid tae be a dancer. 'Oh Christ!' meh father yist tae say, 'Ye'll dance oot this hoose on yir bloody neck some nicht.' Meh father yist tae say, 'Now Eh'm warnin' you lady, if you go to that bloody dancin' the night . . .' Eh'd say, 'Eh'm not goin'.' Eh bloody did. Eh did.

That's whaur ye met a' yer lads lang ago, at the dancin'.

Another woman recalled:

Meh mither wouldnae let me go tae the dancin'. Meh pal poodered her face and there wis nae buyin' oot o' the chemist then, fir yer face. See thay tea pokes . . . they were red, well Maggie aye used tae wet thum 'nd pit it on her cheeks, that's the truth, ye widnae believe that.

Eh wis the only lassie, 'nd meh mither didnae want nothin' tae happen. If ye had a bairn ye'd tae send them oot the toon. She made sure nothin' wid happen tae me: 'You don't need nothin' on yer face.' It's right enough, Ah hid bonny hair awa' doon tae here ken an' it wis auburn. Maggie went tae the dancin', meh mither widnae let me. Eh cannae dance, Eh can hardly walk, meh mither widnae let me dance, 'They're no good that goes tae the dancin', yer not goin'.

Blind fiddler, Nethergait

Just as today, people between the wars spent much of their leisure time in their youth meeting, or at least trying to meet, members of the opposite sex. Monkey parades, weekly Sunday walks in the town centre and elsewhere, the dancing and the picture houses provided opportunities for romance to blossom and courtships to continue.

In the olden days, when Eh started going about with meh wife, we went to a picture house in Rosebank Street, called the Empire. Eh remember distinctly every night we went there we used to buy twelve bars of Duncan's Hazelnut Chocolate, which cost a penny a bar at that time, there were twelve bars between us every evening.

An' then there wis chummy seats. They were at the back o' the hall. That's where we were. That's where the courting couples went.

The cinema, however provided a good night out for people of all ages.

But granny yist tae tak us tae the pictures at night. We yist tae go tae the Rialto, and meh granny wis good. She always hid a sweetie.

Eh remember when we went tae the Oxford now that wis the silent films. We yist tae sneak in there. Somebody wid kerry ye on his back, got ye in for nothin'. Well there yist tae be *The House Without A Key*, an' a this thing, an' *The Green Archer*. Well ye see there wis the silent films and there wir continues [serials], when ye hid tae go the next week. Ye yist tae hurry aboot tae git this penny tae go tae the show. Eh dinnae think we saw the ending o' it, the man run awa wi' the money [laughs].

In the show the dancers wid come on, oh it wis great some o' the local talent. Dancers anathin', we thought it wis great.

Coorse, when ye come oot [of the cinema] ye wir daein' a' yon actions anathin', *The Green Archer*, hidin' up the closes and jumpin' on people.

Dae anythin' tae git back the next week. And of coorse the cowboys; ye yist tae sit on the flair, if it wis packed . . . They put ye sittin' in the aisles, watchin' the cowboys, then screamin' and yellin', and then yid git flung oot [laughs]. Ye yist tae git barred. Tae me ye wir tryin' tae draw attention [laughs].

In later years, once the 'talkies' arrived, the cinema remained as popular.

Well meh mother went every night when we all started workin'. She never got oot afore that, bit when we started workin' she started t' go t' the first hoose o' the pictures. An' if we were good she used t' say, 'Eh'll tak you the night.' Meh mother liked the pictures so much, like we'd a' be arguin' in the hoose, an' she'd put on her coat an' go t' the pictures. It must've been heaven t' sit fir two hours in glamour, cause the pictures in them days were awfy glamorous, they were a' American nearly, an' they wore beautiful dresses. Eh mean it wis another world for twa hours.

Meh father funny enough, he widna go t' the pictures.

And then there were the family outings, a day out for the many who could not afford longer holidays.

We used tae go tae the Stannergate and Broughty Ferry. Well we used tae walk wi' ma dad tae the Stannergate, ye know – Grassy Beach. Oh they used tae go in their huners [hundreds] there an' he [father] would put a' the sandwiches an' a' the stuff in the false bottom o' the pram an' we would walk it, an' ma mother would go on the bus [laughing]. An' we used tae go tae Broughty Ferry . . . that's the only outings thit we got.

186

There was also a great interest in sport in the 1930s. The spectator sports of football and boxing attracted thousands of men.

> How I'm a Dundee United supporter is because I could sneak into Tannadice an' Ah couldnae sneak intae Dens Park . . . The lad that sat beside me at school, his grandfather had a garden in Arklay Street, an' we got in there and climbed over.

The period between the wars also saw an increase in people participating in sports such as swimming, running and climbing. The outdoors were very attractive to men and women who spent too many hours in the unhealthy air of the city. One of the most popular of these outdoor pursuits was cycling, and a number of clubs were established in the city.

> When Eh left the Scouts Ah got a pushbike. Ah used t' go at weekends, and then another chap and Eh used t' go touring. Eh wis in the Corinthians, 'course they're defunk now. Then Eh wis in the Grey Lodge in Wellington Street. Eh did quite a few things in the Grey Lodge, billiards and gyms, running and harrying, cyclin', swimmin' – did a lot o' that.

Others joined clubs:

> Eh wis aboot seventeen when I joined the cycling club, an' that is what Ah did all the time – cycling all over the place. It wis the ILP Cycling Club at that time (that wis the Independent Labour Party), and we cycled all over Scotland.
>   At that stage it wis jist all young lads, bit the club was a mixed club, later on there wis a ladies section. It wis really good, because they wir, och, good class girls, constant, sensible lassies, and, 'cause, they came in through the affiliation t' political things, either because their father or mother wis there.

Religion

Religion in Dundee was an important part of many people's lives. As one older woman speaking about her Edwardian childhood said:

The Stobbie Ponds, c. 1920

> The church was [the] only thing, there wis no television, or no bingo halls, an' things like that in my day, but I loved the church. I still go t' the church.

Apart from the regular religious activity of the churches there were the popular attractions such as the Band of Hope. There were also social movements such as Temperance, which provided support for the Scottish Prohibition Party and saw the election of Edwin Scrymgeour to Parliament. Scrymgeour understood the connection between religion and entertainment, providing events through which he and his followers hoped to

187

lure workers out of pubs. This didn't always go to plan, for example, when the Prohibition Party hired an aeroplane for a stunt, the spectacle ended when the plane crashed onto the roof of a house. Others were attracted to the Spiritualists. However it was the mainstream Churches which continued to receive the largest support. They also brought recreation into religion, especially Sunday School outings and picnics.

Unlike other areas of Scotland there was less bitterness and rivalry between Protestant and Catholic.

> Meh pal wis a Catholic, bit me sister's pals were Protestants. Bit they still come aboot us, an' we went aboot them, thir wis nae difference in oor hoose.

To say that there was a great deal of tolerance is not to say that certain companies in Dundee didn't play the sectarian card of setting worker against worker. Nor is it to say that people failed to notice the differences of approach to worshipping a Christian god.

> Well the Roman Cathlics used tae roll their eggs on a Sunday . . . And the Protestant did the Saturday, that wis recognised in these days.

Many older people can recall Scotch-Irish Day, the patron Saint of Ireland's day, when religious differences were vented in a reasonably good natured punch-up.

> Ma father was Catholic an' ma mother was a Protestant. All ma pals were mostly Catholic. The only day we fell out was St Patrick's Day. We had a fight on St Patrick's Day.

It is also clear that some parents tried to discourage their children from mixing with others of a different denomination, but it is equally clear that these children seldom fell into line.

> Eh palled aboot wi' five boys, an' there wis one o' them, his mother took me aside, Eh think she liked me the best o' the lot, an' she told me she was worried because Patrick was a Catholic an' she was frightened that he would get taken awa' from his faith. See the rest o ' us were a' Protestants. An' that's a thing we never bothered about. But that woman! Even if we went away, when we wis a wee bit older, went to Forfar for a weekend, Pat had t' go and find oot the name o' the priest that did the Mass so's t' tell his mother when he come back . . . which was ridiculous.

Politics

It should not be assumed that the lack of religious bigotry meant that Dundonians were placid souls. It was simply that they used their energies in more positive ways. Trying to live was a

188

struggle itself, and any extra time and energy would be spent on having a bit of fun or in trying to change the way they lived.

Survival was difficult in the days before the establishment of the welfare state and the National Health Service. The amount of deaths from industrial accidents and contagious diseases was higher in Dundee than in many other cities in Britain. Poverty marked the lives of many families. The older people interviewed by the Oral History Project often noted that the city's problems increased with the end of World War One.

Union Demonstration? Bottom of Whitehall Street

In 1918, when the war finished, then there wis the unemployment, that's the first time that the dole came out for the general public. Then things went from that to worse, to the Hungry Thirties, and I can tell you those were very, very hard times. We got very little money. If ye couldn't pay yer rent ye got no help, you were put out on the street. It's not the first time I've seen neighbours furniture put out in the street. When ye signed [on] the burroo ye never knew the minute the Means Test man wis comin' round yer door. Now when he come t' yer house it wis jist like the Gestapo, he put ye through the third degree.

Herbert Baxter* had dealings with Bobby Allan, of the Parish Council.

After meh father died we went on the whit they called the Parish Council Benefits at that time. This Bobby Allan and Mr Woods, they were the Parish Council Inspectors, they were more often in meh hoose than they were in their own. They came in at all sorts of times and they didnae ask your leave, jist opened the cupboard to see whit you hid. Eh've seen them in our house in the middle of the night . . . They had a reputation like nobody's business. But it was a hell of a life to live under it.

Well we only stayed on the Parish Council Benefits for oh maybe about six months. They were issuing clothing, you got issue o' clothing once a year I think it was, and meh brother Bill, the next to me, and me and one sister, we hid to go down to Forester Street to the Parish Council Offices to have this issue of clothing. And meh brother he wis accepting everything that wis offered. When it come to me, 'Eh'm no having that.' Eh turned everything away, and Bobby Allan says to me, 'Eh'll come an' give you a clip in the lug.' And Eh says, 'You'll better no dae that,' Eh says, 'You'll be wrong if you dae that.' Eh wouldnae have him give me a clip in the lug, but I wouldnae accept his clothing, because the clothing was all marked and stamped. This was in case you go an' pawn it, or try and sell it, or something.

Bob Stewart and Mary Brooksbank were members of the early Communist Party in Britain. Both served time in prison for trying to organise the working class. Stewart, who had been a full-time organiser for the Scottish Prohibition Party in 1908, was elected as the Communist Party's Scottish organiser in 1921.

189

Under the Pillars of the Townhouse

Brooksbank is now best remembered as a song-writer, but she did important political work in Dundee for several decades. Her political reputation was somewhat belittled when she fell out with the Communist Party leadership over the Stalinist take-over of the Party in the 1920s.

Not all the demonstrations and strikes in Dundee ended peacefully. Margaret Frews* recalls being caught up in one disturbance in the 1930s.

> It wis like all hell let loose, the mounted police just come right in front o' where we were, an' the batons were swingin' left, right and centre. Oh my God! Now if you were in the way it didna matter who you were, you just had had it. There wis damned big horses comin' beltin' after ye an' the policemen you know. An' Ah wis away up the Wellgate steps an' this great big bloody horse wis half way up the Wellgate steps chasin' the crowd. 'N' the sparks wir flying from its hooves ye know, oh God, Ah wis on the road ti' hell, an' that's something Ah'll never forget [laughing], because it wis like a great big elephant t' me, oh what a size o' a horse. But ye know we were only 'bout eleven years old [laughing]. Oh it wis frightening.

Mr Jackson* was involved in an earlier disturbance. Born in 1895 he joined the police in his twenties.

> The 1921 riots, I wis in them. It all started with some o' the people wirna getting enough money to keep [them], they were idle, no work, an' they went to the Parish Council an' the Parish Council refused to entertain them, they would have nothing to do with them. The Lord Provost was Lord Provost Spence at that time, an' he lived out about Blackness Avenue an' they all went out in a body right up Blackness Avenue, to the Lord Provost an' he wouldna entertain them so they smashed his windows.
>
> An' then it lasted for a good few weeks, night after night they were out. An' they smashed all the windows on both sides of the Overgate, an' different parts of the town. They had the mounted police out, cleared the streets, hundreds were arrested an' thrown in [jail]. The amount of stuff that was stolen was colossal. Birrell's was a big boot-store in the Overgate at that time, Birrell had 'is windows smashed three different times during the time of the riots, an' they were reaching in an' grabbing shoes an' boots, but unfortunately they weren't pairs. An' for weeks after, when we were going round the beat, we were getting shoes, a size nine an' a size seven, lying all round, they were throwin' them away, they had no use for them, 'cos they couldn't get a pair. We had to do a lot of extra duty.

Riots should not be thought to be the norm during this period. Political activity took many other shapes and forms, activity which remains ingrained with pride in the memories of older Dundonians. Margaret Frews* says:

190

I remember when I was a kid 'n' the Spanish Civil War wis on.
And they hud the aid for Spain, of course it wis fir the [Spanish]
workers. That wis in Bobby Allan days. That wis in the days
when if ye'd butter and jam on yer table ye got yer money cut.
In fact ye didna hae butter. And when I used to' go round, they
used t' gie mibbee a tin a Nestles milk or a half a jar o' jam, an'
that stuff counted. That wis a' sent awa' . . .

They'd gie ye thir very last, because they knew what thay
people were goin' through. It wis a real pleasure t' go roond the
hooses, they welcomed ye, because they wir trying t' help. Ah
niver ever mind o' gettin a refusal. I used to go round on a Friday
night, they got their labour exchange money on a Friday.

Another who remembers proudly is Peggy Souter who was
born 1899 and worked as a mill lassie. She was interviewed when
she was eighty-eight years old.

See, we were in the ILP and the older Labour Party men thought
that we were what they call the Militants now, we were militants
in those days! An' they used to say, 'Oh, you'll gain by
experience.' Well, Eh am a militant yet. But Eh'm very happy to
let people know, that Eh'm a Socialist! Just don't say, 'Labour'.
Eh say, 'Eh'm a Socialist.'

Immigration

The Project also collected the life-stories of those born outside
of the city who chose Dundee as a place to live. The earliest
immigrants in living memory to come to Dundee were the Irish
who tended to settle in the Lochee area.

Norman Lyle* born 1911:

The Overgate, c. 1900

Oh ma mother wis an avid, fervent Catholic. She believed it right
up t' the last. She lived as a good person; her background wis very
humble. Meh mother wis born in Ireland, she wis only an infant
when she come here. And she probably come over during the time
of a potato famine. And there was nobody more humble, or
poorer, than these people were.

My grandfather spoke broad Irish. Ye picked up some of the
sayings without ever speaking like an Irish person. Ma grandfather would hear somebody speaking in Dundee, some o' the
kids, and he'd say 'Will ye stop talking that heathen language
[laughing].

There were those who arrived who were escaping not only the
poverty of their native lands, but also persecution. Wolf
Rothman's* family found in Dundee a small but energetic
Jewish community.

Well my mother and father came from a place called Minsk, in
Russia, in 1904 . . . Ma mother and father often conversed in

191

Russian, sometimes they didn't want us to hear what they were speaking about, we were never able to pick it up.

Ma father could read English, but ma mother, she could not read nor write. If she hid tae sign any documents, or anything, she jist hid tae put a cross. An' then the solicitor who wis there would sign it over.

Eh remember one day we had tae go to the solicitors. An' she wis asked tae make a statement, and the solicitor said, 'Repeat after me: I swear to tell the truth the whole truth an' nothin' but the truth.' An' ma mother says, 'Eh swear tae tell the truth, the whole truth an' nothin' about the truth.' [Laughing]. It wis so funny, the solicitor laughed, he couldna help it.

She spoke in broken English, but she wis a super woman. Absolutely super. An' the most marvellous cook, everybody liked her food. Fillet o' the fish was one of her favourites, eh . . . chicken soup, 'n' roasted chicken. There wis a dish called Chaulent, which is made up of vegetables, carrots 'n' turnips, butter' . . . eh . . . raisins 'n' what not.

Well there was about fifty Jewish families [in Dundee] during the war years and now there's only seven. Drastically cut. Well they've either died, or they've shifted to bigger cities with larger Jewish populations. They were concerned with their children – gettin' them married to Jewish people. That's why many of them shifted from Dundee to Glasgow, an' Edinburgh, an' the North of England, an' Manchester. Ma brother, he had six daughters, he went away to Manchester with his wife and six daughters, an' five of his daughters got married to Jewish boys.

Other Dundonians recall settlers arriving from other parts of the world, especially during and after the Second World War when the whole of humanity seemed to be on the move.

We taught the Poles in Meigle to speak English. It was funny one of the children said, 'When we met the Polish soldiers they always say, "Gene Autry"', who was a film star, but it was 'Dzindobry' – meaning 'good day'.

And:

Eh had the same pal fae when we were in primary [school], until Eh got married. Eh wis married aboot two year when the war [World War Two] broke oot. Eh didna lose touch, she came up every Tuesday t' me, at that time, and she met a Pole.

She came up one day an' said she wis gettin' married, would Eh go t' the weddin'. Eh said t' her, 'What t' a Pole!' Oh Eh thought that wis terrible, an' oh she widnae see past him. Eh went t' the weddin breakfast, and they're a' speaking in Polish. Eh says, 'Mary what are the sayin?' She says, 'Eh dinna ken.' Eh says, 'Oh God.' However, they were happy.

Dundonians have shown themselves to be tolerant of out-iders; anti-immigrant feeling, which resulted in fascist activity in Edinburgh, was much less prevalent in Dundee. However the big question remained: Would you marry, or let your sister marry, one of them? Such a question grew in importance, with the Second World War when millions of people found themselves uprooted and some found themselves in Dundee. Bella Keyser tells the story of her marriage.

Eh married a foreigner. Eh met him in the dancin', where many a good woman fell – in the Empress Ballroom [laughing]. All the foreigners were intent on murder 'nd rape in these days ye know, ye really didnae mix. And they had tae give out from the pulpits here, in Dundee, 'Would the girls please speak tae the foreign sailors, 'nd soldiers, they wir very, very lonely.' And these chaps were lonely.

Although as young girls we used tae hae a great laugh, 'nd say, 'Which lot has come intae Dundee this week?' 'A lot of Poles.' 'Well, we'll go down tae the dancin' 'n' get a Pole.'

Then the next week wis Norwegians. 'Oh we'll all go down tae the dancin' and get a Norwegian.' So ye met them on the Saturday, went out on the Sunday, 'nd we'd tae march thim alang tae the grassy beach, [laughing], all in a row. Hae about eight girls 'nd eight sailors [laughing]. It's funny how the crowd all divided up, because one did marry a Norwegian, Eh married a Dutchman, somebody else married an Englishman. But we used tae think this wis a game, but these lads were lonely, 'cause there'd be no place tae go. When they got out the barracks at night there wis no place tae go, and they didnae have much money, so unless people opened up thir homes, and invited them intae thir homes, they wir jist pair lost sowls.

War marriages and relationships were often marked in their early years by separation. Bella's was no different; her fiancé had to return to the Dutch Navy. She eagerly awaited him after a two year absence, they had planned to be married, however, would she recognise him when he arrived back in Dundee?

In the late mornin' the train come in, there wis a lot of pushin' and shovin', wi' people comin' off the trains. Eh'm lookin' up the platform, couldnae see him, Eh wis lookin fir a Dutch uniform, couldnae see him, then the next thing was this navy-blue suit spoke to me, ye know, he says, 'Is that you Bella?' Eh never saw his face, Eh only saw a navy-blue suit. And he took me in his arms, 'nd Eh could smell soap, Sunlight soap, that strong washin' soap, ye know, and it didnae smell like him. As the years passed Eh wis in love wi' that soap, jist soap.

We got married wi' a solicitor. Got all the papers up tae the courtroom. There we wis sittin', meh weddin' finally, beside all the convicts chained tae thir policemen.

After the Second World War, Dundee, like other Scottish cities, attracted workers from all over the world. Gina Rossa*,

193

Continental Foodstore, Hilltown. *Ken Sharp*

born in 1923, along with hundreds of others, arrived from Southern Italy. She was a compositor in an Italian printshop, however the job ended when she contracted blood poisoning from the inks. On going to the local labour exchange she was told that work was available in Dundee, Scotland. It wasn't until later that she found out that the Dundee jute-mill owners were behind recruiting people to work in the mills. Once the immigrants arrived in Dundee they were given accommodation.

> All the Italian girls stay Broughty Ferry, up Panmure Street. I was a year in hostel, they put all Italian girls all together. It was a big, big house, oh lovely, Eh like it, great.
>
> After work finish, paid off. They beena close. All the Italian[s] went away. Everybody got married or went away back Italy.
>
> Eh got my husband first day Eh work in the mill. Eh start work Baxter's. The stoor went on my clothes. When he sees me, him rush in front a me, started clean [the stoor off me], every dinner-time, every night-time. I started friendship. Eh no understand one word he says. He learn Italian so that he can speak to me.

Her future husband was a mechanic in the mill and her job as a spinner often brought them into contact. Although she felt that she had been accepted by her workmates, when she announced she was to marry attitudes changed.

194

Because people wanted [him] to get married [to] a girl from here. Ooh, much trouble. Oh really bad, 'cos my husband every day he gonna bring me something, puts [it] up top of my machine, maybe cakes or maybe clothes, something put every day. One parcel top of da machine where me work. These girls very angry because jealous lot.

First week married I cook Italian, beena cook macaroni. He say, 'Oh I no like.' Eh say, 'Look you no like my food, Eh never goona cook again, che [if] you wanta eat you cook, I eat with you.' He did it his ways always, him cook, he eat again.

My husband died in '64. Thirteen year married, 'avuto [I had] now five children. Been start again work, Eh work Caird's this time . . . Hawkhill. Boss de Caird's comin' up de house, see me, said, 'No use for you to cry your life, him died, no comin' back, you must need to start work.'

Interviewing older people involves certain hazards. On the day I visited Gina she offered me a glass of strega. This home-made, harmless looking, drink, although delicious, is not recommended for those who wish to keep a clear mind. She also makes wonderful Italian meals, but she is a Dundonian. Gina retains her southern-Italian dialect, but she now speaks with an accent that could only be from Dundee. Like other women in the city she has a great strength of character. This strength was also commented on by Bella Keyser when she compared women in Dundee and Holland.

There wis Dutch attitude tae life; the difference between theirs and mine. Eh wis a Dundee woman, and Eh think that says a lot when ye say a Dundee woman, because ye wir a weaver, and the sayin' was, 'Marry a weaver and she could always keep herself'. When unemployment came a weaver could always keep the family. This wis yer value in life, this wis your value as a person, your ability to earn. Eh'm afraid when Eh went tae Holland the women in Holland didnae work. Their value was in bein' able tae knit and tae sew, and tae clean, and tae be a willing servant tae papa. Papa come in from work, and it was, 'Get out o' that chair papa's been earnin' pennies fir us all day papa wants tae sit down.' Now you let papa have his cup of coffee first. And the light goes out, because papa's tired. And when ye spoke tae the women it was, 'Meh man said this, and meh man said that.' Eh said, 'Never mind what yer bloody man said, what the hell do you say?'

And then suddenly they wir very friendly. Friendly people, oh, 'Come intae meh house, we're playin' cards on Sunday.' And Eh thought oh good Eh'll get a game o' cairds. No it consisted o' the men sittin' beside the window playin' cards at the table, and the women sittin' knittin'. And Eh said, 'Oh tae hell we this, if he kin play cairds fir relaxation, Eh'm entitled tae relaxation as well.' Eh dinnae look on knittin' as a relaxation, tae me knittin' wis work, a necessity. So Eh'll hiv a game o' cards wi' the men. Then Eh smoked – oh dear, dear – Eh'm afraid it wis

195

Man destroys the city, the Law is forever.
Joseph McKenzie

only whores and comic singers that smoked in these days in Holland.

And they wir very, very, ashamed o' poverty. We wir brought up in workin'-class districts here [in Dundee], and especially during the last Depression, nobody wis ashamed of poverty, because it wasnae a poverty of thir own makin' it was something that hid been forced upon them. There wis no shame in sayin', 'Eh hivnae got twa bob in meh purse'. Or, 'Eh canna go there 'cause Eh dinna hae the money'. Or, 'Eh canna buy this 'cause Eh dinna hae the money'. There wis no shame attached to it, but in Holland there wis.

Many of us, incomers and natives to the city, love our Atlantis of the North. Wolf Rothman* is no exception.

My ties were here, Eh liked Dundee so much. I've been all over, I've been in Rhodes, Gibraltar, America, Canada, Tenerife, an' there's none can compare t' Dundee. Ah thought Dundee wis super. Eh wouldn't leave it, the wife wants me to go to Edinburgh, but Eh said I wouldn't shift [laughing]. My ties are here, everybody knows me, an' I know them. Every morning I meet somebody that I know, but if I went to another town I'd be lost I'd go down the drain.

196

Wee boy, Hawkhill. *Joseph McKenzie*

Conclusion

Festivals are planned, entertainments designed, a new image is manufactured for Dundee. Recent surveys conclude that the city provides a high quality of life for its inhabitants. There are the aims of attracting tourists, yuppies, and investment, but there is an underlying fear amongst Dundonians that the experts of tourism and promotion may well destroy the very reasons why we enjoy life in Dundee. Frankly I would prefer better housing for Dundonians, for example, than more trendy shops by the river. All we may end up with are circuses and no bread. I know there are those who would claim that the two are connected, however there are memories from when Dundee's suburb of Broughty Ferry contained more millionaires per square mile than anywhere else, and mass poverty and deprivation was rife amongst the people who made the wealth.

For me it is the city's people that makes Dundee worth living in. Dundonians have a dry, deprecating, humour. I've heard brilliant music and seen world-class football played here. The typical Dundee response is that they could have played better. There is a high level of expectation, not only in leisure, but in all areas of life. High hopes are balanced with fears for the future. However, pugnacious, critical, and sharp-witted Dundonians will deal with the future in the same way as they have dealt with the past. They will continue to struggle for a better way of living.

Through Darkening Years

A Personal Account – Dundee 1934-46

by GEORGE BRUCE

'All this time the world was growing darker. . . . The war came at last . . . I got a job in the Food Office in Dundee'
Edwin Muir *An Autobiography*

'We live in a period of transition and disintegration . . .'
William Soutar *Faith in the Vernacular*
The Voice of Scotland Vol. 1 No. 1
(June – August 1938)

When I think my way back fifty-five years, to my time of teaching at the Dundee High School these words come first to mind:

> O my dear heart, young Jesus sweet,
> Prepare thy cradle for my spreit,
> And I sall rock thee in my heart,
> And never mair fra thee depart.
>
> But I sall praise thee evermore
> With sangis sweet unto thy gloir;
> The knees of my heart sall I bow,
> And sing this richt Balulalow.

There are several reasons for remembering these lines from Luther's hymn for Christmas Eve, *Vom himel hoch da kom ich her*. First because thanks to the historian, R. L. Mackie, a former pupil of Dundee High School, who selected fourteen of the twenty verses of the poem translated by the brothers Wedderburn for inclusion in his *A Book of Scottish Verse* (1934), I was able to read them to a senior class. Then there was the further significant association with Dundee of the publishers of Wedderburn's *The Guid and Godlie Ballatis* (1567) being natives of the city.

Without doubt I would have drawn the class's attention to the language being the King's Scots, the language of the community of Dundee from which it gained both authority and homeliness. The idea of community then, as now, was much in my mind, for my stay in the city reinforced my awareness of divisions in our society, and the lack of confidence in our own linguistic inheritance and literature.

c. 1760

William Wallace was not the only famous Scot to be sent to Dundee for his education. The Scots poet Burns described as his 'elder brother in the muse', Robert Ferguson won a scholarship bursary to Dundee Grammar School and spent two years there in the early 1760s, before proceeding to St Andrews University. Here is a passage from one of his poems in English, 'The Rivers of Scotland'.

Where birks at Nature's call arise;
Where fragrance hails the vaulted skies;
Where my own oak its umbrage spreads,
Delightful 'midst the woody shades;
Where ivy-mouldering rocks entwines;
Where breeezes bend the lofty pines:
There shall the laughing Naiads stray,
'Midst the sweet banks of winding Tay.

From the dark womb of earth Tay's waters spring,
Ordain'd by Jove's unalterable voice;
The sounding lyre celestial muses string;
The choiring songsters in the groves rejoice.

Each fount its crystal fluids pours,
Which from surrounding mountains flow;
The river bathes its verdant shores;
Cool o'er the surf the breezes blow.

Let England's sons extol their gardens fair;
Scotland may freely boast her generous streams;
Their soil more fertile, and their milder air;
Her fishes sporting in the solar beams.
Thames, Humber, Severn, all must yield the bay
To the pure streams of Forth, of Tweed, and Tay.

Chorus
Thames, Humber, Severn, all must yield the bay
To the pure streams of Forth, of Tweed, and Tay.

199

This failure of confidence in what should have been part of ourselves was demonstrated by there being no regular place in the curriculum for teaching the Medieval Makars. This was not ultimately the school's fault. The general view, reflected in the subjects selected for discussion in the Higher Leaving Certificate English Literature papers, was that Scottish literature must be treated as subsidiary to the greater merit of English literature. The idea of excellence, not relevance to an inheritance was the test. Although there was also a place for the Scottish ballads and Burns, and in prose Scott and Stevenson, in the Higher, of the middle and late thirties the focus in literature was mainly on the great English writers, Shakespeare of course, the Romantics, and Chaucer. This was splendid material, humanising and enlarging, and, to judge by my relations many years later with former pupils, something of the spirit of this great literature was conveyed at least to some. Still, I felt that, with Mackie's book available, room should have been made for a course beginning from the Medieval Makars. This was allowed for two-years classes after the Highers. There was no compulsion on the pupils to make marks, and so some pupils attended out of curiosity or interest.

At the end of one of my readings to the class, a girl, who had never interrupted or taken part in discussion about literature before – she was to take a science degree – got to her feet and made an explosive protest. I would like to think it came at the end of my reading Barbour's famous apostrophe, 'A! Freedom is a nobil thing,' but I suspect it came after I had uttered lines from Henryson's *Testament of Cresseid*. They come at the point when Troilus, as hero, riding past the group of lepers of which the stricken Cresseid is one, has a flash of recognition of his former loved-one:

And with ane blenk it cam in til his thocht
That he sometime her face before had seen.

'Why,' said the voice of Miss Robertson, loud with indignation, 'did we not have this before?' Why indeed! But not only had the class 'not had it before', but it would not have it again after this year, for study for the Bursary Competition thereafter had to take precedence, and in it there were no questions about the Makars. Neither were there any, I believe, about the greatest poet to attend Dundee High School, Robert Fergusson, who was there on a bursary gained on leaving the High School of Edinburgh. It was Fergusson's achievement to give a renewed vitality to poetry in Scots, to keep in being that strand of spoken Scots which belonged to his people present and past: and which may have spoken to a girl long after we had ceased to have a whole community.

In Dundee I felt the divisions in the community in several ways, as I had not felt them in Aberdeen where, for short

Dundee High School, Athletics Union 1895.
Private collection

Dundee High School. Outdoor Sketching class, possibly Wormit 1896.
Private collection

periods, I had also taught. Aberdeen, and Aberdeenshire more-so, was slow in acquiring those social boundaries regularly referred to as 'working class' and 'middle class'. One reason for this may be accounted for by John R. Allan's phrase, 'Everyone had an auntie in the country'. The city did have the Grammar School which was felt to be socially superior for it was then fee-paying, but only in a small way. I discovered, however, when I was a student at Aberdeen University, that though there was less dialect in the speech than in that spoken in school in my native Fraserburgh, the special Aberdeenshire mode of utterance was used throughout, just as there was a common attitude towards 'education'. Even the 'dunderheads', to use the old-fashioned word, though their energies were directed towards physical pursuits – mainly rugby – respected it. Boring, and out of touch with the realities of life, their teachers might be, but the students did not doubt they believed in what they taught. Not so, to my disenchantment, I discovered in Dundee.

I still remember the shock of the sudden blow delivered with absolute cynical confidence – for so the words felt to me – when a pupil, whom I had met in the street by chance after school, said: 'Shakespeare – I know why you teach Shakespeare: you do it for the money.' I had that afternoon, given my all to demonstrate the marvel of one of Shakespeare's plays. The single defeat was nothing, and the attitude was untypical amongst the pupils, but, I think, it indicated a wider malaise – a belief in money. I recollect now the small boy, whom I did not teach but who knew my habit of leaving the school by a side door and who knew me through an elder brother, would wait in his chauffeur-driven limousine – a Daimler, I think – and then from the back seat lean forward, give a sharp salute, and then nod to the chauffeur, who closed the door, and drove off. There was nothing sinister and no ill was intended, but I and others were being placed in a class. This blindness to our common humanity was in sharp contrast to the general responsiveness and pursuit of excellence allied to respect, and to my surprise, affection, which I was to discover later, during my teaching career at Dundee High School. I did not know then, that a number of these pupils would occupy the highest places in Scotland in the professions of law and medicine, in the Church, as academics and outwith these areas. No one other than themselves can take credit for achievements requiring ability and character, but they attended a school in which there was a general seriousness about learning beyond the requirement of examination passes.

If some kind of wholeness was achieved in the school, admitting a repugnance to the values implied in moneyed quarters, outside, the rift between wealth and poverty in the 1930s was all too evident. Hugh MacDiarmid wrote about the city with characteristic ferocity in 1934:

The Girl's High School. *McKean*

Henry Scrymger (A Dundee Scholar)

Dundee had an established reputation for producing Latin scholars and writers of distinction. Douglas Young – poet, polymath and classicist – here describes the career of Henry Scrymger, one of the great Greek scholars of the later Middle Ages.

George Buchanan is the most famous Scottish Humanist, not only for his mastery of the Latin tongue – he was reckoned throughout Europe the foremost Latin poet of the Renaissance – but for the intrinsic interest of the works he used it for, his polemical history of Scotland and the rest. But in the same year, 1506, in which Buchanan was born, Scotland produced also a greater scholar and a better man, Henry Scrymger, a Hellenist, whose merits have been forgotten because he was less of a publicist and politician than the eminent Latinist.

He was born at Dundee, a city now celebrated for the production of marmalade and jute-products, but in the sixteenth century a centre of the linen trade, with a considerable commerce to the Low Countries and the Baltic. His father was Walter Scrymger, Provost of Dundee, and Laird of Glasswell, near Kirriemuir in the county of Angus, a cadet of the Scrymgers of Dudhope, hereditary standard-bearers to the Kings of Scots, and constables of Dundee. The young Henry went to study in the college of St Salvator in the University of St Andrews, where Greek studies may have been beginning to creep in. Alelxander Stewart, Archbishop of St Andrews, who fell at Flodden with his

201

royal father, had learned Greek from Erasmus about 1508, with whom he visited Padua, Siena, and Naples. Hector Boece, born in Dundee in 1465-6, son of an Angus laird, had also enjoyed the friendship of Erasmus, who dedicated to him one of his works. Another Angus man, George Dempster from Brechin, had been Professor of Philosophy in 1495 at Pavia, one of the Italian cities which paid professors of Greek. So that some interest in Greek may have been kindled in Scrymger already in Scotland. But the first eminent Grecian he came in contact with was at Bourges, whither he had repaired to study law: no less than Amyot, afterwards Cardinal, from whose version of Plutarch North made the famous translation which so much influenced Shakespeare. Through Amyot's introduction Scrymger became secretary to the Bishop of Rennes, ambassador of Francis I to certain North Italian states. At Padua he met the eminent Francesco di Spira, known as The Apostate, who had favoured the Reformation of the Church, but afterwards recanted, only to repent his recantation on his death-bed, in the most terrible agony of spirit.

This encounter put Scrymger about in his religious opinions: moreover, he must have been influenced by such events in Scotland as the burning of Patrick Hamilton in St Andrews for his reformist views, and by the movement of opinion in his native Dundee, which a few years later was to be the first city in Scotland to set up Presbytery. Accordingly he left the service of the Bishop of Rennes, and withdrew to Geneva, where he became Professor of Philosophy. About the same time he published a narrative on the Apostate Spira (Geneva, 1549).

Meantime he came to the notice of the millionaire patron of classical scholarship Ulrich Fugger, of Augsburg, and for ten years collected books and manuscripts at his expense, from Italy, Germany and France, till he had a notable library. His practice was to send collations of manuscripts, together with his emendations and interpretations, to another pensioner of Ulrich Fugger, the publisher Robert Stephanus in Paris, *typographus regius*, and from 1551 in Geneva, who duly printed them in the series of classical texts he was issuing. Voluminous and important authors whose texts owe a great deal to Scrymger include Herodotus, Thucydides, Xenophon, Demosthenes, Strabo, Plutarch, Athenaeus, and Eusebius. His most famous editorial contribution was a recension of Strabo based on some nine manuscripts, a remarkably large number for that period, especially with so lengthy an author. Two generations after Scrymger's death the librarian of the Vatican, Holstenius, wrote to Peiresc (in 1628), that he had never seen a collation of such *diligentia* and never looked at the book without *stupor*. Scrymger seems to have

Dundee is the most appalling example in Scotland of the results of the Manchester School of Economics, the policy of *laissez-faire*. . . . Dundee is a great industrial cul-de-sac – a grim monument to 'Man's inhumanity to man'. In Glasgow the horrible slums are masked by the multifarious activities and bustle of a great city, and Glasgow, moreover, badly hit though it has been, had never 'had all its eggs in one basket' to the extent that Dundee had. There is nothing in Dundee to mask its utter degradation.

The condemnation, up to a point, was fair comment. A young minister who came to Dundee in the late thirties remarked that in the city one week he might be visiting houses with eighteen rooms inhabited by two people, and the following week the pattern was reversed with appalling overcrowding in two rooms, sometimes without wallpaper. In such an area – he was referring to the Overgate, though there were other places – the first requirement was a torch, not for night-use, but on account of the darkness in the houses during the day. In 1935 as I made my way to the High School I saw groups of men at street corners. There was an air of depression and defeat about them. My father-in-law on his first visit was surprised at 'how small they all were'. Arriving at school one immediately felt the contrast, though it was untrue to look on the school as a haven for the wealthy – the range of occupations of the parents (and therefore the range of income) gave the lie to this simplification. Here were minds open to a variety of points of view, and capable of dialogue. But outside, the inequalities and injustice of the society – and the remark goes wider than Dundee – were all too evident.

I had a conversation with a jute-worker. She had been in the mills for forty years and she had never been paid more than £1 a week. MacDiarmid asked me for a poem for this new quarterly, the *Voice of Scotland*. I wrote, 'Jute Spinner'.

> What is it makes that shuttle fly?
> Not ultimately the stroke of a uniformed engine,
> Nor the subtle project of a capital enterprise.
> What is it makes that shuttle fly?
> Not a high voltage,
> Nor current transmitted from a central store,
> But every strand woven,
> Every strand forced in
> Warp and weft
> Moves in its intricacy
> From her nerves and bones and blood.

MacDiarmid wrote me: 'This is just what we want,' but I went no further with this kind of writing, not that I or any other professionals could influence this exploitation.

The people were vulnerabe to other types of exploitation, too. This was the time when attractive 'HP' terms were offered for

Dundee High School, *McKean*

gone much ahead of his time in making a comprehensive accurate recension.

But his chief business was Law, and in 1558 he published over his own name the first volume of an edition of Justinian's Novels (*Novellae Constitutiones*). About 1563/4 he settled again in Geneva, becoming Professor of Civil Law there, and a considerable local grandee. He was in close association with Calvin, whose testament he witnessed. In 1572 the Earl of Mar, Regent of Scotland, invited him to return home and supervise the education of the young king, James VI, but Scrymger declined, his letter in Court Scots to Mar being a most interesting specimen of the literary Scots prose of that day, in which the Bible might have been translated if there had not been already on the market intelligible and relatively cheap English versions. Later that same year, 1572, he died, like Lambinus, of horror at the news of the Massacre of St Bartholomew's Day. How strong he was in law may be judged from the statement of the leading French jurist of the time, Cujas (Cujacius), that he never left Scrymger's company without having learned something from him.

All Scrymger's library, with its manuscripts and *editiones principes*, including no doubt incunabula, came to Scotland, surely the most important collection of the kind ever to reach those somewhat barbarous shores, as a bequest to his sister's son, Sir Peter Young, another Dundee man (1544 to 1628/9), who was then acting as tutor to James VI, and was later, as ambassador to Denmark, to arrange the royal marriage with Anne of Denmark, incurring among other perils the distressful voyage on which Sir Patrick Spens was drowned, theme of the great ballad.

'wireless sets'. One firm got over a hundred pounds for the sale and re-sale of a single set valued originally at £8 to £10, by allowing regular payments to lapse and then seizing the set. All perfectly legal. Another ploy was with carpet cleaners of the Hoover order. One woman was persuaded to buy a carpet cleaner when all she had in her tenement flat was a rug, the other floor-coverings being linoleum. A small body was formed to combat the slick salesmanship. We put leaflets through doors in Hawkhill where the reps. had been active, giving elementary advice: 'Don't sign anything for twenty-four hours after you have been approached', ending with, 'If you are in doubt consult us.' We had a lawyer on the committee. It was a miniscule effort. The social malaise was wide and deep.

Accustomed to freedom of discussion, and actions arising from decisions made on this basis, we felt increasingly impotent and frustrated as we became aware of the autocratic power of the Dundee press as it expressed itself in dictats to employees. Members of staff were not permitted to join the Scottish Typographical Association. Whether or not there was a clause forbidding the publication of writing in any form outwith the press I do not know, but William Blain, a journalist with the press told me that on the publication of his novel, *Witch's Blood*, (now happily acclaimed in Dundee) he was summoned by the boss, rebuked, and told that he would be dismissed if there was any further extra-mural publication. There were surprising restrictions 'within the walls'.

J. B. Salmond, editor of the *Scots Magazine*, was taken with the verse narration I had written for my feature programme, *Buchan Fisherman*, broadcast on the BBC Home Service, produced by Robert Kemp. He asked my permission to publish the narration in the *Scots Magazine*, which I readily gave. Some time later I received an urgent message requesting me to see the editor immediately. Salmond was in a state of abject fear. He had forgotten there was a rule forbidding the publication of any work which had been broadcast. He told me he could lose his job over this, and that at sixty it would be very hard to find work. I calmed him and told him I would not be in the least put-out if the narration was not published. There the matter ended but I found the thought of this good man of recognised ability – he was later to be awarded an LLD from his Alma Mater, St Andrews University – so reduced in dignity, very distressing. He had already written *Wade in Scotland* (1934), a book which is regarded as the standard work on General Wade's roads and bridges in the Scottish Highlands. I had reason to be grateful to him for he gave, in the *Scots Magazine*, the first publication of poems which I was to include in my first collection, *Sea Talk*.

More significant was the material help Salmond gave to Neil Gunn in publishing essays, plays, serialised novels and short stories. He was especially helpful after Neil Gunn gave up his

Civil Service job and became a freelance writer. Lewis Grassic Gibbon also benefited from publication by Salmond, who before this had also published a story by Hugh MacDiarmid. The *Scots Magazine* is not generally thought of as an avant-garde publication, but it made a significant contribution to sustaining the 'Scottish Renaissance'. I find it gratifying to think of an office in Bank Street, Dundee, owned by D. C. Thomson & Co. Ltd, making this provision. Fundamentally the *Scots Magazine* is a popular magazine – a magazine of the people – but when it publishes essays of the quality of Neil Gunn's, their interest as literature remains something to which Alistair McCleery's selection of essays by Neil Gunn in his *Landscape and Light* (1987) bears witness. While the magazine covers a wide spectrum of Scottish culture, it has a special interest in Scottish history. It is itself part of that history and, with the centenary of the birth of J. B. Salmond in 1991, the magazine has cause for celebration.

A main contribution of Dundee to Scottish literature may be in sustaining and popularising literature. The Reverend George Gilfillan, minister of School Wynd Church, included in his *oeuvre* the editing and modernisation of the work of British poets, from earliest times to the mid-nineteenth century. The edition ran to over forty volumes between 1853 and 1866, and included selections of poems by Barbour, Henryson, James I and Gavin Douglas.

Something of the responsiveness of a Dundee audience to poetry came through to me when I was taking an evening-class, under the auspices of the WEA consisting entirely of post-office apprentices. I read them *Tam o' Shanter*. The poem received an ecstatic reception. The liberating function of poetry had possessed them. It was not their Scots they were hearing but the language was near enough to destroy the barriers which formal English put up. They had never heard of the poem before, which surprised me until I discovered from the general manager of Taybank Jute Works that the poem was on the Roman Catholic Index, and therefore banned to members of that Church, to which almost the entire class belonged.

In 1946 Hogarth published *Scottish Nursery Rhymes*, a collection of rhymes and songs made by William and Norah Montgomerie. The collection contained rhymes from all over Scotland but William Montgomerie was a teacher in a primary school in Dundee at the time and this played such a significant part in his interest that he returned many years later to record games and songs in the playground of Hilltown Primary School. The reward was rich in the variety, invention and the sense of belonging in the songs.

When the printer of Dundee High School magazine invited me to suggest a book for publication in 1945, I thought of the uncollected poems of the Aberdeenshire poet John C. Milne who wrote in Aberdeenshire Scots, and so George E. Findlay, 6–8

54 Hilltown. *Dundee District Libraries*

Victoria Road, Dundee, published *The Orra Loon*. At the centre of the book is the 'orra loon', the boy who does all the odd jobs on the farm:

Pu'in *neeps*, wi' hackit hans,	TURNIPS
Scrapin' dubs and *sharny* kye,	SHITTEN
Howkin holes te *beery nowt*,	BURY CATTLE
Reddin' midden-drains forbye.	TIDYING

The dialect may be far removed from Dundee but the appreciation of common humanity and its plight, and of innocence, speaks of the community at the foot of the pile, and draws all together. Such a drawing together is achieved by those whose human concern crosses the boundaries of class or money. Such a one was Neil Leitch, general manager of Taybank Jute Works, one of the Scottish Co-operatives' enterprises, better known in Dundee as 'The Sosh'. Neil had risen from office boy, and as he took me through the works introducing me to whoever was near and momentarily disengaged from work, there was no doubt that here was a community of friends. Neil was an elder in St Paul's Church in the Nethergate, not far from the Overgate, in which it had its Mission. 'Why should there be such a Mission?' I asked. The answer was given that its people felt they could not dress sufficiently well. They did not have the money. They would go as a group, however, which Neil Leitch arranged. This was not the perfect answer, but it was the best that could be done. This the minister, the Very Reverend Dr James L. Weatherhead, understood.

A poem of Rilke's includes several repetitions of the line 'to make *one* thing'. To homologate diverse elements into a single whole or harmony has been a preoccupation of all major artists. It might have been the reason for the sense of peace pervading the atmosphere of the art room in the school, though the pupils had a simpler objective. On one occasion the principal art teacher had put on one of the walls a reproduction of a black and white Picasso print. The Rector entered the room, saw the Picasso, and ordered T. S. Halliday, the artist and Head of the Department to remove what he considered to be 'rubbish'. It stayed where it was until the next class arrived, which was told to 'do something like it in black and white'. They did it with abandon. The Rector returned and found himself confronted by some twenty-five Picassos. 'Could he,' asked Mr Halliday, 'pick out the original Picasso?' It had been moved to take its place alongside the drawings by the aspiring artists. He could. He did. But how far he grasped the presence of genius in the power of the Picasso is not known. Curiously, and sadly, I attended a lecture on modern art given by a journalist-artist. He explained that all the great art in the past had always been eminently saleable – Michaelangelo, etc. So Van Gogh, Cezanne *et al.* were not real artists nor were those who followed them. The great artists of our day were those who made money from their work. He showed as evidence a poster-picture of the 'Gibson Girls'. The audience applauded. I left.

That philistinism existed in this area in Dundee in the thirties was surprising, though it indicates the desire of commercial interests to take over the arts, and to deny integrity to those practitioners who had a different valuation of the objectives of the arts. It was surprising because Dundee was strong in artists of quality at the time. Even MacDiarmid in his defamatory sketch of Dundee noted: 'Dundee has long been the centre of a struggling colony of Scottish artists – men like Stewart Carmichael, Walter Grieve, David Foggie . . .' I restrict my focus to those with whom I associated at the High School, all of whom had distinctive talents. Cadzow was an etcher of such ability that his etchings were acquired by the National Gallery of Scotland. He was followed by T. S. Halliday as Head of the Art Department. Halliday, retired as early as was possible: when he was offered two commissions for stained-glass windows. Five windows in St Mary's Church are by Halliday, and five in St Peter's McCheyne. Halliday's most individual achievement, however, is in sculpture in wood. It is in this art that his ability has been most noticed – in awards and honours from Italy. In 1988 he was elected a Member of the Contemporary Art Society of Milan – '*Accademico d'Italia con Medaglia d'Oro*', the citation reads.

Blackscroft. *Dundee District Libraries*

Colin Gibson was also in the department at the time of my arrival in 1934. He is probably best known in Dundee for his weekly article in the *Courier*, 'Nature Diary', which has run for thirty-six years. This is one way of bringing the country into town. The 'wholeness' of the man was recently acknowledged in an Honorary Degree of MSc from Dundee University. One might see in this, as in other related successes, a symbolic healing of the rifts created by a disintegrated society. By their nature, by their need to be whole, artists – I include all kinds – feel such strains excessively. Certainly, in 1938, Colin Gibson found it necessary to give up teaching for a time. He returned to make *The New Furrow*, a book from his drawings, mainly scraperboard, of the natural world in Angus, drawings of great intensity, and especially an intensity of light, for which I wrote an Introduction in which I said:

> . . . these drawings state a belief in slow natural processes, in the beauty in man's relations with his natural environment. We are at the commonplaces of country life. The balance in the sketches is more than a juxtaposition of objects. It is as well the outcome of an inner certainty.

This was a dawning at a time when the darkness of terrible evil threatened all civilized living. The Perth poet, William Soutar, responded to the abomination of the bombing of Guernica with a poem, 'The Children', which begins: 'On the street they lie.' It was the right, bare language for the ocasion. I met William

207

Montgomerie. We talked about making poems, about the right words, the right idiom. But what could survive? Community. My mind went to my origins, to the community in the port of Fraserburgh of

> Seamen and craftsmen and curers,
> And behind them
> The protest of hundreds of years,
> The sea obstinate aganst the land.

When my first collection of poems, *Sea Talk*, was published, I was a teacher in Dundee. The subject might not have anything to do with Dundee but the tautness and kinesthetic character of the language I had in my ear from my poem 'Jute Spinner'. In any case I was not celebrating something far off but courage, endurance, adaptability. Confidence that I had gone in the right direction, and help in the publication of some of the poems came from Bill Montgomerie. He, too, was engaged in dialogue with himself on issues of style. His solution, I think, came later.

The Montgomeries lived in Broughty Ferry. Norah heard tell of the old fishing community and of the whalers, from a woman whose people had belonged to that community. Bill got to know lifeboat men. He wrote a poem, 'Lifeboat Disaster (April 1960)'. It is dedicated 'To James Coull, Coxswain'. At the end the place is named, Broughty Ferry. It describes the disaster of that year; it commemorates the men who lost their lives: it honours their courage. In this it honours the community which produced them. It was a whole community. In telling the tale – the tale seems to tell itself – it is the right way to do it. Here are a few lines from the poem:

> I have stood by you
> Coxswain James Coull
> at your wheel
> your two hands relaxed
> your knees lax
> would tense like a boxer's
> when the feint and the knock-out come together
> when the feint and the knock-out were two waves
> almost together
> countered on the wheel
> by your hair-trigger fingertips
> ere your brain knew
> a skill coiled and oiled
> in hands and arms
> in thirty storms in twenty-five years
> that brought a hundred lives and more
> ashore
> to hot tea and baps in the kirk hall
> a skill not to be learned in five weeks.

Brown Ochre on the Crumbling Walls. Joe Paterson's house, Taylor's Lane. *Dundee Art Galleries and Museums*

JOSEPH PATERSON'S STORY

Joe Paterson lived in Douglas until his sad death in 1991. His childhood was spent in the city's West End where the poor and the wealthy lived cheek by jowl. That background was explored by Joe in his paintings, his models, his writing, and his words. What emerged from all of these was that very Dundonian mell of nostalgia and stark social realism. In Joe's case it was also infused with love for Dundee and Scotland.

Well, my full name is Joseph Paterson, I was born 28 November 1920, Taylor's Lane, 34 Taylor's Lane. And that was one of the first things I heard as a kid, very, very young – was the mill bummer. That's the hooter calling the people to work. Used to wake up in a darkened room and you could see the chinks of the gaslight through the door as yir mother was preparing to go to work.

Oh how often ma mother told me she's went to work on a cup o' hot water: they didn't even have a drop o' tea in the house, you know . . . Run short of funds halfway through the week sort of thing, marking time until they'd got the wage . . .

My father was an invalid, from the First World War. He was badly gassed; he died when he was 45, you know. There was very few of them reached 50 – the boys, naebody who'd had a bellyful of gas. When I think of ma mother wi oor mob, wi an invalid husband, and she worked as a spinner. And she wasnae unique, I mean there was – I mean six in a family was what you called a genteel, small family. I mean all my mates had masses of brothers and sisters you know . . . We went tae school in bare feet an everything. Well that released the worry of trying to provide footwear for the summer. And I run barefoot from May right through until October one year. And I remember walking down the Blackness Road – ah've told the kids about this, an 'Och, you're kidding Dad.' – 'No, ah'm not kidding.' – I held up meh, my foot and caught a snowflake on it and watched it melt on my foot. And then coming up for the cold weather ma mother would go an put hirsel in debt. We'd all get wellingtons out of some credit-shop, thi were called the packie-man, you know. These were lovely and shiny and I liked the smell of the new rubber off them you know. I remember when I got the first pair one year, when I came back from school ma mother kicked up ructions. 'Wha' ye doing in yir bare feet?' – Ah says, 'Ah don't want to get ma wellies dirty!'

209

The Lichtie Nichts. Joe Paterson. *Dundee Art Galleries and Museums*

First Encounter with the Inevitable 1923. Joe Paterson. *Dundee Art Galleries and Museums*

Food

Ye got a rabbit, wi its claes on, fur thruppence! Then ye got a sheep's head fur, sometimes fur nothing ye got it fur – we often had that. An then uh a great part of wir diet was Icelandic dried fish. It came in slabs, square slabs, tied with white string – it was a sort of reddish colour, and that was as hard as a brick too, you know. They jist threw you a block over the counter.

Very rarely got cakes except they were aulders. An that was the – the aulders were when ye went to the baker – the baker in oor area, Neave, was open at half-past four fur, as we called them, the aulders, the old stuff. An they dished out all their yesterday's an the day before's confectionery an bread an everything. It depended on the size of the receptacle you brought wi ye, ye could get it full, you know, some pillercases, baskets. They just brought in these boards an heaped it all in. Ye got angel-cakes that wer' so fossilised ye could belt them off the wall withoot chipping them, you know. But she, our mother seemed to have a magic touch at rejuvenating the bread and athing you know.

School

We're sitting there bare feet, shivering – they were nae very well heated these schools either you know.

An 'Now boys,' she says; she wheeked out the map and showed us a map of Scotland. First she says, 'Now this is Scotland.' 'Oh that's fine we're nearly as big as England ken.' But she says, 'Although the land area is comparable to England,' she says, 'there's more sheep than people. An she says, 'From here, from the Tay upwards,' she says, 'it's literally a desert, no good for anything.'

Well I felt deflated and angry you know. An then she shows us the map and says, 'All the bits marked red belong to us.' And I says, 'How am I sitting here taking side leaps with hunger if that's the case?' you know. [Laughs] The Empire! – The only contribution we were allowed to make was the unemployed get dressed up in kilts and go out the Khyber Pass!

Sense of community

As ah say, thir was an awful lot that was bad about the period, as far as actual conditions were concerned, you know. Nobody would like to see a return to that, but we've lost a lot on the way.

Well in these days, Dundee was, in my opinion, a collection of villages. And wir village wis, as far as we were concerned, stretched say from the Sinderins to Bellefield, (Beyond that was another community.) And south towards the Magdalen Green and north towards Blackness Road. And everybody if they didn't know one another by name they knew the person by sight, as you would in a village, you know, fair-sized village.

Oh as I say – in this drawing here – the *Lichtie Nichts when Neebor Wives coloquered.* After they had their evening chores done, an it were a good night, they'd all be out sitting on the stairs roond about. Och I remember them getting the pipes out on the back green and the old gramophone and doing the old shoteesh and reels. And sometimes there'd be a drunken rammie now 'n' again to liven the place up, an – but never anything vicious ye know – usually sorted out alright.

And then the beggars of coorse. Ye had the beggars that came up, and quite a lot of them were ex-servicemen. And thi were very rarely given enough money – people didn't ha money to give them. Ah've often come from school and seen a beggar sitting in the lobby wi a bowl of soup and a piece of bread that my mither's given him, ye know.

So it was a pretty close community, and pretty deprived, but we didn't think we were particularly puir cos everybody was in the same boat. It was only when ye sort of wandered into the more salubrious parts of the town ye realised just how poor ye were.

Illness

And uh you had this periodic visitations of diphtheria. An ah remember a couple o kids dying wi it, ye know, yir wee contemporaries, taken o'er to see them, ye know, lying in a wee white coffin. Ah remember a wee Polish girl died o' TB . . .

I wisnae even at the school at the time, I was just a toddler. And I used to be allowed to sit in the lobby. My father rigged me up and put me oot there. She used to come out the stairhead toilet ye know. And her and I became great friends.

I thought she was a woman, I thought she was a 'wifie' – she was only fourteen! She was emaciated, ye know, thin. And when my father released me I used to run along an jist barge in there, an she'd be in bed on her own. And that's how poor that room was! There was the bare minimum – a bed, couple o' chairs, a wee kitchen table, a fire, a ring, an whit have ye. And it was tiny. That was actually underneath the garret stairs, so part of this bed recess was sloping, ye know. So I used to talk away to her, an everything.

211

And uh my mother says to me, 'You'd better stop going to see yir Mary.' . . . I was a wee bit hurt as if I'd done something wrong, but I let it pass an forgot about it. An then I don't know how long it was after that, it couldn't have been all that long: uh, I was playing out, my mother picked me up. She says 'You of all people should see this.'

So she brought me in and here's Mary lying on the bed like that – oh, beautifully dressed. It was the first time I'd ever seen a dead body, you know . . . It was a south-facing window, and the light coming through – this was the family crucifix, it was the best-looking thing in the house, lovely piece of wood and a lovely sculpted brass figure of Christ. Oh I was shivering a bit because the light from the window hit the brass and it was reflected up into her face and – oh, yellow ken, what. And I shuddered a wee bit you know. But as I say, that was the first time I'd ever seen a dead person and realised [that you had to die].

Looking back

Ah remember one bloke was discussing these things, an this, strangely enough, red-hot Tory upholsterer, working-class man, he says, 'You're not exaggerating a wee bit, Joe?'

Ah says, 'Ah'm not exaggeratiang in the least.' Ah says, 'It's your type,' Ah says, 'You prefer to forget that, an pretend it never happened. You think there's some sort of stigma attached to it.' Ah says, 'Ah'm bloody proud of it, to think I survived it.' Ah says, 'Ah'm proud of it!' Ah says, 'when I look back,' Ah says, 'to survive, and never have to put a foot wrong, if you like, as far as getting in trouble with the law, or being able to lead a fairly honest, straightforward, down-to-earth life even after all that!'

Joe's Dundee childhood between the wars is summed up in this poem:

Land Fit for Heroes

The empires licht shone roond the globe
Yet the open midden reigned
While trauchled wives and shillpit bairns
Wi' money ills were pained,
The 'but an' ben' and the 'single end'
Were the order o' the day,
The heroes o' the 'fourteen waar'
Could'na mak' a pay.

Throughoot the lan' sneaked the means-test man
Tae tally ilka maik,
Leavin' a trail o' fear and woe
Tremblin in his wake
Twas the day o' the backcoort chanter
And the drinker o' the 'feak'
The begger at the 'beggers door'
His bowl o' soup tae seek,
Yet a' the while the barefuit bairns
Played merrily through the wynds
Sae young sae young, sae ower young
Tae really fash or mind.

maik – halfpenny   *feak* – 'meth' spirit
trauchled – troubled   *fash* – bother
shillpit – under-nourished   *'but an ben'* – two
                            rooms

Joe Paterson at home in Douglas, 1990. *Ken Sharp*

212

The Lochee Factor?!

Sport in Dundee

by JIM WILKIE

Liz McColgan is a deceptively-tall young woman whose fashion style could easily be mistaken for that of an advertising executive or banker. Grinding as such jobs may occasionally be, however, they surely cannot compare with the professional routine of athletics, a discipline so exacting, its ultimate rewards are usually received in a physical and mental haze as the human body goes faster – in her case – than that of any other female distance-runner in the world.

Liz's parents come originally from Lochee, a self-contained, hard-working community whose independence from Dundee is still assiduously maintained, 150 years after its industrial transformation by the jute-owning Cox family. Such was the level of Irish immigration that part of this 'dark village' became known as 'Tipperary' and, as late as the 1930s, Liz's father was the only child of an immigrant family *not* to have been born in County Sligo. By a curious coincidence, the mother of another world-beating athlete, Daley Thompson, also came originally from Lochee. In recent years, we have heard much of the predominance of the African genetic factor in world athletics. In times to come, will sporting historians be compelled to examine the Dundee, sorry, Lochee factor?

Liz McColgan, back home after winning the Commonwealth Gold, 1990. *Copyright D. C. Thomson & Co. Ltd*

I gave up my own sporting ambition some time ago. In the late fifties and sixties, however, it seemed that in my immediate circle of friends we thought about little else. Our arena was Baxter Park and we were there at every available opportunity, dawn till dusk, playing football mostly, an occasional game of cricket, and tennis in summer at the corporation courts which boasted a thriving club in those days. Sport was very democratic. There were territorial allegiances, of course, largely determined by which street you came from or which gate you entered the park by. But as different sides were picked every night on merit, class distinction counted for little and I can think of a whole range of boys from the area who went on to play football at a senior level. The park also had a way of introducing us to the natural world. The glorious smell of new-cut grass, or the sight of great flocks of birds heading south for the winter, could virtually stop a game in progress. This was surely the Greek ideal – a healthy mind in a healthy body – and there was no reason for us to think that such an idyllic existence would ever end.

Even when we progressed to the more cynical world of spectator sport, Dundee still appeared to hold the aces. George Kidd was a world wrestling champion, Dick McTaggart was declared the greatest amateur boxing stylist in the world at the 1956 Melbourne Olympics, Dundee United got promnotion to the First Division in 1960 and, within three years. Dundee FC had won that League and reached the semi-final of the European Cup. Patrick Barclay, a Dundonian and leading football correspondent with the *Observer* newspaper, is fond of quoting a remarkable statistic – that only two British cities, Glasgow and Dundee, have provided two semi-finalists for that great competition. Not Liverpool, Manchester or London, you will notice, and one can also reflect upon the complete failure of Bristol or Bradford's two clubs to reach the heights of even domestic football, never mind the European game. (Indeed, Bradford Park Avenue disappeared altogether, some years ago.)

The story of organised sport in Dundee really begins around the 1870s. There is a marvellous story of Dundee whalers playing a game of football in the Davis Straits in 1875 and being scattered by a brown bear which proceeded to eat the sealskin ball but, generally speaking, organised games had been the prerogative of 'good' schools and universities. With the advent of political, industrial and educational reform, however, the working classes began to find themselves with more leisure time on their hands and more thought to use it creatively.

Initially, the geography of Dundee was not suited to sport, but flat land was being sought for industrial premises, and land reclamation became the policy of the Harbour Board and Town Council. Athletics was popular at this time and closely associated with the newer sport of cycling. Dundee Hawkhill Harriers were founded in 1889 and are still going strong 100 years later. And, on one of the few occasions when the Scottish athletics championships were held outside Glasgow or Edinburgh, in 1892,

Footballers from SS *Active* on Arctic ice, 1894. *Dundee Art Galleries and Museums*

they came to Dundee. Unfortunately the event ended amidst allegations of official corruption.

Once it had separated from the older game of rugby, it was football which captured the imagination of the masses. It was played at every level – East Craigie, for example, are the oldest Scottish junior club in continuous existence – and by the 1890s it had been adopted as the national game, professionalised and subjected to a kind of religious fervour.

Initially, it was the leading team from the city's Irish community, Dundee Harp (f. 1879) which enjoyed most success. However, in 1893, two of its 'Scottish' counterparts – Our Boys (f. 1877) and East End (f. 1877) – amalgamated as Dundee FC and, for the next thirty years, professional football in the city and Dundee FC were synonymous, whilst the 'Irish' team drifted out of existence until it was reconstituted as Dundee Hibs

(f. 1909). Dundee FC had a number of players capped at the turn of the century, won the Scottish Cup in 1910, and by the 1920s boasted an outstanding administrator, William MacIntosh, who became SFA Treasurer. By that time the team had vacated their celebrated Carolina Port stadium (which also played host to cycling and athletics) and moved to their present ground, Dens Park, literally across the street from Tannadice Park, where the Hibs played. This unique state of affairs has been the subject of great interest in the football world ever since.

It is an important point that neither club was ever sectarian in its choice of players and in the 1920s the Tannadice side began to move away from its Irish tradition by appointing a well-known Scottish internationalist (and Protestant), Jimmy Brownlie, as manager, and by changing its name to Dundee United. Dundee responded by raising the stakes commercially.

MacIntosh approached a number of the city's jute barons seeking investment in ground improvements for Dens Park. This further established them as a big club, but the move was ultimately detrimental, for the jute merchants insisted on control and eventually ousted MacIntosh, who proceeded to cross the road and take up a shareholding with United.

The thirties saw Dundee FC in a period of serious decline. In the years which followed the Second Wold War, however, controlling interest passed to a local accountant named James Gellatly and he began to transform the club both in footballing and financial terms. With George Anderson installed as manager, Billy Steel was signed for a Scottish-record transfer fee in 1950, the League Cup came to Dens twice in that decade, and, by the time they had won that League title and reached the semi-final of the European Cup, they were Scotland's most successful club outside the Old Firm of Celtic and Rangers. In a sense, however, they became victims of their own success. A number of ex-Old Firm players were tried as managers and coaches, and a League Cup victory in 1974 has been the only glimmer of light in what has proved to be a very long, dark tunnel for the club. It was financially restructured by chairman Angus Cook in the late eighties – there was even an attempt to 'amalgamate' with United by buying their shares – but all to no avail, and the chairmanship has now passed to a Canadian businessman, Ron Dixon.

United, meanwhile, have rarely had delusions of grandeur. They have gone for continuity of staff, with ex-players becoming directors, and managers being given time. They were quick to appreciate the benefits of club football pools. And they were never blinded by local rivalries. In 1971 they appointed a relatively-young Dundee FC player – Jim MacLean – as coach and assistant to long-term manager, Jerry Kerr. MacLean, who became the longest-serving club manager in British football (and chairman to boot), approached the task by scouring the district for local talent and then developing that talent to its full potential within a flexible team-plan. At one point in the 1980s, they could supply four players to the Scottish national side (Sturrock, Gough, Narey and Malpas) who had cost the club nothing, and their success in European football is legendary. They reached a European Cup semi-final in 1984, and a UEFA Cup final in 1988, following which the club received a special fair-play award.

When Jerry Kerr took over Dundee United they had recently finished in the bottom four of the Scottish Second Division. The ground had a wee wooden stand which pre-dated the First World War and caused at least one fan to vacate his seat because 'every time the ba' hut the roof, ye got covered wi' forky tailies!' For them to have reached the top four in Europe is a remarkable achievement of which all Dundonians should be extremely proud, and the only major Scottish trophy to elude the club, the Scottish Cup, was finally brought to Tannadice by Jim MacLean's successor, Ivan Golac, in 1994.

Alex Stuart is someone who knows a great deal about local rivalry in what he calls this 'football-mad city'. An Aberdonian by birth, he played for both Dundee and United in the sixties and, following ten years in football management, took up the newly-created post of Sports Officer in Dundee, in 1980. 'Both then and now,' he says, 'I could fill all the local facilities with football. There has, however, been a developing public awareness of the place of sport and fitness in society in the last ten years, and more leisure time. It was the will of the local politicians to cater for these changes.'

This meant new facilities, and leisure centres have been built at Kirkton, Lochee and Douglas. Lochee Baths were converted into an exremely popular sports/health centre and squash courts have been built at Finlathen. A new running track was constructed alongside the old model at Caird Park and since Stuart's philosophy – largely shaped by what he had seen in Scandinavia – was to educate and build from the broadest possible community bases, the employment of coaches was also encouraged. In one particularly ambitious move, it was decided to employ Liz McColgan as a Sports Officer; besides acting throughout the world as a sporting ambassador for the city, she is able to offer regular coaching assistance to Dundee youngsters.

Stuart also pays tribute to the local Sports Council which brings together representatives of local sports clubs on a monthly basis. 'Many sports people are blinkered and tend to keep themselves to themselves. The Sports Council, however, has provided the town with a pool of enthusiastic administrators whose assistance has been invaluable for events such as the Kellogg's Cycle Race and the Dundee Marathon.'

Dundee's achievements in community running have indeed been notable. In Jenny Wood Allen they have a world-champion marathon runner in the over-seventies age group, and many's the time I have looked at the racing field in events in other parts

216

of Scotland, or in northern England, and marvelled at the Dundee representation. There have been benefits, too, for the rural hinterland. Forfar Roadrunners, for example, originated from participants in the Dundee events who subsequently organised their own races.

Dundee District coaching now extends to a wide range of sports but there is also great pride in the achievements of the independent clubs, in tennis and golf, hockey, swimming, rugby, bowling, the martial arts – the list of distinction is a long one. The North American influence has also seen the birth in the town of professional ice-hockey and, more recently, American football. Ice-hockey was made popular throughout the UK by Canadian servicemen during the Second World War. Dundee's largely Canadian team – the Tigers – went into decline in 1954, but the sport experienced a resurgence in the seventies, and, in the early eighties, Dundee Rockets won the British Grand Slam for three consecutive years. Ice-hockey (which encourages junior as well as senior participation) has suffered from inadequate facilities and business machinations in recent times, and must resolve these, possibly with District Council assistance, if its undoubted local popularity is to be restored.

Dundee Whalers, on the other hand, the American football specialists, are a much more recent phenomenon. Founded in 1987 as a result of the interest created by television coverage of the sport, they are strictly amateur and rely heavily on the enthusiasm of the local players, each of whom must find at least three hundred pounds to kit himself out, and make a contribution towards the cost of each game, which requires statisticians, five national-league referees, and an ambulance in attendance. They won the Scottish Thistle League in the first year of their existence and have managed to secure a home base at Caird Park.

Whatever one's choice of sport, the pursuit of excellence remains the primary goal. Dundee has produced world-class athletes in a number of sports – David Leslie in rugby, Ian Blyth and Ruth Gilfillan in swimming, Fergus Murray and the little-known Thistle Harrier John Suttie Smith in distance running, and wrestler, George Kidd. However, two Dundonians, in particular, stand out as having reached the absolute pinnacle of sporting achievement.

I saw Dick McTaggart box 'live' once, at a Caird Hall exhibition in 1957, shortly after his triumphant return from the Melbourne Olympics. I saw him again in 1990, this time in his capacity as Scottish National Boxing Coach, at a glittering event – Scotland versus the USA – staged at the Angus Hotel in Dundee by Frank Henry's St Francis Club. The 'Oor Wullie' haircut had gone but the lean physique, which had mesmerised fans and opponents alike as it ghosted around the ring, was still intact, and his introduction received the greatest ovation of the night. Dundee has produced a few boxing champions, Fred

Dick McTaggart is greeted in Dundee following his triumph at the Melbourne Olympics, 1956. *Copyright D. C. Thomson & Co. Ltd*

Fred Tennant

217

Fred Tennant's Story

Jobs in the 1920s and 1930s were scarce for men over the age of eighteen, and the city's employment market did not favour unskilled men. The more adventurous would join the armed services rather than be idle. The most adventurous might try to make it as professional boxers.

Dundee was as fight crazy a city as Glasgow, perhaps even more so. Dundee, and in particular the Hilltown area, produced some of Scotland's best boxers. There was Jim Brady, the British Empire champion, Jim Cowie, Gilbert Johnston, Dennis Cahill, and later Bobby Boland. But it was the Overgate that produced one of the best-loved boxers: Fred Tennant, who became the Scottish Flyweight Champion in 1938.

Fred Tennant was actually born in the Fife mining village of Lochgelly in 1913, however, for almost all his life, from 1914 until his death in late 1987, he lived in Dundee. I remember Fred for his kindness, his energy, and the time he gave in helping with my research into boxing booths. He was also self-effacing and could tell a good tale. While working on a film about booth boxing, Billy Kay asked Fred if he ever became big-headed, because of his fighting success. Fred replied:

Oh naw naw. Nobody could say that I ever got that way. No. Ah'm no trying tae tell ye this because it's being taped, Ah'm bein' frank wi' ye. I never did anything to give me a big head. Never at the end of my fights would I say, 'That wis fantastic, I'm the greatest.' 'Cause that would have been daft . . . [laughing]. You've got to be frank about this and I'm being frank.

Here is a small part of Fred's story.

Ah'm talkin about the 1930s an' . . . eh . . . the early 1930s when the conditions in this country, you guys won't know about it, but conditions were shocking, shocking. My mother had five kids underneath me, there was six of us, and my father and my mother got five shillings a day to keep us. Just think now, five shillings a day to keep us for five days o' the week and on a Saturday she got a pound. That was my mother's wages. That was to keep eight o' us in the hoose, an' my father had to get the best steak and the best mince.

He was full of his own importance. Everything had to be the best. The best steak, the best sausages. Ma mother and the rest of the family we had to take what was left, you know, the leavings. Oh meh father was a hard man. My mother died when she was thirty-odds, my father died when he was eighty-six.

Tennant, Jim Brady and the brothers from Lochee, Daniel, Dennis and Frank Gilfeather, for example, and witnessed a few bizarre sideshows – like the initiation of black world-heavyweight champion, Jack Johnson, into freemasonry! There was nothing, however, to compare with the career of Dick McTaggart.

He was born on 15 October 1935, in Wilkie's Lane. His father came from Glasgow and was probably of Irish extraction, and his mother from Dundee. She gave birth to eighteen children, only nine of whom survived the ravages of infant mortality and premature death, and Dick – the second son to be given that name – was the fourth-youngest child. When he was a year old, the family was rehoused at 73 Dens Road.

He attended St Mary's Forebank School and was good enough to play football for a school team which included Jimmy Briggs and James Coyle (brother of Johnny), but he had no other sporting ambitions until his elder brother Peter joined Belmont Boxing Club.

I was about eight or ten and we were pushed into it in a way, to keep us off the streets. There were plenty boxers then, and ten or twelve clubs in Dundee. After the Belmont I went to George Kidd's club in Carnegie Street, then the Hawkhill Club where the professionals trained under Jocky Smith. We appeared on a Johnny Victory Show at the Palace [theatre], sparring and skipping, and the fee was a packet of crisps and an ice-cream! Then I went to the Dunhope Castle Club, under Frankie Quinn.

I was winnin' a' my fights, but no' championships. My brother Peter beat me in a Midlands final and the trainer says, 'Why did you no' hit him?' I says, 'Because he'd hit me when we got hame!'

The sport was a hobby for McTaggart, until he joined the RAF in 1953. He had worked as a butcher's boy with Alex Munro in the Overgate, and was employed in that line of work in the forces. He steered clear of boxing until a minor incident occurred in the barracks with an unfortunate Englishman, and thereafter he was propelled to five consecutive RAF championships and a place (ironically) in the English national team before he was honoured by Scotland.

'I never, ever thought I had special talent,' he says with typical modesty. 'People told me I was gifted wi' something and my trainer once said, "Nobody can teach Dick. It goes in one ear and out the other, and the things he does – I wouldn't teach anyway!" My hands were down, I was a southpaw who could change to orthodox, and I could do things on the ropes like sidestep and make opponents slide. Things that Muhammad Ali did later on.'

The analogy with the great heavyweight is an interesting one, and the style McTaggart concisely describes probably accounts in large measure for the success of both boxers. McTaggart went on to win the ABA championships in 1956 and booked his place for the Melbourne Olympics.

218

'I went as an outsider, but thought, myself, that I had a chance. I had won in Finland, and in Moscow against the Russian champion.'

Dick won each of his fights in Australia, by the unanimous decision of five judges. The performance was to win for him the prestigious Val Barker Trophy for the outstanding boxer of the games, and his homecoming was a great event. He was met at the station by a large crowd and taken through the streets in an open-topped car; he paraded his trophies at Dens Park and was given a civic reception; the BBC filmed and interviewed him (although they later gave the Sports Personality of the Year award to Olympic steeplechaser, Chris Brasher); and his wax effigy was given a place at Madame Tussaud's in London.

This period of celebrity, however, was not to last. Dick had assumed that work would be easy to find on his return to civvy street (in 1958), but Dundee was an unemployment blackspot with one-fifth of the working population still exposed to the vagaries of the jute trade, and McTaggart was forced to alternate between menial jobs and the dole queue. He did have the option of turning professional and at least one well-known Scottish manager made him a substantial offer, but Dick was distrustful of professional management, believing that he would no longer enjoy boxing if large sums of other people's money were to become involved. 'In spite of what some "experts" say, I think I'd have done reasonably well as a pro,' he ventures. 'I had more than 600 fights and only lost twenty-four as an amateur, and some boxers I'd consistently beaten, like Johnny Cooke, did well professionally. I didn't want my heid battered for two hundred pounds.'

Such social and financial conflict brought intolerable pressure to bear on his first marriage, but life improved when he was offered what nowadays might be called a public relations job, with the *Daily Express* in Dundee. For domestic reasons, he decided to take his new family to Glasgow, and he continued to enjoy success as an amateur boxer – Olympic Bronze in Rome, European Gold in Belgrade – although employment opportunities remained a problem. A naturally gregarious and dignified man, however, he eventually managed to find a maintenance position with Rolls Royce, and he pays tribute to a company which has allowed him to remain involved in boxing throughout twenty years of employment.

Following a period out of the game, he was appointed National Coach in 1983, a position created with the assistance of the Sports Council. He was also awarded the MBE around that time, and tells a story not untypical of the British establishment at work. Apparently the civil servant responsible phoned the Scottish authorities and asked for (sporting) suggestions for a gong. 'What about Dick McTaggart?' said the man. 'Dick McTaggart?' exclaimed the official, 'I thought he was dead!'

Like most youngsters Fred would go to the shows or fair each year that they came to Gussie Park.

And the most common thing in Dundee, when the Gussie Park [shows] was on, the booths would be on. They [people] went to the football match first, Tannadice or Dens, and then walked along, five minutes along the road, to Gussie Park. So they came from the football match into the boxing. Monday to Saturday was a . . . well Monday, Wednesday, Friday and Saturday were the most popular nights.

Eventually I asked Woods's [fairground booth owners] if I could get a job with them. I wasnae havin' it very good at that particular time. I was flung out by my father on numerous occasions and I knew I would be happier away. That's when I went wi' the booth. I got offered fifteen shillings a week and my keep, that was my wages. Fifteen shilling a week, seventy-five pence [laughing].

It was really an escape for me, getting away from the arguing, earning a living for myself, keeping myself. An' off that fifteen shillings I sent five shillings home to my mother. Every week I always sent that, got a five-bob postal order and sent it home to my mother.

If it had been my father I wouldnae have sent any money home to him. At that time when I went away with the booth I was the oldest of six [children] and every penny was very necessary in our house.

In the mill there was the jute and the dust and oh dreadful shocking conditions, well in the booths you're outside, you're working outside.

Ah thought Ah was earning good money. When I boxed at Dundee Ah boxed at the Coup [along Riverside] first for Woods's booth. I got five shillings for six rounds.

I was away from the home, away from the house. Nobody had a gun at your head. Oh it was a great life, I loved it. [laughing]. Oh I was in the booths among people for five or six years; every summer I went wi' the booths. I used to box in the halls in the wintertime.

Fred developed his own views of boxing.

If you try hard, people like that. You see, you go into a hall and you lose a fight without trying, whose gonna come back and watch it? But you go into a hall and it's a good fight, even although you lost they'll come back and see you again. That's the way I looked at it. If you try hard you make it look good, people will come and see you again. So that's what makes you a draw [an attraction].

Winning wasn't important, because the amount of fights I hid. I've just been looking at some of my fights here, the dates. There's loads; I'd about six fights in the month. I boxed a lot more than that. I mean that's apart from aw these fights that are official contests. Oh hundreds o' fights. I boxed six times in two days at Nottingham Goose Fair. You boxed two fights on the first night and four fights on the main day.

It couldnae happen now. Men wouldn't do that now and the wages, the men wouldn't take their jacket off for two pound – you got two pounds for ten rounds – they wouldn't do it.

But I was a local hero. Local hero, boy makes good. The Dundee people they knew the local boys.

Amongst the highlights of his career was fighting Benny Lynch, world champion.

Oh Lynch was a topper. He was a smashing fellow. When I first boxed him I beat him on points in Glasgow. An' Ah lost at Dundee an' Ah lost at Edinburgh. Five times Ah boxed him. Ah lost three, won one, and a draw. Although Ah beat Lynch, Ah don't put myself in his category. He was first, superior you know.

Fred recalls his own time in boxing with a wry smile.

Boxing for my highest purse was boxing for ninety pounds. Imagine, ninety pounds! At Dundee, when Ah boxed Jackie Patterson for ninety pound, oh Ah thought it was a fortune, it cost two bob tae speak tae me. Ninety pounds aw tae masel'. Yes that wis the highest purse Ah ever got. Ah boxed for five shillings, an' Ah boxed for ninety pounds. Right through the whole spectrum.

Liz McColgan was born into a sporting family and attended St Vincent's and St Saviour's schools. Around the age of eleven she was spotted in a class run by a PE teacher who was a running enthusiast, and entered for the Dundee Schools Cross Country. She did not win that event, but performed well enough to want to join a running club, and at Hawkhill Harriers she made an important contact in coach Harry Bennet.

'At that time, myself and a girl called Caroline Stewart were quite even,' says Liz, 'but I seemed to have more appetite for training.' Within a month she had outstripped her rival and, at the Scottish Schools Championships in Edinburgh, she took silver in an under-fifteen's two-mile event.

Leaving school in her Fourth Year, Liz was at first unemployed before gaining a YOP place in a jute mill in Perth Road. The experience obviously concentrated her mind, for, when it finished, she began to train twice and sometimes three times a day. She won her first senior event – the Scottish Cross Country Championships – at the age of seventeen and, two years later, in 1983, was offered a one-year placement at Rick's Junior College in Idaho, USA. 'I had never been away from Scotland, and decided to turn it down. The scout, however, then phoned Harry, and he accepted! It was the best move I could have made. I got more time to train and within a year had run out of competition.'

At the Idaho college she met future husband, Peter, himself a talented runner, from Strabane in Northern Ireland, and jointly they decided to move to the University of Alabama, something which was to offer her personal stability and widen her educational horizons. Unfortunately, Harry Bennet was not to witness the great success he had both predicted and contributed to. He died in 1984.

Liz took the Commonwealth Gold medals over 10,000 metres in 1986 and 1990, established a world (road) record at the same distance in Orlando, Florida and just failed to win an Olympic Gold at Seoul in 1988 when the Russian, Bondarenko, overtook her in the final stages. Her coach from that period, John Anderson, believed that, as an endurance athlete, she would eventually become the finest distance-runner the world had ever seen. Long-term injuries in the 1990s unfortunately disrupted her training but her career continues at the highest level, and it is gratifying at least to know that her experience and expertise have been passed on to children from Dundee.

Don't Forget the 3J's City!

Dundee Soul

by DONNY COUTTS

A Saturday Night, 1981 London School of Economics Union.
Paul Young & Q Tips, supported by Dundee's Mafia:
   Paul Young – 'How come all you jocks can sing soul?'
   Donny Coutts – 'Come to Dundee and find out!'

For years I knew my native city had character and heart, and that its people, young and old, were kind, adaptable and gregarious. That aspect of their 'soul' shone through many an adversity, often accentuated by the city's traditional place in the pecking order of Scotland's four cities – last! Glasgow and Edinburgh disputed first place, and Aberdeen as an established university town and 'Capital of the North' as third. Dundee, with its dismal industrial image was an understandable last thought, just making up the numbers. It was also a natural for the phenomenon of blues and soul music – the working man's protest and source of inspiration in similar cities in America. Until I was in my late teens that fact was, however, lost to me.

Dundee people have always wanted to sing. In pubs, clubs and at parties (and particularly at New Year) most need no second asking. Some unaccompanied versions of old traditional Scottish favourites, perhaps not appreciated in my early life, strike me now as being full of soul. There is an analogy, however tenuous, between the poor black man toiling all day for a pittance in the heat of the sun, and the wee Dundee man or woman slaving away in the heat and noise of the mill. Poverty and unemployment have affected Dundee's people over the years. Any enjoyment in life was self-made and, inevitably, there were songs, delivered with the full emotion required to reflect the situation. Whatever you call that special ingredient, and to me, 'soul' is as good a word as any, Dundee's singers have it, and belt-it-oot with feeling, even raw aggression if required, but always, straight from the heart.

The following scenario could have taken place in a Detroit ghetto, but actually happened in Dundee. A young singer, living for his music, but short of money and opportunity, was offered a pair of shoes by a friend. When asked what size he took, he replied poker faced, 'Anything fae a three 'til an eight, dependin on how many pairs o' socks eh'm wearin.' In comparison, I had a somewhat sheltered upbringing, my parents sacrificing everything to send me to the fee-paying Dundee High School. I was

221

unaware of the real poverty in the city and of the conditions in which families lived, and survived. The traditional industries were in decline, and whilst sterling efforts were being made by the local authority (including the attraction of American companies, like Timex and NCR), there was not a lot of money going round. Music, however, survived, and the phenomena of skiffle, rock 'n roll, trad, and jazz captured Dundee's young people like others in the country. I was amongst them but, for some reason, my taste ran to what were eventually termed R 'n' B and soul music, played by black American artists and found on obscure import record labels, deep in the stockroom of Low's Record Store in Crichton Street, where I worked on Saturdays. I was unaware that I was not alone in Dundee.

One evening I was dragged along by a friend to 'Robbies' in Well Road, off Hawkhill, owned by the famous Duncan family. The occasion was the culmination of a twist marathon by Cathy Connelly, who was striving to beat the world record. The crowd, however, was more interested in the band who were providing the music, and so was I. The Hi-Four, including Dundee soul don, Dougie Martin, were playing soul and R 'n' B numbers which I had previously only heard on the American Forces Network, and what's more, the crowd was singing along with them. The Hi-Four had played with American bands in US bases in Germany and had picked up the songs along the way. The performance was very 'black' and on a par with the American soulsters. That group was a forerunner of many groups in Dundee at the very start of the Merseybeat era. Dundee's heritage and tradition, coupled with the Hi-Four influence, was to ensure a continuing love affair between the city and soul music and produced an apparent conveyor belt of soulful singers to the present day.

In the halcyon early days of soul music nationally, when to some it was admittedly the flavour of the month, I always felt that Glasgow and Dundee, in particular, as truly industrial cities, had more affinity with Tamla Motown and Stax than, say, Edinburgh or Aberdeen. I know from working in a record shop that if a local chart had been compiled at that time there would have been more of the Four Tops, Temptations, Supremes, Otis Redding and the like than appeared in the national charts in which Merseybeat and British cover-versions of American hits held sway.

In those exciting years of the early to mid-sixties, Dundee teenagers attended venues as diverse as the Caird Hall (2,750 capacity) to the Trade Café which held about fifty people at a push. Other venues included the Top Ten Club, the JM, the Continental, The Haparanda (God Bless, Ciano!), the West End Palais (Robbie's) and a plethora of youth clubs in church halls. Kids danced and drank soft drinks to the music of the Hi-Four, the Poor Souls, the Honours, the Vikings, the Durelles, the

Staccato Five, the Mystery Men, the Executives, Cleo's Mood, the Paladins, the Earle Blue Stars, the Black Diamonds, the Wise Brothers, the Syndicate and many more, too numerous to mention. Yes, the music scene really was that healthy at the time.

Of course traditionally, the inevitable happened: something else came along, and was championed by the music press, and soul music no longer dominated the market. In Dundee, however, soul survived flirtations with other types of music. Sometimes the survival is mainly evident in the manner in which songs are delivered, but you can still hear all the old standards in some pub, somewhere, any weekend.

Many Dundee musicians have achieved national, and international recognition over the years and in different spheres of music. The story of Nat and Ron Gonnella in jazz and fiddle music, respectively, is well known, as is that of Dennis Clancy in Scottish music, and the brilliant and fascinating career of flugelhorn player Jimmy Deuchars, a world-class jazz musician. In the popular music stakes the list is topped by the Average White Band whose original line-up included two sons and two adopted sons of Dundee. Roger Ball and Robbie McIntosh, tragically one of the music business's many casualties, were the sons, and Allan Gorrie and Malcolm (Molly) Duncan the adopted sons (both attended Dundee's Duncan of Jordanstone College of Art). Subsequent line-ups included keyboard player Michael Fraser, also from Dundee. International success peaked in 1974 with a No. 1 album and single in the USA, and a No. 1 single, the still popular, 'Pick up the Pieces', on this side of the Atlantic. Their brand of black American funk apparently prompted the American band Wild Cherry to write the classic soul hit 'Play that Funky Music, White Boy!'

Glasgow band Deacon Blue have as their singer and principal writer, Dundee's Ricky Ross. The band have had a string of hit singles, and two hit albums. Their highly acclaimed material contains thoughtful, and thought-provoking, lyrics. The soul influence on them is obvious. Listen to 'Fergus sings the Blues' from the album 'When the World Knows your Name'. The lyrics read

> Homesick James, my biggest influence
> Tell me why, James and Bobby Purify
> I'm lost in music, Sweet Soul Music
> This is my country, these are my reasons

(a reference to James and Bobby Purify who recorded the soul classics 'I'm your Puppet', 'Oh! How Happy', 'Morning Glory' 'All the Love I Got', and 'When Something is Wrong With My Baby'). The lyrics continue:

223

From the Campsies over Christmas
I still dream of Memphis
'Cause, I look in the mirror
And it throws back the question
And I whisper the words
That beg an answer,
Tell me, can this white man sing the blues?

Can Fergus sing the blues? Well, if he comes from Dundee he certainly can, nae bather at a'!

The Associates, originally Allan Rankine from Edinburgh and Dundee's own Billy McKenzie, have recorded several highly acclaimed albums. McKenzie's voice with its soaring range and quality, a hybrid of Sam Cooke and Jackie Wilson, is recognised as one of the finest in the popular music business today. I heard him at a local wedding, singing a traditional Scottish song, full of emotion and soul. A rare experience indeed, and not as incongruous as one might imagine.

More recently, Danny Wilson, a three-man Dundee group, have achieved success in Britain, Europe and the USA with the singles 'Mary's Prayer' and 'First Summer of Love', taken from two successful albums. In their early days, Gary Clark, the vocalist, displayed maturity beyond his years both in his writing and his vocal delivery. Supplemented by the solid and inventive bass-playing of Ged Grimes and the vision and energy of Kit Clark, they became a formidable force, touring round the world.

Michael Marra, one of Dundee's most loved musical sons, released records with Skeets Boliver, a highly successful Dundee band of the mid-seventies, before embarking on a solo career. Skeets Boliver had many good qualities, but it was Marra's voice which added the polished finish to the product. Gravelly and low, the rough edge also had sensitive delivery, a perfect recipe for a good old Scottish soul stew! He has recorded three albums: one for Polydor, one 'bootleg' cassette during a period of management problems and a third, *Michael Marra and the Gaels Blue Orchestra*, containing original songs most of which refer to Scotand and its history.

The Gaels Blue Orchestra was essentially a group of Dundee musicians (around eighteen in number, at times) who backed Marra in his traditional Christmas concerts in Dundee's Bonar Hall. All sharing similar musical tastes, Marra wrote, and included on the album, the song 'Gaels Blue', a tribute to Scottish soulmen and their affinity to their American counterparts. The chorus lyrics read:

Gaels Blue
We've been weighed up and found to be true
'though we never had the Chevvies or the Baptist Church
We had a choice of colours for a broken crutch

We'll do
Whatever it is that we do
You can ask the driver on the Glory Train
We'll sing it up to Heaven and home again
Gaels Blue.

Marra's songs are extremely clever: good melodies, with entertaining, yet meaningful lyrics. A great many relate to his beloved Dundee, or to his own local musical heroes and friends. Songs about Dougie Martin and Peter McGlone spring to mind, as does his tribute to Dundee United's Hamish McAlpine, in which Skeets Boliver's Gus Foy also gets an honourable mention. And, again, the beautiful 'Peggy Peace', written of his wife.

Peddie Street and Brown Street, Dundee, respectively inspired the melancholy 'Pity Street' (changed from Peddie Street because some English record producers have 'nae ehdea') and the belligerent 'Hey Jimmy, do you know the way to Brown Street'. Marra is now achieving wider acclaim, having written 'Mother Glasgow' which he performed together with Eddi Reader, of Fairground Attraction, in front of 200,000 people at Glasgow's Big Day. He has gained prominence as a musical director for John Byrne's TV series *Your Cheating Heart*, and also secured the role of the butcher in the film production of McIllvaney's *The Big Man*. However there will

Michael Marra. *Ken Sharp*

Dougie Martin, Donny Coutts and Gerry McGrath giein it laldy in Chambers.
Ken Sharp

always be music in Marra somewhere, and there is plenty left in his bag of goodies for us all to savour.

Dougie Martin, well, where do you start? I suppose by saying that his shoe size is anything from a three to an eight! Dougie has been described by coloured soulmen like Jimmy James, as Dundee's only white negro! In his thirty-five years in music, Dougie has had his ups and downs, but being 'streetwise' straight from the pram (he was the youngest of 'seevin bairns fae Fleemin' Gairdens'!), he has overcome all adversity. Many offers of greater things along the way, from the post of head of A & R at Polydor Records to a chance to join Manfred Mann and Jim Mullen, the highly respected jazz and soul guitarist, have been turned down and his finest hours have been spent with the Hi-Four, the Poor Souls, and the Mafia. Mafia gained a huge following in Scotland and London in the late seventies and early eighties for their live set of Motown and Stax soul standards. A solid rhythm section enriched by a horn section including Peter and Allan McGlone (the Fountain-blowers!) was the backing for the vocals of Dougie, Gerry McGrath and myself. Dougie's harsh to velvet tones, *à la* Teddy Pendergrass of Harold Melvin's Bluenotes, doubled with Gerry McGrath's spine-tingling, often electric, vocal

226

quality on lead vocals. The blend of voices is something of which I will always be proud to have been a part. Dougie is an institution in Dundee, loved and respected by the three or four generations of musicians with whom he has played, and all the punters of soul music.

Solo singers abound, but the best are Lorna Bannon, Frances Carlin and Lloyd Anderson. Lorna Bannon's voice can be gentle and soft one minute, raunchy and powerful the next, and her confident style and delivery has seen her tour and record with London chart-funk outfit, Shakatak. Frances Carlin has a fine soulful voice – the range superb, but with a smoky feel in the lower register, reminiscent of Ketty Lester of 'Love Letters' fame. Lloyd Anderson is a singer who promises much but has yet to fully deliver. With a voice reminiscent of the early Stevie Wonder, he has already been in great demand for well-known brand commercials.

Lorna Bannon

Visits to Dundee by established American soul acts are regrettably few and far between. However, the Caird Hall, Greens Playhouse, the JM, the Whitehall Theatre, De Stihl's and the Palais have played host to the Four Tops, Martha and the Vandellas, Mary Wilson's Supremes, Edwin Starr, Mary Wells, Thelma Houston, Chaka Khan and the Drifters. All the performances were memorable nights, but one occasion in particular stands as a testimony to Dundee soul.

The Four Tops were appearing at Greens Playhouse in 1982 and had the crowd in the palms of their hands, having created a tremendous atmosphere in the hall. (The knowledgeable and willing Dundee crowd had, of course, played their part.) Halfway through the set, the band launched into the opening pulsating rhythm and bass riff of 'I Can't Help Myself' when a man at the front could contain himself no longer. He jumped up and down, clapping and waving his hands, his face a picture of joy and happiness, experiencing a most natural high. Levi Stubbs of the Tops noticed and reacted by simply handing him the mike, inviting him to start the song. Without hesitation he went for it, singing the familiar opening verse, 'Sugarpie honeybunch/You know that I love you/I can't help myself/I love you and nobody else.' I saw him after the show, still on cloud nine, shouting over to a friend: 'Did you see uz? Did ye? Did you really? Eh, wuz the Fufth Tap, wuz uh?'

When Martha and the Vandellas stayed at the Angus Hotel after a gig in Dundee, several Dundee musicians talked to them into the small hours, about Dundee and soul music. When they became hungry they were persuaded to try what is probably Dundee's equivalent to soulfood – a 'piece 'n' chips wi plenty sahce'. They stopped short of 'peh on a roll', perhaps understandably.

So there are many links between Scottish and American musicians in the soul field. Apart from the inheritance from each

227

other of characters and traditions, producing in each a love of the
history and heritage of the other, another factor exists. In the
fifties and sixties, it was accepted that black blues and soul artists
could sing and play to middle age and beyond, whereas amongst
white pop musicians you were past it at twenty-five or if you got
married. In music today it is acceptable for all artists to remain
successful, regardless of age. In Dundee that has always been the
case. Many of the fifties and sixties brigade have kept playing
and they and their brand of music are identifiable to more than
a couple of generations. Call in nowadays to Chamber's, Bar
Chevrolet, Scott's, the Rendezvous, the Marquee, the Underground, the West Port Bar, amongst other pubs and clubs in
Dundee, and you'll be able to hear one band or another or a collection of musical worthies from four decades jamming together.
There's bound to be a healthy dose of soul or R 'n' B in there,
somewhere. The older musicians have the respect of the newer
breed. There is no contempt for those who blazed the trail, and
who, for their part, are only too happy to pass on what they have
learned.

The venues may have changed over the years, some may no
longer be with us in name, some no longer with us physically and
we may have forgotten TFM's, the Windmill, the Top Hat and
the Tayside Bar, but the memories of great nights there remain.
The number of venues, including pubs, clubs and discos offering
live music, continues to grow, and there is a vast choice of entertainment, and not just at the weekend. The opportunities for
musicians to work regularly are good and the music scene
remains extremely healthy and vibrant.

Paul Young did come to Dundee – with Q-Tips in 1983. The
gig was thronged with Dundee soul punters. As he readily
admitted afterwards, Paul was left in no doubt that Dundee had
more than enough soul to go around and that local musicians
were lucky to have that kind of environment in which to play.
Maybe that's one reason why we 'Jocks' can sing soul, but I think
a couple of hundred years of working-class history along the way
has had a lot to do with it as well!

A Dour Gentleness

Writing in Dundee

by MATTHEW FITT

Let's face it. Dundee is not the Left Bank or Greenwich Village, with a dozen poets' cafés and publishing houses ready to sign you up. Writers in this city make their own luck. The Dundee poet nowadays, looking for a publisher, an audience and a living, must be as intrepid as the Scottish–American prospector of the last century and possess integrity as tough as a whaler's hands. Sacrifice, frustration, exile; the creeping temptation to gie up – these, on the dark winter nights, are the Dundee writer's unwanted companions. William McGonagall knew the territory well. Pursued through the streets by Dundonians armed with cobblestanes and foostie tomataes, the infamous rhymester eventually took the huff with the city and plied his dubious trade elsewhere. And as early as the sixteenth century, James Wedderburn's brittle satires against the Catholic Church so nipped the heids of the town's burgesses that the author was best advised for his own safety to retire from Dundee to France.

Harsh critics the people of Dundee may be, but they are equally the most willing and generous of patrons. The Poet's Box, a shop in the old Overgait owned by the brawly-named Lowden MacArtney, peddled ballads and occasional songs to the Dundee public who, fair taen up with the idea, made it one of the most thriving wee businesses of its day. More recently, a book-launch at James Thin's by Kate Armstrong or Eileen Ramsay, two Tayside writers, is as likely to draw as large a crowd as for any national celebrity. Dundee folk have made every Dundonian play staged at the Rep Theatre a box-office smash. And starved of their own culture on television, they simply cannot get enough of perennial publications, such as *So Ye Think Ye Ken Dundee?*, *The Scheme Hopper's Guide* and *Dundonian for Beginners*, not to mention the Furst Fut Scroll or the annual rammy of Dundee calendars. There is a considerable audience for local writing within the city but it is aye an uphill struggle for the writer, working alone, to reach that audience. And yet at a time when patronage of the arts is particularly thin on the ground and the written word itself is under attack from the million-channel cartoonery of satellite entertainment, it is strange (or perhaps characteristically thrawn) that Dundee in the 1990s has struck a rich vein of literary talent and that Dundee writers are making their voices heard inwith and furth of Scotland.

One of these writers is Don Paterson, whose first collection of poetry, *Nil Nil*, drew praise and acclaim from many quarters.

The Fisher Lassie
(after Heine)

Ma bonny fisher lassie,
Bring ye the boat tae laund,
An come tae me, come sit ye doon
An tak me by the haund.

Lay yer wee heid ower ma hert.
Be na sae feart o me
When ilka day ye trust yersel
Fearless tae thon wild sea.

The sea has storms an wathers;
Ma hert's the very same,
An mony a pearl ye'll find sae braw
In airts ablow the faem.

Kate Armstrong

229

Winner of the Arvon Poetry Prize and one of the most visible figures on National Poetry Day, Don's reputation as a bold new player continues to grow. A stint as writer-in-residence at Dundee University brought him back to the city of his birth. His first innovation was to howk poetry out of its academic cubbyhole by relocating the traditional university readings to the more conducive and commercial setting of Waterstone's Booksellers in the city centre. He booked the top names on the circuit to come and perform, and the result was a satisfying increase in the number of Dundonians listening to live poetry.

Don's own poetry is as absorbing as it is enigmatic. In *Nil Nil*, the poet is a traveller reading new and familiar landscapes with instinctive irony and a poker face. There is a polished wryness in his style and evidence sometimes, in his choice of situation, of a brooding darkness around the heart. His vision, inherently cosmopolitan, relentlessly pushes to expand its own parameters.

> One day we will make our perfect journey –
> the great train smashing though Dundee, Brooklyn
> and off into the endless tundra,
> the earth flattening before us.

The language is an intriguing blend of the scientific and the vernacular, keying into a unique vocabulary of brand names, medical terms and loan words, all shot through with a pocketful of Scots. Witty and often disturbing, Don Paterson's is a name the city will be hearing more of in the future.

As Dundee as they come, Ellie McDonald has earned the respect of many in the Scottish writing community. She is a poet blessed with rare ability and a wicked sense of fun, and when it comes to poetic integrity, the River Tay itself is more likely to change course than Ellie. Her lyric poetry, fashioned in classical Scots, is often so hauntingly beautiful it can send a shiver the length of your spine. And yet when roused, her anger at stupidity and neglect can cut like a blade. But the elemental current that drives Ellie's poetry is a force most Dundonians would recognise in themselves: that of a dour gentleness. The tone in her collection *The Gangan Fuit* can sometimes be hard and unflinching –

> Me – fashed? I dinnae gie a docken
> ye thrawn, carnaptious
> misbegotten deevil o ill-luck.
>
> Ye pickt the wrang lass
> gin ye thocht I'd shaw the warld
> a sair begrutten hert.

– but underneath the implacable exterior there beats a hert o corn –

Forby

> tulziesom tykes aye hirple hame
> an fine I ken, at the hinner end,
> I'll hae ye back – ye scunner.

10 Year On

10 year on

an Merch hauds nae bield
heich on the hill o Balgey.

A puckle trees hae blawn doun,
thir ruits lik hurtit bairns' herts
crucify my een.

I ettilt tae scrieve
til ye then.

Min hou the leaves
reishelt abuin our twa heids,
sae close,

I thocht shair the soun
wis frae yer mou.

Whaur the tree-line ends
houses ligg nou,
huggeran the hill.

Aathin's happit up
fornenst the haar –

An me, trawlan owre
siller-green seas
tae gaither iodine

bareheidit i the weet.

Ellie McDonald

Eloquent and with both feet firmly on the ground, Ellie is now one of the most important figures involved in the revival of the Scots language. She carries the scars of campaigning for Scots at a time when no one else gave tuppence for it and now that the Mither Tongue is being re-established in the schools, Ellie McDonald should be given a position of influence in order that her skill and experience with the language be recognised and passed on to the next generation.

A. L. Kennedy is a young Dundee novelist from whom we can anticipate great things. The heroes of her spellbinding stories are ordinary people, often characters who are uncomfortable in their environment or in uneasy relationships which threaten to derail those involved. She confronts the familiar realities of modern living with savage calm and works into her style a seeming ambivalence which masks sterker emotions running below the surface of her tales.

> I've been listening here all day and I can hear for miles. I told that to someone this morning and got no answer. Perhaps I muttered. People have told me I mutter from time to time and it has never been important because I have never had anything very much to say. It doesn't matter today if no one heard me because I was mainly speaking only to myself. I know what I know and what I know is the idea that came into my head that there is a clearness up here for listening far away to dogs and motors and children which are all down there.

When her debut collection of short stories, *Night Geometry and the Garscadden Trains*, was first reviewed, the critics of serious fiction both north and south of the border were uniformly up to high-doh. Her first novel, *Looking for the Possible Dance*, disappointed no one, and a second book of short stories, *Now That You're Back*, confirmed the arrival of a major writer. A. L. Kennedy has won the attention of the establishment, not to mention a whole bouquet of awards, and her unusual style of fiction has attracted a healthy following among the reading public, especially in Scotland.

John Glenday's *The Apple Ghost* is a fine collection of lyrics, each one a demonstration of a poet of very high calibre. He locates with ease the beautiful metaphor and in the rhythm of his elegant, modern style there is more than a hint of the old border ballads. A place or a town can sometimes leave a profound mark on a writer and it is interesting to note that John Glenday, born in the Ferry, brought up in Monifieth and now living in Carnoustie, returns again and again in his poetry to the processes of the sea.

> The waves have come
> in their borrowed coats.

The Drowning Pool

This is the pool
from which
I shall not arise

water as black as love
will draw me in
water is dark

is dark
but in her eye
turn greater darknesses

feel how my skin
is white
she whispers

here
against my thighs
and winds herself

around me
I breathe in
but she covers my mouth

my nose
my ears
my eyes

this
is the pool
in which I cannot swim

John Glenday

231

Jute Mill Sang

Baxters Upper Dens Mill, a hauf mile roun
o muckle stane waas and iron yetts.
The bummers quaet this lang while syne.
Nae siller nou in jute an niver wis
for them that wrocht twal hours a day,
but gied a creshy linan tae the bosses pouch
an biggit railroads hauf across America.

Ilka day, ilka day, ilka day, the hemmers
ding doun the waas o Baxters Upper Dens.
Naebody kens whit's tae be pitten in its place,
naebody greets for its demise.
An stour blaws frae the houkit out wame o't
sclairtan the cars and buses that birl awa
tae concrete fields of spacelessness.

Ellie McDonald

They shelve to the ocean's
imperceptible decline;
then gently fall away
like other people's lives.

Like other people's
lives, unfolding
in curves of silence,
searching for an end.

We only hear them
when they break against
our world.

John, a drugs counsellor in the city, is a poet of rare intuition and talent. His reputation has taken him abroad as a creative writer on the Scottish-Canadian Exchange Fellowship but his most vital role has been in Dundee as a director of poetry readings and workshops and as a pamphleteer and publisher of local poets. Formerly an editor for Blind Serpent Press (whose catalogue boasts *Darkness and Snowfall* by Andrew Fox and Margaret Gillies Brown's *Looking Towards Light*), John Glenday has been selfless in his promotion of good Dundee writing.

The most successful poet to emerge from the Blind Serpent stable is Kate Armstrong. Published widely and a kenspeckle

Baxter's Upper Dens Mills today.
Good housing, art, and urban renewal –
the new Dundee. *Ken Sharp*

face among local writers, Kate's contribution to Dundee's literature is considerable. She has worked tirelessly with writers' groups to promote quality writing in the city and her own creative agenda, which can be seen in her volume of poems entitled *Wild Mushrooms*, is bound strongly to the sights and sounds, concerns and problems of the town in which she bides.

> Sudden, frae oot the kirk's dark maw
> is spewed a lassie, dirled like a huiled pea
> amang the hird, in a cotton sark an a cardie
> flaffin tae ilka souch. The mithers smile at the braw
> spinnaker time alane sall haud. Her muckle wame
> fykes sherp an true ablow oor sixty faulds o dwam.

Wild Mushrooms is a sympathetic and intelligent keek at modern experience, viewed from a shairply pragmatic north-east perspective. There are several beautiful owresettans of German poems into Scots and a number of wry epigrams of city life in English, but Kate's most prosperous and rewarding pitch is her original poetry in Scots.

W. N. Herbert, a prolific and energetic representative of a new generation of Scots poets, has taken the parochial yardstick by which his native Dundee is habitually measured and broken it owre his knee. His several volumes of poetry are testimony of a writer no feared of new, untried concepts of literature and language. Although an accomplished writer of English verse, Herbert's most adventurous experiments have been with the Mither Tongue. In his book *Dundee Doldrums* and his later collections *Forked Tongue* and *Anither Music*, he has taken Dundonian (a dialect of Scots often rejected as oarie and coorse, the very utterance of which has been known to black affront the most liberal of purists) and he has sold it to a UK audience.

> Whaur ur yi Dundee? Whaur's yir Golem buriit?
> Whaur doon yir pendies lurks it?
> Broonbrick, eldscoorit, timedustchoakit,
> blin windies – whaur's MaGonagall's hert?
> Creh o seagulls echoes through the closies' lugs:
> nithin but 'iz hertsherds, shatterit, deidtrootdreh,
> nithin but vishuns o lehburers deean.

W. N. Herbert has chapped at doors, punted his message the length and breadth of the country, tholed and persisted with his innovative yet unconventional style and finally won through. Having already held a number of writing fellowships in Scotland and England, Herbert is now a respected mover on the UK poetry circuit. A versatile composer of elegies, eulogies, sci-fi poetry and audacious poetic sequences, he is also a shameless promoter of things Dundonian. The vision of the city on offer in Herbert's *The Testament of the Reverend Thomas Dick*, based on the raivelled imaginings of a Dundee astronomer, is a treat which no one of Dundee birth can afford to miss.

The resurrection in Broughty Ferry

In Barnhill Cemetery my grandfather feels
the soil with his new-grown hands
that nonetheless remember
the darkness in its yield.
His wife, who never hoped to hear
herself called Susie anymore
(her proper name is Isobel)
has much to tell
of the years between their deaths.
His sister comes
between the stones
to walk them to the harbour.
The families weave their generations
through each other as they go
like the Celtic chains
on his headstone.

In the hills, like worms pushing
their noses out at rain, the ancient dead
pull their thoughts out of the earth
in perfect tangles, nets that cradle
their catch of years.
Angels tug the sluggish up like gulls
and lug them to the harbour.

Like invasive seals that lifeboat crew
that capsized in 1959
tramp up the pebbles, empty
out their oilskins. Others shoal
the shallows, drowned Norries,
lost Lorimers and Ferriers,
the thirteen fishing families amass
and watch the heavens with
familar gestures.

W. N. Herbert

233

Writing in Dundonese is an art with a long tradition. It is a skill which requires a rare lug for language and one which the late Norman Lynn had in abundance.

> 'Eh weesh the factor wid dae somethin' aboot they bunged-up cundies,' Mum sighed. 'Efter a heavy rehn the coortie's like the Swanee ponds. It micht be rare fun fur you lads, makin' dammies, but it disna dae meh licht shoes much guid trehin' ti git in an' oot the closie.'

Norman Lynn's 'Row Laddie' books, from which this extract is taken, give an entertaining and valuable insight into life in the city earlier this century. And David Phillips, author of *The Lichty Nichts* and the newspaper column 'Meh Dundee', was also in his own lifetime a popular literary figure. His stories, anecdotes and witty recollections of local folk are written in his own charismatic brand of 'Dundonesian'. Of that same generation, the unpretentious character of Mary Brooksbank's poetry is a style which schools in the area would do well to study. Mary wrote in honest Dundonian, illustrating without nostalgia the spirit of a Dundee long since gone. And nowadays, aye cairryin the torch for the dialect, is the man-aboot-toon writer and playwright Gordon Burnside. His tale *Wullie's Turn*, about a bookie's runner, is an enterprising collaboration with Duncan of Jordanstone College of Art which interweaves period illustrations with Burnside's energetic dialogue. Dundonian's unique sounds and turns of phrase are the result of the collision last century between the languages of rural Angus and Irish immigrants coming to work in the jute. It is an accent of great linguistic vigour and with a wealth of expression many writers have exploited to their advantage over the years. Here is Gordon Burnside let loose on the Mither Tongue:

> 'Na, that's no' Wullie's knock. He aye chaps twice. Hud on a meenit! Git iz mi teeth, an' shut the curtains on they dishes. Look at the state o' this hoose! Yi didny hear "Coal" did yi? Turn that werrliss aff an gie' the fyir a rake. Move yir erse fur Goad's sake! An' pit the light on, dae yi waant thim ti think wi've hid the electric cut aff.'

It will be interesting to see if the next century can produce as many fine practitioners of 'Dundonesian' as this present century undoubtedly has.

There are three more books worthy of a mention, all of which are required reading for the discerning Dundonian. The first, *Sword and Pen*, edited by Bruce Pandrich and Hilda Spear, is an anthology of poetry composed by soldiers from Tayside who fought in the Great War. The poems are not masterpieces but knowing they were written by local lads, many of whom were to be killed in action, lends an eerie pathos to the whole collection. Nigel Gatherer's *Songs and Ballads of Dundee* is another treasure kist. Primarily a record of traditional and original works by

Dinna speak tae me o' the guid auld days,
For wha mair than me kens better;
Wha run barefitted in ragged claes
In summer days and winter.

Guid days they were for some, nae doot,
But never for me or mine;
Puir, hard-working, aye daein' withoot,
And hungry mony's the time.

Mary Brooksbank

Mary Brooksbank

Dundee folksingers, it is also a history of the city in song. A poignant entry in the collection is Catherine Smith's 'Pull Doon the Chimneys', set to the air 'Bonnets of Bonnie Dundee'.

> Come pull doon the chimneys and close a' the mills,
> Demolish the fact'ries where'er ye will,
> Remove the West Port and soon ye will see,
> There's naethin' at a' left o' Bonnie Dundee.

The splendid anthology *Caa Doon the Mune* is also worth a keek. This collection of Scots poetry for Angus bairns brings together the talents of Mary McIntosh, Lydia Robb and Jan Natanson, and features a gallus tale by Doris Watt recording a close encounter of the third kind in Baxter Park.

> An affy size o a thing it wis, this spaceship, like a big sasser wi a cup turnt upside-doon on it – ken, like the weh ye pit yer cup when ye're waitin tae git the tea-leaves read – and there wis a big licht on tap o it, shinin like the sun comin owre the Caledon shipyaird.

The city has been host to many guest writers. Some of these have come into the community, like itinerant traivellers, to serve as creative writing fellows at the University or at Duncan of Jordanstone. Sean O'Brien, Anne Stevenson, Donald Campbell, Carl MacDougall, John Byrne, Kathleen Jamie and Liz Lochhead – it is a prestigious leet. Others have made this area their home, flitting here and bringing with them their expertise and enthusiasm for literature. Harvey Holton, Douglas Dunn and Rosamunde Pilcher have all become writers-in-residence of indefinite tenure.

Dundee produces writers of quality and character. It needs to. To thrive in the hostile environment of publishing media requires durability, vigour and enterprise. That Dundee lacks the cultural frills of larger cities has been no obstacle to its poets. They have gone out and impressed the socks off the heid yins of the literary world or established presses of their own within the town. Too often Dundee is dismissed as provincial. But I would argue that the city has become the unofficial headquarters of Scots poetry. In a recent television production about Scots, four out of the six poets invited to the studio were from Dundee. And a quarter of the writers presented in *A Tongue in Yer Heid*, a collection of prose in Scots, were Dundonian. The town's poets have likewise been snapping up the top prizes in major competitions both in Scots and in English. Success, though, for the Dundee writer is hard won. It is the efforts of selfless individuals in local writers' groups, the professional advice available from visiting poets and the independence of the Dundonian spirit (to no leh doon when sumdy's kickin ye) that have brought about this overdue recognition of Dundee's writers. Lang may the city's literary lums reek.

ken

o jeannie, eh'm sluppin awa
– eh, eh ken
mrs zieman's affy no weel
– eh, eh ken
sheena sehs she's awa doon the murraygait
– eh, eh ken
breenie cannae see the wudd fur the trees
– eh, eh ken
the word for cundie in bulgarian is okap
– eh, eh ken
the bairn didnae half gie his granfaither a fleg
– eh, eh ken
ivan golac is serbian an no croat
– eh, eh ken
firmly insert the spurtle an gie hit a guid shauchlin
– eh, eh ken
dundee districk cooncil – putting the heart back into the city
– eh, eh ken
thon liz mccolgan's a real tonic
– eh, eh ken
what i wouldn't give to be if i was mary's prayer
– eh, eh ken
o beautiful silvery tay
with your landscapes so lovely and gay
along each of your waters, to Perth all the way
– eh, eh ken
fehve peh suppers oot the deep sea, mario
– eh, eh ken
an an ingan ane an aa
an an ingan ane an aa
'Dundee Man Bound For Australia'
– eh, eh ken
'Dundee Man Bound for Saudi Arabia'
– eh, eh ken
'Dundee Man Bound Over (dash) Failure To Pay Fines'
– eh, eh ken
there's alan and alan and alan gilzean
– eh, eh ken
buzz tellt sniff he wus gonnae gie us some
– eh, eh ken
takkin you hame's nae problem, lassie
the problem's the wife
– eh, eh ken
the memorial on the law has been illuminated
– eh, eh ken
the timex gates have now been closed
– eh, eh ken
they crucifehd wis, they crucifehd wis
o jeannie, eh'm sluppin awa
– eh, eh ken
o jeannie, eh'm sluppin awa
Matthew Fitt

Art in Dundee

by DR JOHN MORRISON

There is a notion prevalent south of the Tweed that Dundee is a mere mushroom city of yesterday, wholly given over to commerce and manufactures . . . This is a total mistake . . . As to the position of Dundee in the world of Art, it is sufficient to say that for many years it has held premier rank in Scotland for the sale of pictures at its exhibitions. Since these exhibitions were established some thirty years ago, the totals of annual sales of pictures have exceeded those of either Edinburgh or Glasgow; and indeed there is no English provincial town, save Liverpool, that can show larger results than Dundee.

So wrote A. H. Millar in the magazine *Art Journal* in 1898. Millar was trying to correct the late nineteenth-century impression that Dundee was a cultural backwater. That impression was wrong in 1898 and is equally wrong today. In the last 150 years Dundee has been the home not only of highly successful exhibitions, but has also housed numerous high-quality private collections, produced many accomplished artists herself and been home to still more. Duncan of Jordanstone College of Art, since its founding in 1892, has become the largest of the four Scottish colleges of art and design and possesses a role of staff and alumni which it is hard to better. This chapter can only scratch the surface of Dundee's more recent claims to artistic fame but hopefully it will help to create a better appreciation of the city's true position in the arts in Britain.

Portrait of J. C. Bell by G. P. Chalmers. *Dundee Art Galleries and Museums*

The Nineteenth Century

As Millar suggested, Dundee in the nineteenth century was a hive of activity in artistic terms. There were so many notable private art collectors in Dundee and the quality of their collections was so high that the *Dundee Advertiser* produced a series of articles on them which ran for over two months. Reviews of these collections appeared not infrequently in the national press. One of these collectors, John Charles Bell, formed three separate collections during his lifetime.

Bell was a successful and highly respected businessman in the flax and jute trades. He had come to Dundee in 1832, as a fifteen-year-old, to learn 'the methods of commerce'. His family had for generations lived in Berwick-upon-Tweed, so his background was perhaps less commercial and industrial than his later life

237

would suggest. Although successful, he was never a rich man judged by the standards of the day. His home at 7 Cowgate, was a modest one, yet he managed to form collections which were both financially and artistically valuable. Since he chose to live in an unostentatious style, he had more money available to purchase paintings. His first collection, begun in the 1840s, was formed at a time when a man of moderate means could still acquire works by distinguished painters. He was a contemporary of Sam Bough and Horatio McCulloch and possessed fine examples of their work. By the time the next generation of Scottish artists, the Scott Lauder pupils, appeared on the scene, Bell was a recognised collector and became very much their patron.

It was this first collection which came up for sale in 1877 when Bell was sixty-one. Possibly its sale allowed him to continue to collect during his retirement. There was a large crowd at Dowell's auctioneers on the day the collection was sold, including buyers from London, and the pictures fetched £11,000. At the time this was the largest sum ever realised for a modern Scottish collection and reflected the rising popularity of contemporary painting.

Bell had a good appreciation of artistic merit so the sale included early works by artists who subsequently gained high reputations. His collection was not exclusively Scottish but he did have fine examples of the work of William McTaggart, Hugh Cameron, John Pettie, George Paul Chalmers and W. Q. Orchardson. McTaggart's *Willie Baird* fetched £245 at the 1877 sale and works by Bough, Pettie, Cameron and Chalmers made similar sums, which amounted to, in some cases, over five or even ten times the original price. This phenomenal rise in the price of paintings illustrates the rapidly growing fashion for collecting modern pictures and demonstrates that Dundee was at the heart of Scottish art of the period.

Bell could not long exist without paintings in his home and he soon began the formation of a second collection which now included examples of the work of J. L. Wingate, J. Farquharson, W. D. McKay, and others. Bell's example, which influenced other prominent Dundee businessmen to form collections, many larger than his own, was further promoted by the encouragement he gave to the exhibition of paintings in Dundee. The first exhibition to be held, in the Drill Hall in Dundee, was in 1867 on the occasion of the visit of the British Association. It owed much to Bell's cooperation with J. G. Orchar, T. S. Robertson, G. B. Simpson and W. Ritchie, Simpson's business partner. Bell lent all the finest works in his possession for the exhibition and thereafter took an active part in all subsequent local exhibitions. He was a prominent member of the Fine Art Committee which directed the frequent exhibitions held in the Albert Institute.

Circumstances led Bell to dispose of his second collection in 1890, but almost immediately he began to build up a third collection. The economy was considerably less buoyant by this time and this undoubtedly had an effect on the sale of paintings. Nevertheless, before his death at the age of eighty-one in 1897, Bell had once again acquired the basis of a sound contemporary collection of Scottish painting. Like other major collectors in Dundee, he had warm, friendly relations with the artists, whose work he purchased directly rather than through exhibitions. G. P. Chalmers regarded Bell with great affection and the portrait he painted of the collector, claimed at the time to be one of the finest portraits ever painted in Scotland, reveals much of the quality of the sitter. Chalmers's diary recorded Bell living and dining with him during work on the painting.

A year after Bell's death in 1897 another major collector in the area, James Guthrie Orchar, died and left the whole of his art collection to be retained for the benefit of the burgh of Broughty Ferry and for public exhibition. In 1979 the Orchar Gallery at Beach Crescent, Broughty Ferry closed. It had housed the collection since 1929 but lack of funds for looking after the gallery and its contents adequately, meant that the collection was handed over to Dundee District Council Art Galleries and Museums. Although there is insufficient space to hang all of the more than 400 items in the collection, a significant part of it can now be seen in the handsomely refurbished Victorian room of the City Art Gallery.

Orchar's collection had begun in the 1860s. He was very much a self-made man from the 'virtuous peasantry'. His father, a country joiner and wheelwright, had a small business at Craigie outside Dundee while his grandfather had farmed at West Ferry. Early training as a joiner led subsequently to engineering first in Dundee and later in England. Returning to Dundee, he later entered into partnership with William Robertson, another noted collector, to form the Wallace Foundry. Once the business was securely established both men went on to play a prominent part in public affairs. As chief magistrate, later Provost of Broughty Ferry, Orchar was a popular local figure. His reputation was that of an eminently social man with a fund of old Scottish stories which he told superbly. Although a man of many interests, the dominating influence in Orchar's life was art. He was himself an amateur painter and was considered to be a reasonable draughtsman. From a modest beginning as a collector when a young man, he gradually built up an extensive collection of contemporary art. While his taste was not narrow – he owned examples of work by the Dutch artist Josef Israels, by Sir John Millais, and a selection of etchings by J. M. Whistler – his collection was mainly Scottish and predominantly the work of artists such as G. P. Chalmers, William McTaggart, Hugh Cameron and their contemporaries.

Like Bell, Orchar had a genuine interest in the artists whose paintings he acquired. He was always prepared to give generous support to young artists or to those who were ill or infirm. A particular friend was Chalmers and it was his painting *Old Letters*, which founded the Dundee Permanent Collection. When the gallery first opened in 1874 this painting, the gift of Orchar, was its only possession, all the others being loan pictures. Orchar's example induced others to follow. Like Bell, Orchar played a leading part in the organisation of the first fine art exhibition held in Dundee, in 1867. As was the case with Bell, Orchar was keen to lend out his pictures to exhibitions. With twenty-five works, he was one of the largest single lenders of pictures to the 1867 show. Similarly he was one of the motivating forces behind the inaugural 1873 exhibition which celebrated the opening of the permanent gallery.

Orchar gave much time to setting up exhibitions in Dundee. With T. S. Robertson, he acted as joint-convenor of the managing committee of the series of highly successful artists' sale exhibitions begun in Dundee in 1877. It is indicative of the number of Dundee collectors that the average sales over a twenty year period, till 1895/6 when the last exhibition was held, were about £5,000 a year, a result far surpassing that of any other fine art exhibition of the time in a city of comparable size.

It was Orchar who put forward a proposal that new galleries be specially built for the annual exhibitions. J. M. Keiller's donation of £10,000 made the project viable and other collectors such as T. S. Robertson and I. J. Weinberg lent their support. The scheme was formally launched in 1887 and the first exhibition was opened in late 1889. The new exhibition space, an extension to the Albert Institute (opened in 1867 in time to house the meeting of the British Association), was named the 'Victoria Galleries'. Its establishment marked Dundee's commemoration of the golden jubilee of Queen Victoria in 1887.

Bell and Orchar are just two of the large number of major collectors who lived in Dundee in the nineteenth century. However, the fact that these men had their homes or places of business in Dundee would not merit a great deal of discussion in terms of the history of art in the city were it not for one other important fact. Pictures from these collections did not simply hang on the walls of the houses of their rich owners. Almost all of Dundee's collectors lent their paintings for public exhibition at every opportunity. Residents of Dundee had repeated chances to view large parts of these collections on quite a regular basis. At a time when public collections were only just beginning to be established this gave the community a chance to see celebrated works of art. The willingness of these men to give freely their collections for display is demonstrated by a remark made by a reviewer of I. J. Weinberg's collection. He noted that although Mr Weinberg's pictures were of very high quality, they were so well known due to their frequent public exhibition that they were barely worth writing about.

The Twentieth Century

The turn of the century heralded the end of the era of the great
Victorian collectors and marked a change in artistic terms for
Dundee. With the demise of the Dundee Fine Art Exhibitions
in 1896 Dundee ceased to be a regular venue for the exhibition
and sale of paintings of the highest quality. However, artistic
activity in the city continued to prosper in other areas. At the end
of the nineteenth century the painter John Duncan came to prominence. Duncan produced graphic works for the short-lived
magazine The *Evergreen* and the same mystic spirit of the Celtic
revival is present in his later, large-scale paintings. At the heart
of a good representative collection of the artist's work Dundee
City Art Gallery possesses one of the very best pieces Duncan
produced: the 1911 *Riders of the Sidhe*. John Duncan's studio at
31 Albert Square was shared for over a year by George Dutch
Davidson. Under the influence of Duncan, and taking much
from the Glasgow-based Scottish Art-Nouveau movement,
Davidson produced a number of works which showed great
promise. Tragically he died at the age of twenty-one. With John
Duncan having already left the city by this time, the chance for
Dundee to establish itself as a major force in Scottish art of the
time faded away.

Riders of the Sidhe by John Duncan. *Dundee
Art Galleries and Museums*

241

Autumn, Kinnordy by J. McIntosh Patrick.
Dundee Art Galleries and Museums

The Dundee Art Society's history makes for happier reading. The society dates back to 1890 when a Graphic Arts Association was founded in Dundee. In 1904 the Association's name was changed to its present title. Its biennial exhibitions have attracted interest and comment from the start, and, since the acquisition of the ground floor of 17 Roseangle in 1947 and its subsequent remodelling into the Roseangle Gallery, the Society has had a custom-made home. Over the hundred years of its existence Dundee Art Society's exhibitions have displayed the works of many distinguished artists and also demonstrated the continuing high level of interest in art in Dundee. Two of the true stalwarts of the society's exhibitions, from the start until well into the 1940s, were Stewart Carmichael and C. G. L. Phillips.

Phillips was mainly a painter of landscape and occasionally of subjects from history, although there are a number of portraits and drawings of the city by his hand also. Stewart Carmichael was for many years a well-known figure in Dundee. Certainly his habit of dressing in a flowing cloak and long black boots made him a memorable sight but his painting too makes him worthy

242

of remembrance. He was the first honorary president of Dundee Art Society and some of his work, a lot of it religiously-based, has found a permanent home in one or other of the city's churches. After the artist's death in 1950, an exhibition of his work was held at the City Art Gallery. When the show closed, the artist's sisters offered many of the larger paintings to churches and other organisations. It is fitting that a man who lived and worked in Dundee for most of his eighty-three years should be represented in more than a dozen local institutions.

Carmichael was well known on the local Dundee stage. Undoubtedly, however, Dundee's most renowned painter of the twentieth century in national terms is Dr James McIntosh Patrick. Patrick was born in Dundee and although he trained at Glasgow School of Art from 1924, he has lived in Dundee for most of his life. Initially gaining renown as an etcher, it is on his ordered and rhythmic landscapes, often of Angus and Perthshire, that his reputation has been built. Works from the 1930s and 1940s such as *Autumn, Kinnordy* and *Winter in Angus* (both Tate Gallery, London), with their flowing linear drawing and precise control of paint, provide a record of the artist's cool, rather detached view of the world. The graphic quality of these earlier paintings probably derives from the artist's contemporary work in the linear medium of etching. Later works are more freely handled and rather more bold in colour, with the watercolours in particular evoking a sense of place, air and atmosphere. The retrospective exhibition of Patrick's work held in Dundee City Art Gallery during the summer of 1987 had the highest attendance of any show of paintings in Dundee this century.

With the rise of the Painting Department in Duncan of Jordanstone College of Art, several significant painters have made their home in Dundee. Alberto Morrocco, though inevitably popularly remembered for painting a portrait of the Queen Mother, is seen at his best in the bold exuberant still-lifes and latter-day genre scenes of his Italian heritage.

David McClure, a near contemporary of Morrocco's, paints pictures that reflect the long-standing artistic relationship between Scotland and France. A painting such as *Orange Studio*, while superficially reminiscent of earlier twentieth-century French painting, is really pure McClure. The well-known objects – female figure, sheet music, blue and white jug, painted kist – appear here suffused in a rich, warm glow. What comes across most is a love of colour, and, despite the stillness and isolation of the objects in the painting, a feeling of intense and joyous emotion.

Recently Duncan of Jordanstone has produced a number of artists who are right at the forefront of British and European art. In 1987 the *Vigorous Imagination* exhibition at the Edinburgh Festival celebrated the emergence of a new, vital force in

243

Girl in Orange Studio by David McClure.
Dundee Art Galleries and Museums

Scottish art. Analysis of the show, and indeed part of the cata-logue itself, tried to create the impression that this force emerged from Glasgow. In fact, more than a third of the artists in the exhibition were trained in Dundee. Among them was the sculptor David Mach who builds giant playful constructions often out of old newspapers or car tyres; works which aim to make us quest-ion our own assumptions about things that we take for granted.

A close contemporary of Mach's at Duncan of Jordanstone was the illustrator Keith Brockie. After graduating, he achieved almost instant success with his 1981 *Keith Brockie's Wildlife Sketchbook* and has since produced two other volumes. The most recent book is a record of the wildlife in and alongside the river Tay from headwaters to estuary. Brockie now has a fine reput-ation as a wildlife artist, with his tremendous attention to detail attracting a lot of praise. His work is far more than an accurate record of markings and behaviour, however. The sense that the creatures he draws and paints breathe the air and feel the rain of their environment is more vivid in Brockie's work than it ever

244

could be in a photograph. Brockie does not so much document the flora and fauna he chooses to depict as recreate them as life for his audience.

Without resorting to a simple list of names it is impossible to credit all the designers, painters, sculptors and even writers that have been produced by Duncan of Jordanstone. However, among many others, the achievements of Calum Colvin in photography; Ian Hughes, Phillip Braham, Ian Scott, Keith McIntyre and Eddie Summerton in painting; Stephen French in design; and David Cane in writing, all deserve recognition.

It would be impossible to conclude any discussion of art in Dundee without noting the innovative and original work done in Dundee in the field of public art. In 1982 two public art schemes were founded in the city – the Blackness Environmental Arts Team (BEAT), funded by the Manpower Services Commission and sponsored by Dundee District Council Art Galleries and Museums, and the Blackness Public Arts Programme (BPAP), funded jointly by the Scottish Arts Council and the Scottish Development Agency. Both projects aimed to relate the visual arts to the local community as directly as possible. The original co-ordinator of both programmes was Liz Kemp, at the time the assistant curator of art at Dundee City Art Gallery. Under her initial leadership, schemes were undertaken which aimed to brighten the urban landscape of the Blackness area. An early BPAP scheme, which won a prestigious Saltire Society award, involved the use of bricked-up windows as the site for a series of five low-relief ceramic panels. These panels are a perfect example of what public art is about. An old building is put to a new use and different demands are made of it. But, rather than have these demands lead, as so often happens, to unsightly conversions and alterations, they are here made the starting point of a decorative scheme which, while remaining faithful to the spirit of the original building, transforms the old into the new and enhances and improves the built environment.

Both BEAT and BPAP were about humanising the city and asserting the value of the artist to society as a whole. The very close ties of art to people, and the spirit of the artist in the service of a community are very well demonstrated by the story of the creation of Maggie Milne's tiled, mosaic entrances for three blocks of flats in Polepark Road. While the flats were being renovated in 1982, BEAT took over an empty flat as a workshop. From there one of the group conducted a door-to-door survey to try to find exactly what the community as a whole wanted to see. The result was the three bright, sunny mosaics that now light up the entrances to the buildings. Even on a dull Dundee afternoon in January, Milne's multicoloured groups of birds, chattering and squawking or soaring coolly on the wind, bring life and warmth to what previously had been a series of rather dull, empty spaces.

Drawing from *The Silvery Tay* by Keith Brockie. *Dundee Art Galleries and Museums*

245

Mural by Maggie Milne, Polepark Road.
Ken Sharp

After sixteen projects in three very successful years BEAT and BPAP merged in 1985 to become the Dundee Public Art Programme. Five years further on, and now working throughout the city, more than forty projects have been completed. Dundee was one of the very first cities to have a permanent public art programme. The experience and expertise of those involved is now much sought after as other schemes get underway in other parts of the country.

The above is only a brief summary of Dundee's artistic achievements over the past 150 years. Inevitably many interesting and noteworthy artists, exhibitions and ideas have been omitted, or mentioned only in passing. While this is unfortunate, it does illustrate the tremendous wealth of artistic endeavour in the city. Dundee has nurtured, and continues to nurture, art and artists of the highest quality. Very recently there have been significant changes in art in the city. On 1 August 1994 Duncan of Jordanstone merged with the University of Dundee. Such an alliance ought to ensure that the art college continues to produce graduates of high quality in years to come. Without complacency, all of the above achievements deserve to be celebrated.

246

The Community Strikes Back

Theatre in Dundee

by DAVID WILL

On 8 April 1982, Dundee Repertory Theatre moved into a new permanent home in Tay Square after a nomadic existence of almost two decades. Visitors to the new 'Rep' were to discover that the walls of its public lavatories were papered with reproductions of old posters. In lavishly processed black and gold, these showed a number of the most glorious past productions mounted during the forty-three previous years of the Rep's existence. The productions chosen for this hagiographic treatment are informative: they demonstrate the standards of excellence by which the Rep had judged its past.

All seven of the productions up on the walls featured actors and actresses who had gone on to become national (i.e. British) stars of stage and screen. In chronological order they are: Ian Carmichael (1946), Virginia McKenna (1950), Nicol Williamson (1960), Glenda Jackson (1961), Jill Gascoigne (1964), Michael York (1964) and Andrew Cruikshank (1975). Only one of the seven plays is by a Scottish author (Andrew Cruikshank's own *Games*). While two are 'classics' – one by Shakespeare, one by Shaw – the others are, to put it charitably, of slight literary worth. (Has anything more been heard of *He Wanted a Cream Front Door* by A. R. Whatmore or *Black Chiffon* by Lesley Storm?)

In fact, these 'glorious' productions are an ill-assorted rag-bag but they define what the Rep of old saw as its finest hours. The reason for this can only be the presence of stars whom the Rep helped on the road to greater things. The Rep got its kudos from the *reflected glory* of the West End stage, or television screen, rather than from anything intrinsically valuable about the productions staged there. A similar phenomenon occurred a couple of years ago in even starker form. In a BBC series about small cities, the English actress Joanna Lumley spoke about 'her' Dundee. Her credentials were that she had played Hedda Gabler at the Rep and thought that Dundee was a super place! Needless to say, all the other cities in the series were represented by real natives, but apparently the BBC believed that Dundee had to be shored up by someone more substantial than a mere Dundonian. Similarly the Rep had to justify its existence by claiming its historical links to stars of the British stage.

The cast of the second run of *They Fairly Mak Ye Work* at Dundee Rep. *Spanphoto*

The eighties have changed all that. Were the walls to be repapered today, a very different selection of posters would result. Without exception, the major productions of the eighties did not boast a single minor star, let alone a star of stage and screen. But, far from being an ill-assorted rag-bag, they all had similar concerns for the history of Dundee and the experience of the Dundonian working class. And, of course, they were all examples of new Scottish drama. These plays were: *They Fairly Mak Ye Work* (1986), *Witch's Blood* (1987), *Witch's Blood 2* (1988) and *A Man at Yir Back* (1989). What emerged in the eighties was a sense of theatrical identity which was committed to the community but in a way which avoided the common traps of Scottish populism: there was neither tartanry nor kailyard on display. (See *Scottish Myths* edited by Colin McCarthur, British Film Institute, 1982 for a good account of tartanry and kailyard.)

Most of these new productions emerged from the Community and Youth Theatre Projects at the Rep, initiated by Alan Lyddiard in 1983. The interest and direction of these projects were very different from those of the traditional repertory theatre and there were tensions at times between them and the 'theatrical' side of the Rep. The traditional theatrical productions staged in the eighties were the usual mixture of classics, farces and safe contemporary plays. Some were worthy, some meretricious but few, if any, were outstanding. It was the new theatre, orientated towards the community, that made an impact, both in Dundee and beyond.

The first of the new community productions, Billy Kay's *They Fairly Mak Ye Work*, created a sensation when it opened in April 1986. The play traced key episodes in the history of working-class Dundee, linking them through their impact on the life-story of Sarah Craig, whom Billy Kay had met while researching a radio documentary on the jute industry. The play starts in 1913 with the build-up to the First World War, moves on to the early twenties and a period of intense industrial unrest in the city and ends with the Depression. Grippingly directed by Alan Lyddiard, Kay's play is both thoroughly located in Dundee – its use of the Dundee vernacular is always precise and sharp – and yet not parochial. Kay is concerned to demonstrate the relationship between national (and international) events and local experience, in a way that makes the relationship between the two understandable.

This dual aspect of the play – both local and universal – had an extraordinary effect on its audiences. At the start of the play the audience was entranced by the recognition of their city, their dialect and themselves on the stage. However, Kay and Lyddiard built on this recognition effect, so that the audience became progressively more unsettled once the major catastrophes of the period – the First World War, the Depression – started to affect

248

the characters. Instead of the precise evocation of Dundee becoming a focus for nostalgia, in the play it becomes a stimulus for reflection, not just about the past, but about the present and future. In short this production was a consummately successful example of neo-Brechtian theatre.

The dual nature of the play was further reinforced by Michael Marra's musical score. Marra is usually described as 'Dundee's Randy Newman' and his score displayed a biting wit and a range of styles whose eclecticism precisely mirrored the interplay between past and present in the play. The collaboration between Marra and Lyddiard which continued with subsequent productions, led to some unforgettable theatrical moments.

Such was the success of its first run that *They Fairly Mak Ye Work* was repeated at the Rep in August 1986. Unfortunately the production did not tour elsewhere. It was invited to the Mayfest in Glasgow in 1986, but such was the nature of the set, which was based on three enormous rotating towers, that the problems posed by transporting it were insuperable. There was, however, no possibility of the next community production being invited to tour: *Witch's Blood* was literally rooted in Dundee.

This play was based on William Blain's pulpy historical novel about a Dundonian family. (Blain spent most of his life working on comics at D. C. Thomson's.) It traces the family's progress from rags to riches beginning with the matriarch's burning at the stake as a witch in 1660 and ending in the mid-nineteenth century with the family in the forefront of (what else?) the jute industry. Pulp novels, as Hollywood has known for many years, often make great spectacles and *Witch's Blood*, staged in July 1987, was no exception.

The production was in two parts, the first of which was literally a guided tour through simulated history. The audience, which had gathered at Dudhope Park, was placed in buses and then driven round to various sites in the city to witness scenes from the history of Dundee, before being driven back to Dudhope Castle to watch the second half. On each bus, a 'courier', dressed in period costume, acted as a narrator/guide. The buses stopped at a number of sites where the audience were able to walk into historical scenes, in which key moments in the novel were dramatised. These scenes included passengers disembarking at West Ferry from a boat carrying the plague; a riot in Balgay Park; and a chilling reconstruction of a seventeenth-century street complete with filthy children, beggars, manure and a 'witch' in the stocks, berated by a crowd who were clearly anticipating her imminent immolation with considerable pleasure.

As with *They Fairly Mak Ye Work*, *Witch's Blood* avoided the traps of easy nostalgia. The most obvious problem with this type of project is the tendency to produce a certain kitsch, tartan nostalgia when trying to recreate Scotland as it was. (A problem

249

Witches Blood II at the Coup, Riverside Drive. *Spanphoto*

endemic in many folk museums, for example.) However, here the experience was unsettling rather than nostalgic. For example, the sheer squalor of the seventeenth-century street and the stench of manure that pervaded it, afforded few opportunities for a rosy glow of nostalgia. Similarly, the experience of actually being in the scene oneself is a bizarre one. In some cases, the actors ignored the presence of members of the audience and acted as if they were not there. This technique gives the audience an experience of being an intruder/voyeur in a way that does not occur with conventional theatre. And, paradoxically, this can mean that actually being in the scene makes the audience feel more alienated from it.

In other scenes, actors, usually playing minor parts, addressed members of the audience as if they were 'really' in the scene. For example, a beggar would ask the audience for alms or a drunk would shout insults. Once again, this is a potentially alienating experience, since it tends to increase the audience's self-consciousness. *Witch's Blood* provided one of the few theatrical experiences of this sort of 'participation effect'. Indeed, outside of the spectacles provided on a Universal Studios tour, it is hard to think of an equivalent experience. The overall effect was to produce images of the past that were uncomfortable rather than cosy.

Michael Marra's music, which was relayed through the bus on the couriers' ghetto-blasters, enhanced this lack of cosiness. Its sharp harmonies and jagged melodies were quite the antithesis of the background music (lilting folk songs, melodic laments) usually provided for ceremonies of Scottish nostalgia. Once again, Marra's music played a key role in what I can only call the 'alienation machine' underpinning *Witch's Blood*.

The final component of this machine was Neil Murray's set for the second part, outside Dudhope Castle. Murray, who had also designed the giant towers for *They Fairly Mak Ye Work*, created a phantasmagoric graveyard, crammed with bizarre tombstones and distorted statues. For the audience, leaving the buses to take up seats in the outdoor auditorium in front of Dudhope Castle, it was like stumbling into a surrealist *tableau vivant*. The play that followed, written by John Harvey, was difficult to follow, not only because of its rather abstract nature, but also because it was being performed in a gale. However, the impact of the spectacle as a whole was very powerful. At one moment, near the end, a strikingly red-haired singer was passionately singing one of Michael Marra's most eerie songs as the wind whistled through the castle. I caught myself wondering if I was really in Dundee. Surely this was the kind of thing that went on at Italian music festivals in places like Bologna? *Witch's Blood* undoubtedly changed ideas about what was possible in Dundee.

Witch's Blood 2 (1988), built on *Witch's Blood* and, like its predecessor was the centre-piece of the Dundee Community

250

Festival. This was Alan Lyddiard's last production in Dundee. He left to work in Glasgow where *City*, his Glaswegian version of *Witch's Blood*, was staged in 1990.

The challenge to provide theatre reflecting the culture of the city, established in the 1980s, fortunately has been met in the 1990s. The production of *A Man at Yir Back*, the first play written by Dundee dramatist Gordon Burnside, clearly demonstrated the local demand. The Rep reported that the first night could have been sold out three times over and there were letters in the *Evening Telegraph* accusing city councillors of obtaining too many complimentary tickets! Burnside's play was also well received by several national critics. It is also authentically rooted in Dundee and, like *They Fairly Mak Ye Work*, brilliantly captures Dundonian dialect. That unique dialect has been exploited in the various translations of Molière's plays into Scots which have found great success at the Rep. The mell of Molière's timeless wit and actor Kern Falconer's riotous local humour gave the large audience a memorable night out.

There have also been welcome additions to the theatre scene recently. Under the guiding hand of John Harvey, the company Theatre Touring Tayside have achieved critical success performing in town halls, small theatres and prisons. Their production *Not Walking on the Cracks* won a prestigious Fringe First award at the Edinburgh Festival of 1994. Taking its name from the extinct volcano which dominates the town, the La' Hull Theatre Company was formed in 1993 by Jock Ferguson and Leslie Gray. Their main production was of Dundee's lost 16th-century masterpiece, *The Complaynt of Scotland*, by Robert Wedderburn. They also put the city's long history on video with their production *Dundee: Burgh of Discovery*. Other plays, including *Even the Good Times Were Bad* and *Slaters*, were performed on low budgets in small local venues. Run by Ed Steel, Secret Theatre is a special-needs group which receives council support.

The flagship theatre in the area remains the Rep. Under the directorship of Hamish Glen and Michael Duke, it has gone from strength to strength in the 1990s. Plays by local writers on local themes have continued to be sought out: The World War I drama set against the backdrop of local junior football rivalries, *The Harp and the Violet* by Lochee's Frank Gilfeather, and the Dundee Arctic whaling tale, *Toshie*, by Stuart Brown, being the most significant. Prestigious co-productions with other theatre companies have helped confirm the Rep's reputation as a major centre for Scottish drama. It has also shown itself to be firmly rooted in the community it serves, proving that if the creative spirit is there, there need be no tension between the desire to be local, national and international.

251

The City and Estuary 1966, at the time the road bridge was opened. *Joseph McKenzie*

ON BEING AN ESTUARY BIRD by Douglas Young

*Dundee's influence extends well beyond the city, with people from communities all around having strong con-
nections with the place. The villages strung along the Tay opposite Dundee, Tayport, Newport, Wormit and
Balmerino – memorably described by Graham Ogilvy as Dundee's Left Bank – have the best of both worlds;
a beautiful, often idyllic setting combined with instant access to a bustling city centre. The writer and painter
John Byrne, the poet Douglas Dunn, the painter Neil Dallas Brown and the photographer Joseph McKenzie
are just a few of the artists who have chosen to live in the area. It was also home to Douglas Young, one of
the leading figures in Scottish literature and Scottish nationalism this century. He wrote this in praise of the
area, in the* Glasgow Herald, *in 1953.*

Why, people ask me, why have you stuck yourself in Tayport, an obscure hole in an out-of-the-way
corner of Fife? Because, I tell them, Tayport is the pleasantest place to live in that I have found in
Europe.

From Athens in the South to Stockholm in the North, I have gone questing; and from Dublin in
the West to Moscow in the East. But for a place to live in I have never yet found any to equal Tayport.

The most important aspects of a place for living were set out long ago by the founder of scientific
medicine, the Greek Hippocrates, whose oath our medical men yet swear. He wrote a treatise 'On
Airs, Waters, and Places,' in which he stressed the importance of site and climate and of the local
presence of waters. In all these I find that Tayport is most pleasant, most temperate, best balanced.
And all this follows from its being, not only on an estuary, but on the best of all estuaries, and at
the best point of the estuary.

A little reflection shows that estuaries form the environment most suited to the human personality
on earth, with the finest intermixture of variety and stability in the surrounding scene that confronts
the eye, the master-organ of sense.

The worst sites are in marshes – Minsk, for example, the capital of Byelo-Russia, is never likely
to contribute largely to the elevation of human culture. Only less bad are the great plains and
plateaux, as at Milan. A sizeable river flowing through a town is, to be sure, a redeeming feature,
even on a flattish landscape like the Danube at Budapest or the Neva at Leningrad. And there is much
merit in lakes, as at Geneva and Zurich. Even a valley is an advantage, as for Innsbruck between
its mountain walls, or Heidelberg in its wooded hills.

But rivers and valleys imply a one-way movement, a monotonous rhythm in a single direction,
whereas a tidal estuary implies the majestic recurrence of complementary impulses, an enantiodromic stability deeply symbolic for human life. A mere tide, as on any sea coast, is hardly enough,
for it may be barely perceptible, as at Copenhagen by the Baltic or at Venice on its brackish lagoons.
Estuaries give you most markedly the feeling of being poised between two elements and two movements, the sense of the interaction of sea and land, of life and death and rebirth.

Life came on this earth, from the sea. Our globe's surface began as a sea of fire, and will end as
a sea of ice. It is by estuaries that we live closest to the eternal verities, the ebb and flow of mortal
things, the Heraclitean flux, what Chinese philosophers call *yin* and *yang.*

Coventry Patmore put the tidal rhythm tellingly into some verses:

> Here, in this little bay,
> Full of tumultuous life great repose,
> Where twice a day
> The purposeless glad ocean comes and goes . . .

He concludes by expressing the feeling of estuary-dwellers that we may have confidence in the
ultimate rightness of the sum of things:

> For want of me the world's course will not fail.
> When all its work is done the lie shall rot.
> Great is the Truth and shall prevail
> When none cares whether it prevail or not.

Those who live by the outflow of great tidal rivers attain thereby a sense of balance and tranquillity.

It was by rivers that the oldest civilisations arose; higher forms of civilisation sprang up by seas;
and the more tidal the seas the higher the development of the civilisation. Tidal firths indeed afford
the perfect site for civilised living. The geopoliticians appear so far to have overlooked the probability
that it was precisely because Scotland is so rich in estuaries that our discriminating ancestors chose

253

it to settle in. As was remarked in the Arbroath Declaration of 1320, the Scots originated somewhere near the Caucasus, at the eastern extremity of Europe, and traversed thousands of miles, examining different territories, before wisely resolving to colonise Scotland.

Now we have many and notable estuaries, from the Solway and the Clyde, round by the white sands of Morar to Ythan, as far south as the Tweed. But, after personally inspecting most of them, I am convinced that eastward-opening firths have a general superiority to those that flow west, north, or south. For the flow against the sun's course better maintains that sense of enantiodromic equilibrium, of constant variation within a stable frame of reference, that makes the special emotional quality of estuary-dwelling.

The Tay, moreover, is our greatest river, drawing down from among the little red saxifrages on the snow-fed screes on Ben Lui, swelled by a myriad burns, flowing by historic places, to culminate at Tayport and join that world-encircling highway of brine, the open sea.

Mere eastward expansion is not enough: the actual size and proportions of a firth are very important also. And in these aspects the Tay estuary is perfect, as viewed from Tayport, and above all from my own study window. On Solway the disproportion is too great between the firth at ebb and the flooded estuary; on Forth it is too small; at Morar the river meandering through the white sands is a mere trickle at low tide compared to the full basin, and the same objection may be urged against the Esk at Montrose; the surrounding landscape of the Ythan is too paltry.

But here, at Tayport, it is just a mile of glittering strait from our harbour mouth to the old castle of Broughty on its Angus promontory; and then, eastward, the firth expands to some three miles in glorious sweeping bays of golden sand and green links, when the tide floods up and the basin brims full, shining in the sun, gleaming in the moonlight, a myriad different shades as the seasons and days shift and the clouds wander over.

And when it ebbs, twice in a day and night, Tay does not dwindle too far, but remains a majestic stream a mile and a half wide, between expanses of richly hued alluvial soils, patterned with endlessly varying pools and streamlets. On one side lie the wooded hills of Angus, backed by the splendid curves of the Sidlaws, and the purple ranges beyond of the Mownth, which tourists call the Grampians from a misprint in Tacitus. And here on our Fife side are moors and forests reaching to the Eden, and the last spurs of the Ochils running down among woods and farmlands to the rocks and sands.

No landscape, no seascape can compete with firthscape, the inter-animation of both elements, ever changing and conflicting, but always with the fundamental reconciliation that brings a saining to the soul.

NOTES ON CONTRIBUTORS

Billy Kay is a writer and broadcaster who lives in Newport-on-Tay.

Joe Austen writes for television and is a writer and illustrator of children's books, including the *Magic House* series. Born and brought up in Dundee, he now lives near St Andrews.

G. W. S. Barrow is the former Professor of Scottish History at the University of Edinburgh. Publications include *Robert Bruce* and *Kingship and Unity: Scotland 1000–1306.*

Chris Whatley is a reader in Scottish History at Dundee University. Publications include *The Life and Times of Dundee* and *Bought and Sold for English Gold? Explaining the Union of 1707.*

J. S. G. Blair is a surgeon in Perth and Honorary Senior Lecturer in Surgery at the University of Dundee. He is author of the book *Ten Tayside Doctors.*

Charles McKean is Professor of Architecture at the Duncan of Jordanstone College, Dundee. He is the author of *Banff and Buchan* and co-author of *Dundee: An Illustrated Introduction* and *Central Glasgow.*

George Rosie is a freelance journalist, writer and broadcaster who lives in Edinburgh. His books include *The Ludwig Initiative* and *Hugh Miller.*

Graham R. Smith organised the Dundee Oral History Project, and is completing his PhD for Stirling University. He is Scottish Network Organiser for the Oral History Society and Community Historian for Tayside Regional Council. He lives in Dundee.

Jim Wilkie is a freelance writer and musician. He has written a history of Dundee football, *Across the Great Divide*, and the story of Scottish rock music, *Blue Suede Brogans.*

David Will is a psychiatrist who lived in Dundee for most of the 1980s. He wrote about cinema and theatre for *Radical Scotland*. He now lives in Edinburgh but still gets his coffee sent from Braithwaite's in Castle Street.

Matthew Fitt is the second holder of the Brownsbank Writers' Fellowship. He writes poetry and prose in Scots.

Dr John Morrison is a lecturer in art history at the University of Aberdeen. Publications include *The First Hundred: Dundee's Art College 1892–1992.*

George A. Stout is visiting Professor in the Department of Accountancy at Dundee University. Until 1988 he was Joint Manager and Director of the Alliance Trust. He lives in Monifieth.

Ellie McDonald is a poet who writes in Scots and promotes awareness of the language. She lives and works in Dundee.

George Bruce is a poet who lives in Edinburgh. He was an arts producer for the BBC from 1946–70. His publications include *Collected Poems* (Edinburgh U.P.) and *Perspectives: Poems 1970–1986* (Aberdeen U.P.).

Graham Ogilvy is a journalist and features writer who runs the Dundee Press Agency. He is the author of *The River Tay and Its People*, and his second book, *Fife and Its Folk*, is to be published shortly. He is currently writing a historical novel inspired by the life of George Mealmaker and the activities of the United Scotsmen.

Bruce Pandrich is a teacher of English in Perth. He is co-editor of *Sword and Pen: Poems of 1915 from Dundee and Tayside.*

Ken Sharp is a freelance photographer who works mainly for London-based magazines and papers. He still works in London but has moved the family home back to Dundee.

Joseph McKenzie was born and brought up in London. He came to Dundee as the lecturer in charge of Photography at Duncan of Jordanstone Art College in 1964. He retired in 1985 and lives in Tayport. He has made several important photographic studies of Dundee. His books include *Pages of Experience* and *Gorbals Children.*

Donny Coutts is a town planning consultant, golf fanatic, United and Dundee HSFP fan and is still Dundee soul Brither Nummer Ane. This Donny Coutts is the real Donny Coutts.

BIBLIOGRAPHY

Armstrong, Kate, *Wild Mushrooms*, Blind Serpent Press

Bruce, George, *Collected Poems 1940-1970*, Edinburgh University Press

Buchan, James, *The Expendable Mary Slessor*, The Saint Andrew Press (1980)

Burnside, Gordon, *Wullie's Turn*, Duncan of Jordanstone (1989)

Caa Doon the Mune, Angus District Council (1993)

Cameron, James, *Point of Departure*, Oriel Press (1967)

Cockburn, Lord, *Circuit Journeys*, Byway Books (1983)

Defoe, Daniel, *A Tour Through the Whole Island of Great Britain*, Penguin (1971)

Donaldson, William, *Popular Literature in Victorian Scotland*, Aberdeen University Press (1986)

Douglas, Sheila, ed., *Fair Upon Tay*, Tayside Regional Council (1993)

Elliot, Walter, *Adventurer's Coast or The Two Sides of the Tay*, Oliver and Boyd (1954)

Fraser, Eugenie, *The House by the Dvina*, Mainstream (1984)

Fraser, Eugenie, *A Home by the Hooghly*, Mainstream (1989)

Gatherer, Nigel, *Songs and Ballads of Dundee*, John Donald (1986)

Gibbon, Lewis Grassic and MacDiarmid, Hugh, *Scottish Scene* (1934)

Gilbert, J. C., *A History of Investment Trusts in Dundee*, P. S. King (1939)

Glenday, John, *The Apple Ghost*, Blind Serpent Press

Hay, William, *Ancient Dundee*, William Kidd (1886)

Herbert, W. N., *Dundee Doldrums*, Galliard (1991)

Herbert, W. N., *Anither Music*, Vennel (1991)

Herbert, W. N., *Forked Tongue*, Bloodaxe (1994)

Herbert, W. N., *The Testament of the Reverend Thomas Dick*, Arc (1994)

Heron, R., *Scotland Delineated, 1799*, The Mercat Press (1975)

Hume Brown, P., *Early Travellers in Scotland*, David Douglas (1891)

Kay, Billy, *Tae Be Yersel: Investigating the Scots Language*, Tayside Regional Council (1995)

Kay, Billy, ed., *Odyssey: Voices From Scotland's Recent Past*, Polygon Books (1980)

Kay, Billy and Maclean, Cailean, *Knee Deep in Claret*, Auld Alliance Publishing (1995)

Kennedy, A. L., *Night Geometry and the Garscadden Trains*, Phoenix (1990)

Kennedy, A. L., *Looking for the Possible Dance*, Secker & Warburg (1993)

Kennedy, A. L., *Now That Your're Back*, Cape (1994)

Kennedy, A. L., *So I Am Glad* (1995)

Kerr, W. G., Scottish Capital on the American Credit Frontier, Texas State Historical Association (1976)

Kidd, William & Sons, ed., *Dundee Past and Present* (1909), *The Chartist Agitation in Dundee*, both William Kidd.

Lindsay, Maurice and Mackie, R. L., compiled by, *A Book of Scottish Verse*

McDonald, Ellie, *The Gangan Fuit*, Chapman (1991)

McDiarmid, Mathew P., ed., *Hary's Wallace*, Scottish Text Society, Blackwood (1968)

MacDiarmid, Hugh, ed., *The Voice of Scotland* (1938-39)

McKean, Charles and Walker, David, *Dundee: An Illustrated Introduction*, Royal Incorporation of Architects in Scotland/Scottish Academic Press (1984)

Maxwell, Alexander, *The History of Old Dundee*, William Kidd (1884)

Milne, John V., *Poems*, Aberdeen University Press

Montgomerie, Norah and William, compiled by, *Scottish Nursery Rhymes*, Chambers (1990)

Montgomerie, William, compiled by, *From Time to Time*, Canongate (1985)

Morrison, J., *The First Hundred: Dundee's Art College 1892-1992* (1992)

Morton, H. V., *In Search of Scotland*, Methuen (1929)

Murdoch, W. G. Burn, *From Edinburgh to the Antarctic*, Longmans, Green and Co. (1894)

Myles, James, *Chapters in the Life of a Dundee Factory Boy*, William Kidd (1887)

Myles, James (under the pseudonym Simon Straps), ed., *A Feast of Literary Crumbs*, Valentine (1948)

Ogilvy, Graham, *The River Tay and Its People*, Mainstream (1993)

Paterson, Don, *Nil Nil*, Faber & Faber (1993)

Paterson, Tony, *Churchill: A Seat for Life*, David Winter & Son (1980)

Pearce, W. M., *The Matador Land and Cattle Company*, University of Oklahoma Press (1964)

Phillips, David, *My & Meh Dundee*, David Winter (1971)

Scott, Andrew Murray, *Discovering Dundee*, The Mercat Press (1989)

Shelley, Mary, *Frankenstein*, Penguin Classics (1985)

Southey, Robert, *Journal of a Tour in Scotland*, John Murray (1929)

Spear, Hilda D. and Pandrich, Bruce, *Sword and Pen: Poems of 1915 from Dundee and Tayside*, Aberdeen University Press (1989)

Tayside Environmental Education Project, *A Pictorial History of Dundee*

Tennant, Charles, *The Radical Laird*, The Roundwood Press (1970)

Walker, David, *Lean, Wind, Lean*, William Collins (1984)

Whatley, C. A., Swinfen, D., and Smith, A., *The Life and Times of Dundee* (1993)

Whatley, C. A., ed., *The Remaking of Juteopolis: Dundee c. 1891-1991* (1992)

Wilkie, Jim, *Across the Great Divide*, Mainstream (1984)

Young, Douglas, *Chasing an Ancient Greek*, Hollis & Carter (1950)

Young, Douglas, *A Clear Voice: Douglas Young, Poet and Polymath*, Macdonald Publishers (1974)